PSYCHOTHERAPY & DRUG ADDICTION, I:
Diagnosis & Treatment

Papers by
Charles P. Cohen, S. Robinson, Reginald G.
Smart et al.

MSS Information Corporation
655 Madison Avenue, New York, N. Y. 10021

Library of Congress Cataloging in Publication Data
Main entry under title:

Psychotherapy and drug addiction.

"Collection of articles previously published in
various journals."
CONTENTS: 1. Cohen, C. P. and Robinson, S. and
others. Diagnosis and treatment.--2. Silverman, I.
and Garber, R. S., and others. Community and
institutional care.
1. Narcotic habit--Addresses, essays, lectures.
2. Narcotic addicts--Rehabilitation--Addresses,
essays, lectures. [DNLM: 1. Drug abuse--Collected
works. 2. Drug addiction--Collected works.
3. Psychotherapy--Collected works. WM270 P974]

RC566.P7   616.8'63   73-11097
ISBN 0-8422-7143-0 (v. 1)

Copyright © 1974
by MSS Information Corporation
All Rights Reserved

TABLE OF CONTENTS

CREDITS AND ACKNOWLEDGEMENTS

Baumann, Franz, "Hypnosis and the Adolescent Drug Abuser," *The American Journal of Clinical Hypnosis*, 1970, 13:17-21.

Berzins, Juris I.; Wesley F. Ross; and Jack J. Monroe, "Crossvalidation of the Hill-Monroe Acceptability for Psychotherapy Scale for Addict Males," *Journal of Clinical Psychology*, 1970, 26:199-201.

Cohen, Charles P.; Elna H. White; and Joseph C. Schoolar, "Interpersonal Patterns of Personality for Drug-Abusing Patients and Their Therapeutic Implications," *Archives of General Psychiatry*, 1971, 24: 353-358.

Cuskey, Walter R.; Arthur D. Moffett; and Happa B. Clifford, "Comparison of Female Opiate Addicts Admitted to Lexington Hospital in 1961 and 1967," *HSMHA Health Reports*, 1971, 86:332-339.

Cuskey, Walter R.; T, Premkumar; and Lois Sigel, "Survey of Opiate Addiction among Females in the United States between 1850 and 1970," *Public Health Reviews*, 1972, 1:6-39.

Dahlberg, Charles C.; Ruth Mechaneck; and Stanley Feldstein, "LSD Research: The Impact of Lay Publicity," *American Journal of Psychiatry*, 1968, 125:685-689.

Davis, William N., "The Treatment of Drug Addiction: Some Comparative Observations," *British Journal of Addiction*, 1970, 65:227-234.

Foulks, Edward F.; and Russell Eisenmann, "An Analysis of a Peer Network Using Psychedelic Drugs," *Psychiatric Quarterly*, 1969, 43: 389-395.

Freedman, Daniel X., "Implications for Research," *Journal of the American Medical Association*, 1968, 206:1280-1284.

Glatt, M.M., "Psychotherapy of Drug Dependence: Some Theoretical Considerations," *British Journal of Addiction*, 1970, 65:51-62.

Griffiths, Sheldon H., "Video Recordings," *Nursing Times*, 1970, 66: 1208-1209.

Kolouch, Fred T., "Hypnosis in Living Systems Theory: A Living Systems Autopsy in a Polysurgical, Polymedical, Polypsychiatric, Patient Addicted to Talwin," *The American Journal of Clinical Hypnosis*, 1970, 13:22-34.

Kraft, Tom, "Treatment of Drinamyl Addiction: Two Case Studies," *The Journal of Nervous and Mental Disease*, 1970, 150:138-144.

Maddux, James F., "Current Approaches to the Treatment of Narcotic Addiction," *Journal of the National Medical Association*, 1969, 61: 248-254.

Ottenberg, Donald J.; and Alvin Rosen, "Merging the Treatment of Drug Addicts into an Existing Program for Alcoholics," *Quarterly Journal of Studies on Alcohol*, 1971, 32:94-103.

Robinson, S.; and H.Z. Winnik, "Motivation for the Addiction to Amphetamine and Reducing Drugs," *The Israel Annals of Psychiatry and Related Disciplines*, 1969, 7:213-222.

Serber, Michael, "Drug Dealing Paranoia," *Psychological Reports*, 1971, 28:529-530.

Smart, Reginald G.; and Dianne Jones, "Illicit LSD Users: Their Personality Characteristics and Psychopathology," *Journal of Abnormal Psychology*, 1970, 75:286-292.

Suinn, Richard M.; and Jackie Brittain, "The Termination of an LSD 'Freak-Out' through the Use of Relaxation," *Journal of Clinical Psychology*, 1970, 26:127-128.

Taylor, Robert L.; John I. Maurer; and Jared R. Tinklenberg, "Management of 'Bad Trips' in an Evolving Drug Scene," *Journal of the American Medical Association*, 1970, 213:422-425.

Wikler, Abraham, "Diagnosis and Treatment of Drug Dependence of the Barbituate Type," *American Journal of Psychiatry*, 1968, 125: 758-765.

Wilmer, Harry A., "Drugs, Hippies, and Doctors," *Journal of the American Medical Association*, 1968, 206:1272-1275.

Wilmer, Harry A., "Innovative Uses of Videotape on a Psychiatric Ward," *Hospital and Community Psychiatry*, 1968, 19:129-133.

Wilmer, Harry A., "Use of the Television Monologue with Adolescent Psychiatric Patients," *American Journal of Psychiatry*, 1970, 126: 1760-1766.

Wolpe, Joseph, "Commentary on 'Treatment of Drinamyl Addiction'," *The Journal of Nervous and Mental Disease*, 1970, 150:145.

Wurmser, Leon; and Herzl R. Spiro, "Factors in Recognition and Management of Sociopathy and the Addictions," *Modern Treatment*, 1969, 6:704-719.

PREFACE

This volume on the diagnosis and treatment of drug addiction presents studies on the personality of drug abusers, their motivations and psychopathology. Also included are theoretical discussions on the psychotherapy of narcotic addiction, and comparisons of treatment for addicts and alcoholics. New techniques including the use of video-tape and recording equipment in drug treatment are among the topics discussed.

A companion volume, *Psychotherapy and Drug Addiction, II: Community and Institutional Care*, deals with the current use of therapeutic communities including Phoenix House, Synanon, the Laguna Beach Experiment, and the California Rehabilitation Center Program. Other papers deal with the success of intensive, short term treatment in out-patient clinics, in-patient treatment centers for heroin addicts, emergency psychiatric treatment for drug users and attrition rates in out-patient detoxification programs.

Personality Patterns of Addicts

Interpersonal Patterns of Personality for Drug-Abusing Patients and Their Therapeutic Implications

Charles P. Cohen, PhD; Elna H. White, PhD;

and Joseph C. Schoolar, PhD, MD

Despite increasing national concern about drug abuse, there are still few formal studies dealing with the drug-abuser seeking help along with discussion of therapeutic possibilities. Previous studies have focused on the psychological effects of lysergic acid diethylamide (LSD)[1,2] with no concern about the personality of the individuals taking the drug. Where there has been an interest in the question of psychopathology, studies have utilized *volunteer* drug-takers[3-6] and have emerged with conflicting findings. Other studies have relied on clinical observation[7,8] with groups which were very small and which were not compared to any control group.

This paper is part of a continuing study by us which attempts to describe the multidrug-abuser who has come to a drug-abuse clinic seeking help. Utilizing Leary's[9,10] system of Interpersonal Diagnosis of Personality, we presented in earlier studies (White et al[11] and Schoolar et al, unpublished data) some descriptive statements about the drug-abuser. The following picture has emerged thus far:

1. The drug-abuser generally behaves in a dominating and critical manner to an extent significantly

greater than a matched population of outpatients with non-drug-related problems. Keeping in mind that the members of both groups had come to a clinic for help, it is noteworthy that the symptomatic behavior of drug-abusers tends to alienate sources of help by provoking feelings of competitiveness and resentment in the would-be helper. This pattern of open defiance of authority figures was recently confirmed in a study which found that LSD-users behave in a socially nonconforming manner and have more authority problems than non-drug-users.[5]

2. The drug-abusers and their non-drug-using counterparts both perceive their behavior as socially undesirable, indicating an awareness of the feedback they are eliciting. The meaning of this feedback may vary for the two groups because of significant differences in the values they endorse. Drug-abusers clearly differed from controls in expressing a wish to be passive and suspicious. Thus, while the drug-abuser functions routinely in an action-oriented manner, he would prefer to not engage in striving behavior for which he will take personal or social responsibility. In effect, he rejects traditional values and expresses an ideal of distrust and nonconformity. It is difficult to ascertain whether responses endorsing values of passive aggression and dependency are merely another means of expressing defiance to perceived authorities symbolized by the tests. On the one hand, the drug-abuser may truly see no redeeming features in the values espoused by the society-at-large. On the other hand, he may not see himself as capable of achieving these values and so rejects them to avoid the frustration of inadequate performance. Such a view would suggest that the drug-abuser is trying to ward off the depression which

some workers[8] regard as a common factor among this population.

3. A third finding of considerable importance involved the drug-abuser's basic intentionality or "underlying character structure" (Schoolar et al, unpublished data and Leary[9]). At this level of personality the drug-abuser is significantly devoid of socially desirable or "healthy" orientations. Essentially, the ground from which his public behavior emerges and becomes figural can be described as angry, suspicious, and self-doubting. This constellation has been noted in another study[12] where the authors saw "paranoia" (persecution complex) as "a characteristic part of the reaction."

4. Finally, another noteworthy result of our previous study (Schoolar et al, unpublished data) indicated that drug-abusers described their parents as self-reliant, responsible, and generally behaving in a socially desirable manner. This was similar to the way parents were described by nondrug-using patients. In effect, our data did not support the hypothesis that the parents of drug-abusers were uniquely different than other parents.

Proceeding from the above descriptions of some individual levels of personality, we now propose to analyze the potential conflict patterns between different personality levels. The present study is thus intended to explore the possibilities for therapeutic intervention with drug-abusers and their implications for the therapist. As in the previous studies, the Leary Interpersonal System[9,10] has been used to describe these interlevel differences. Again, a comparison will also be made with a control group of outpatients matched for age and sex but presenting no drug problems.

Method

Subjects.—The drug-abuse popula-

Table 1.—Variability Indices of Drug-Abusers (in Frequency)

Verbal Definitions of Indices*	Amount of Discrepancy														
	00	23	26	41	44	48	62	66	68	81	84	91	105	114	No.
A. Interlevel conflict															
Self-deception	15	4	1	7	12	2	2	3	0	15	5	0	10	4	80
Conscious self-acceptance	20	2	0	5	13	0	0	6	0	13	3	3	9	3	77
Identity diffusion†	12	1	0	4	15	1	0	4	0	15	7	1	16	4	80
Self-actualization	8	3	1	0	15	1	1	4	0	18	5	2	11	8	77
B. Identification with parents															
Mother	10	4	0	3	11	1	0	4	0	16	3	3	15	6	76
Father	8	3	2	4	14	1	0	5	0	15	5	0	13	4	74
C. Internalization of parents†															
Mother	9	1	0	2	6	0	0	2	0	19	4	2	17	14	76
Father	7	0	0	3	16	0	0	5	0	16	1	2	18	6	74
D. Idealization of parents															
Mother	6	2	1	4	15	0	0	4	0	9	3	3	13	13	73
Father	14	0	0	4	9	1	0	1	1	11	7	1	13	9	71

* Operational definitions of these indices are given in the Leary manual.[9]
† These indices are new to the Leary framework.

tion consisted of 80 patients who had sought or been referred for help at a clinic established for this problem. The group consisted of 53 males and 27 females, ranging in age from 14 to 33, with a mean age of 19.2 years. The control group, matched for age and sex, were obtained in random fashion from the University of Houston Counseling Service and the Child Guidance Center of Houston. Thus, both groups were seeking professional help but differed in the nature of the problem which they presented (drug vs nondrug).

Procedure.—The Minnesota Multiphasic Personality Inventory (MMPI) and Interpersonal Checklist were administered to both groups and scored according to Leary's system.[9,10] After scores on each of the different tests are located in one of the indicated octants (see Schoolar et al, unpublished data, for a description of this procedure), the next step is to consider the relationships among the levels connoted by these measures. These interlevel relationships are called variability indices and reflect the amount of discrepancy between (1) different diagnostic levels within an individual; (2) self-diagnosis and ratings of parents; (3) the conscious ideal and ratings of either self or others; and (4) nonconscious aspects of personality and ratings of self and parents. The latter have not been part of the traditional Leary system and represent an extension of the personality dimensions that can be explored within the system.

The first of these two new measures is derived from Erikson's[13] discussion of ego identity and has been defined here as "Identity Diffusion." Following the idea that children and adolescents need to maintain inner sameness and continuity matched by the sameness and continuity of one's meaning for others, the possibility of "identity diffusion" becomes salient when role confusion occurs. Behavior at that point can be seen as a means of precluding such a catastrophe and preserving some sense of identity. Operationally, "Identity Diffusion" is reflected in a high discrepancy between self-description (IIS) and basic intentionality (IIIMM). The second new measure is derived from the psychoanalytic concept of "introjection."[14] Psychologically, this refers to a process of assimilation whereby "objects presenting themselves are absorbed by the ego into itself."[14] Erickson has commented on the importance of this mechanism for ego development and noted that the "primitive 'incorporation' of another's image depends for its integration on the satisfactory mutuality between the mothering adult(s) and the mothered child."[13(p159)] Without this experience of initial mutuality providing a safe pole of self-feeling, the child will have difficulty reaching out for love objects, and a foundation for experiencing alienation may result. In the present study this measure has been labeled as "Parental Assimilation" and is operationally defined as the discrepancy between ratings of each parent (IIM and IIF) and basic intentionality or underlying character structure (IIIMM). Rejection of some parental quality may be said to exist where a significant discrepancy occurs between IIM and IIF vs IIIMM.

There are 14 possible discrepancy scores, ranging at unequal intervals from 0 to 114. If the discrepancy between two measures, eg, public behavior and self-description, is one octant or less, than no significant degree of conflict is considered to be present. A discrepancy score of more than 44 defines a difference of more than one octant between ratings and indicates a significant degree of conflict. The maximum score of 114 is obtained when the two ratings being compared fall into opposite octants, ie, 5 and 1, 8 and 4, 6 and 2, 3 and 7.

Results

Table 1 summarizes the drug-abusers' interlevel conflicts and identification with parents, as well as idealizations and assimilations of them. Section A of Table 1 gives the distribution of discrepancy scores obtained by the drug-abusers on self-deception, conscious self-acceptance, identity diffusion, and self-actualization. Data for the control group are similarly presented in Table 2.

As stated earlier, a low score (under 48) means that the octant ratings being compared are very similar, whereas scores above 44 indicate that the ratings are significantly different. Inspection of Section A in Tables 1 and 2 show that 50% and 38% of the drug-abuse and control groups respectively, misperceive their public interpersonal impact. Where this occurs, it is generally in the direction of emphasizing their submission and affiliation and being self-deceptive about their assertive and oppositional behavior.

Although both groups are divided evenly in their conscious acceptance or rejection of themselves, the latter takes a different form for each group. Thus, self-rejecting drug-abusers tend to prefer being more passive and dependent than they see themselves, while the control group wants to be more assertive and self-reliant. This difference between groups is significant ($\chi^2 = 6.115$, $P < 0.02$) and indicates a different source of discomfort for each. Even more striking is the fact that two thirds of drug-abusers and controls fail to behave in ways that achieve their ideal goals. Here again the two groups differ significantly ($\chi^2 = 7.941$, $P < 0.01$) in the way they achieve low self-actualization scores. Controls are evenly divided in wanting to actualize dominant or submissive behavior, while the symptomatic assertive and arrogant qualities of the drug-abusers are almost the exact opposite of the passivity and dependence which they idealize.

Comparing the sense of identity in both groups reveals a significant difference between them ($\chi^2 = 7.243$, $P < 0.01$). Fifty-nine percent of the drug-abusers show a significant discrepancy between the way they see themselves in relation to their basic orientation toward life. This conflict usually takes the form of drug-abusers seeing themselves as stronger and more affiliative than their basic intentionality would in-

Table 2.—Variability Indices of Control Group (in Frequency)

Verbal Definitions of Indices*	Amount of Discrepancy														
	00	23	26	41	44	48	62	66	68	81	84	91	105	114	No.
A. Interlevel conflict															
Self-deception	15	2	5	5	23	1	2	4	1	9	2	0	8	3	80
Conscious self-acceptance	10	5	0	6	18	1	2	2	0	13	4	2	11	5	79
Identity diffusion†	18	2	0	9	22	0	0	2	1	8	3	1	11	3	80
Self-actualization	8	4	0	2	12	0	2	2	1	15	4	1	15	13	79
B. Identification with parents															
Mother	5	4	1	5	22	5	2	4	0	9	4	0	10	9	80
Father	5	2	1	4	17	1	1	3	3	17	3	4	8	9	78
C. Internalization of parents†															
Mother	10	2	1	7	21	1	0	2	0	16	1	0	11	8	80
Father	5	1	0	3	13	1	0	1	0	14	5	2	19	14	78
D. Idealization of parents															
Mother	7	1	0	6	23	1	0	4	0	11	6	0	16	4	79
Father	11	1	0	2	24	1	1	5	0	12	3	1	11	6	78

* Operational definitions of these indices are given in the Leary manual.[9]
† These indices are new to the Leary framework.

dicate. Contrasted with the drug-abusers, only 36% of the control group reveals a significant discrepancy between self-perception and basic intentionality. It is noteworthy that when the controls have this conflict it is more likely because they see themselves as hostile when their basic orientation is affiliative. In effect, when the drug-abuser experiences a conflict of identity he is faced with a sense of isolation and doubt about "belonging." On the other hand, the control group has a basic trust and attachment to other people. Their conflict is in terms of risking exposure of tender feelings and becoming vulnerable to some form of rejection.

Section B of Tables 1 and 2 show the distribution of discrepancy scores for the conscious identification indices. Inspection of the data reveals that more than one half of both groups are "disidentified" with their parents. While both groups see their parents as "healthier" and more responsible (Schoolar et al, unpublished data), the basis of these "disidentification" patterns are somewhat different. Subjects of both groups view their mothers as more loving and affiliative than themselves, but fathers are rated more competitive and oppositional than the subjects rate themselves. Thus, both groups see themselves as weaker than their parents, but more hostile than their mothers and less so than their fathers.

Section C of Tables 1 and 2 presents the distribution of discrepancy scores for the "assimilation" of parents. These data reflect a striking difference between the two groups ($\chi^2 = 11.448$, $P < 0.001$) in their perception of mother and its relation to their basic orientation. Seventy-six percent of the drug-abusers show a high discrepancy between the two ratings (IIM and IIIMM) while only 49% of the control group have discrepancy scores greater than 44. In effect, the data of the previous section take on more meaning and allow us to look at "disidentification" from two vantage points. For the control group it appears to be based on a more recent sense of feeling different from their mothers. The drug-abusers, however, apparently have lacked any strong ties from an earlier stage of development. Interestingly enough, both groups have failed to assimilate the image of father, a not too surprising finding in view of their perception that father is strong, aloof, and not readily available for an affiliative relationship.

Section D of Tables 1 and 2 gives the distribution of discrepancy scores for the idealization indices. Inspection of these findings indicate that more than one half of the drug-abusers and controls devaluate their parents. This result for the drug-abuser seems to be the difference between his wish for a passive-dependent or rebellious role and the responsible, managerial qualities attributed to his parents. The picture for the control group is less clearcut and high discrepancies among them are evenly distributed across all of the octants.

Comment

The data in this study extend, and in some cases modify, our previous findings (White et al[11] and Schoolar et al, unpublished data) of interpersonal behavior patterns in drug-abusers. The focus of the present study was on conflict areas defined by the Leary Interpersonal System[9,10] and the implications for therapeutic intervention. When compared to a group matched for age and sex who were not abusing illicit drugs but had also sought professional help, neither group was significantly self-deceptive. Drug-abusers in particular, impress others as strong, narcissistic, and hostile with self-ratings which correspond to this description. This combination suggests a help-rejecting stance which is not conducive to a good prognosis. Leary states that "help rejectors do not stay in treatment because they present themselves as hypernormal people not consciously bothered by emotional symptoms and stressing their healthy internal adjustment."[9]

The above picture receives further confirmation when one examines the level of conscious self-acceptance. Only 48% of the drug-abusers are significantly discrepant in the way they view themselves and what they aspire to be. Such a finding would indicate that as a group, drug-abusers are not expressing significant discomfort of the kind usually present when professional help is sought. Thus, even as the drug-abuser behaves and describes himself in a socially undesirable manner, he does not want to take responsibility in asking to be helped. In fact, intervention which is explicitly defined as "help" threatens his self-reliant facade and raises the spectre of being manipulated and exploited.

In a hypothetical interaction between professional therapist and drug-abuser, it is likely that the latter would use his superficial strength to engage in a competitive power struggle, criticizing the therapist as a manipulator who really has nothing of value to offer. Given the drug-abuser's stated desire to be passive he counts on opposition to such a goal since it would be viewed as socially undesirable. Such an interaction would either (1) allow the drug-abuser to leave the therapy situation feeling vindicated in his assessment of the other or (2) if he remained in it, the result would be a mutually frustrating stalemate with both "adversaries" contending that the other is afraid to try something different. Given this possibility it is not surprising that drug-abusers will usually ask for help in an indirect way by requesting treatment for a "bad trip" or in some other impersonal form which refers to the "condition" rather than to themselves. Our control group, on the other hand, expresses a desire to be stronger and more responsible. This conforms to the expectation of what a "good patient" should want in the way of change and also confirms the role image of the therapist.

The issue of identity is one of the most critical findings in our study. Drug-abusers reveal a significant discrepancy between their self-ratings and basic intentionality. This would suggest experiencing much tension without necessarily being able to provide a cognitive scheme or label for it. The fact that this basic intentionality is not socially desirable and is loaded in the passive-hostile octants (Schoolar et al, unpublished data) connotes a serious gap in development which has apparently been of long duration. Our control group, on the other hand, differed significantly from drug-abusers in not having particular conflict in this area. Thus, the problem of identity diffusion described by Erikson[13] is particularly salient for drug-abusers. Their oppositional behavior may well be an attempt to establish a "negative identity" rather than face the anxiety of having no sense of who they are or what they mean for others. The notion of "competence"[15] may be of value here in understanding the abuse of illicit drugs. On the one hand, engagement in this activity allows for expression of curiosity needs. Furthermore, it permits the drug-abuser to gain a sense of power by "blowing his mind" through the process of treating his body as an object whose sensations can be altered. Finally, he renders himself, for the time being, impotent in the social world but can now declare what had been a liability to be a virtue.

The drug-abuser's desire for "expanded consciousness" may actually be viewed as a desperate search for a sense of belonging, even if only attained in imagery. When he speaks of a "greater identity" this is more accurately translated as a desire for an identity. Earlier it was noted that this can be achieved to the extent that society frowns on his behavior and thereby provides him a place in the real world, albeit a negative one. An added aspect of reality common to much deviant behavior is the drug-abuser's discovery of a subculture. Here, others in the same position provide him consensual validation for his feelings of alienation. It is, indeed, a paradox that this focusing on and sharing of feeling different and unacceptable to the larger society mitigates the tension such feelings originally aroused.

The identity problems of the drug-abuser are seen in bolder relief when one analyzes the data regarding assimilation of parents. While both groups fail to assimilate the image of their fathers, drug-abusers are also lacking in material assimilation. This contrasts significantly with the control group whose perception of mother is not markedly different from their basic intentionality. This has important implications for understanding the disidentification with both parents mentioned earlier. Whereas the controls currently see themselves as different from their mothers, their basic orientation is similar to the dominant and nurturant qualities attributed to their mothers. Drug-abusers, on the other hand, are not only consciously "disidentified" from their mothers but are also significantly discrepant in their assimilation of maternal qualities.

What are the maternal qualities which have not been assimilated? Fifty-nine percent of the mothers are described as strong, managerial, and narcissistic (Schoolar et al, unpublished data). This would suggest that drug-abusers have experienced a gap in the tender, sensuous aspect of life while being exposed to a model of efficiency within a prescribed goal orientation. When the description of father is taken into account, a picture emerges of a family where both parents are seen to behave in a "symmetrical" relationship[16] where little interdependency is exhibited. Thus, we have a situation where both parents are self-reliant, behaving adequately by societal standards, and living their lives in the pursuit of socially approved goals. By no means would such a home be described as "pathological" in the commonly accepted sense. Underlying this image however, is often a family characterized by *emotional environmental deprivation* and communication deficiencies.[17] In such a family there is a minimum of displayed affection and even then it is often perceived as false by the child. Furthermore, this type of family has difficulty communicating their feelings or being responsive to those of their children.

What are some of the possibilities for a child growing up in the type of family system described above? One is for the child to emulate the parental model of social responsibility and strive toward socially approved goals. If, however, the child cannot formulate meaningful goals, lacks confidence in his ability to compete successfully, or questions that closeness in this family is even attainable, he may renounce the former and seek the latter elsewhere. This still poses problems since he has not experienced intimacy in his earlier development and is fundamentally at a loss as to how it occurs. The anxiety provoked by this situation must then be circumvented since the child has learned not to exhibit fear or acknowledge weakness. Abuse of illicit drugs may then becomes one route for appearing strong and self-assured while

feeling a pseudointimacy with others engaging in the same behavior.

Generally, the drug-abuser presents a highly complex and challenging situation. Although he behaves in a socially undesirable manner he appears to experience little discomfort as a consequence. Further, he expresses an ideal of passivity from a criticizing and suspicious stance which is designed to provoke resentment and rejection from others who have been defined as helpers. In terms of therapeutic intervention, perhaps one critical factor must involve recognition of the drug-abuser's severe identity problem. In effect, it becomes necessary to disregard what he says at the outset and be more attuned to the intention of his communication. Although it has a paranoid-rebellious quality, it nevertheless reflects a help-accepting stance.[9] Basically, a therapist would have to be aware of the drug-abuser's underlying despair about making an impact in a world perceived as critical, success-oriented, and unresponsive to needs which cannot be logically justified or even articulated directly.

A critical feature of therapy with the drug-abuser would be the necessity of creating situations where he is in a position to offer something valued by the therapist. Inherent in this would be the latter's willingness to present himself as a model who can risk exposing his tender feelings and the potential of experiencing rejection. By no means does this imply that the therapist forsake his role of authority since it will be needed in providing a new model of adulthood. He must, however, be ready to assume a position which allows him to empathize with the drug-abuser's feeling of isolation and impotence. In this way the drug-abuser may learn of his ability to make an impact on the therapist without resorting to a power struggle and eventually learn to trust himself and others.

Focusing on drug abuse itself would seem to be contraindicated for two reasons: (1) basically it is not a problem which the patient can speak about in a logical cause-and-effect manner and he has learned to use words as a barrier to genuine communication; and (2) emphasizing one aspect of his behavior rigidifies his negative identity and restricts his possibility for the future to simply that of a non-drug-abuser. This would confirm his feelings of being an object in an impersonal world and the therapist would be reduced to the status of problem-solving technician. Such a role would preclude any chance of revealing the more tender and nurturant aspects of human living.

Given the drug-abuser's action orientation, therapy on an outpatient basis will require a long-term commitment. Not only is this inherent in severe identity problems but there will be many resistances to involvement combined with acting out, designed at some point to test the genuineness and stability of concern exhibited by the therapist. In some respects, the challenge to the psychiatric community seems almost overwhelming. How does one move unflinchingly into an arena where he is made to feel unwanted, incompetent, and even malevolent? To assume the role of nurturant mother, understanding father, punching bag, and student in relation to one sent for help is indeed the compounding of many contradictions. And yet, it is only through the willingness to engage in these varied interactions over a length of time (6 to 12 months at a minimum) that the drug-abuser may still achieve an identity with integrity. Perhaps the question is not whether we should try a seemingly impossible task but, rather, whether we can afford the potential waste of human life which would result from not trying.

References

1. Katz M, Waskow I: Characterizing the psychological state produced by LSD. *J Abnorm Psychol* 73:1-14, 1968.

2. McGlothlin W, Cohen S, McGlothlin M: Long-lasting effects of LSD on normals. *Arch Gen Psychiat* 17:521-532, 1967.

3. Blum R (ed): *Utopiates.* New York, Atherton Press, 1965.

4. Hartung J, McKenna S, Baxter J: Body image and defensiveness in an LSD taking sub-culture. *J Project Techn* 34:316-323, 1970.

5. Smart R, Jones D: Illicit LSD users: Their personality characteristics and psychopathology. *J Abnorm Psychol* 75:286-292, 1970.

6. Welpton D: Psychodynamics of chronic lysergic acid diethylamide use. *J Nerv Ment Dis* 147:377-385, 1968.

7. Blacker K, Jones R, Stone G, et al: Chronic users of LSD: The acidheads. *Amer J Psychiat* 125:341-351, 1968.

8. Hekemian L, Gershon S: Characteristics of drug abusers admitted to a psychiatric hospital. *JAMA* 205:125-

130, 1968.

9. Leary T: *Multilevel Measurement of Interpersonal Behavior*. Berkeley, Calif, Psychological Consultation Service, 1956.

10. Leary T: *The Interpersonal Diagnosis of Personality*. New York, Ronald Press Co, 1957.

11. White E, Schoolar J, Cohen C: Communication and drug abuse, in Wittenborn JR, Smith JP, Wittenborn SA (eds): *Proceedings of the Second Rutgers Symposium on Drug Abuse*. Springfield, Ill, Charles C Thomas Publisher, 1970.

12. Smith L, Cline M: Changing drug patterns in the Haight-Ashbury. *Calif Med* 110:151-157, 1969.

13. Erikson E: *Identity: Youth and Crisis*. New York, WW Norton & Co Inc Publishers, 1968, pp 128-160.

14. Freud S: Instincts and their vicissitudes, in Riviere J (trans): *Collected Papers*. New York, Basic Books Inc Publishers, 1959, vol 4, p 78.

15. White R: Motivation reconsidered: The concept of competence. *Psychol Rev* 66:297-333, 1959.

16. Haley J: *Strategies of Psychotherapy*. New York, Grune & Stratton, Inc, 1963, p 11.

17. Freudenberger H: Treatment and dynamics of the "disrelated" teenager and his parents in the American society. *Psychotherapy* 6:249-255, 1969.

Motivation for the Addiction to Amphetamine and Reducing Drugs*

S. Robinson and H. Z. Winnik

ABSTRACT

The psychodynamics of two cases of drug addiction are presented. Conflicts connected with the ties to the mother image and separation from the mother in early infancy are seen as a background from which the addiction arose.
The noxious influence of the drug and the addiction to it leading to mental disorders are discussed.

INTRODUCTION

Amphetamine is a sympathomimetic amine, first synthesized in 1887, which however, came into use only in 1932 as an inhalant, and in 1935 in the treatment of narcolepsy [10, 18]. Since then the drug is extensively used against various ills: obesity, fatigue, Parkinsonism, depression, epilepsy, intoxication of the central nervous system caused by depressants, and it is also recommended in behavioural disorders of children with brain injury.

Administered orally, a 10–30 mg dose generally induces alertness, mood elevation, euphoria. Considerable doses taken over an extended period of time are usually accompanied by complaints such as depression, fatigue, headaches. Cases of addiction are reported where the tolerance reached up to 1700 mg daily.

One of the first who pointed to the dangers of amphetamine addiction was Gutman, (1937) [11]. Young and Scoville (1938) [26] described paranoid psychosis ensuing as a complication of benzedrine sulphate treatment against narcolepsy. A report from the U.S.A. (1966) showed that in 201 out of 242 addicts, symptoms of psychosis appeared after the use of the drug for a period of 5 years. [4]. The magnitude of the dose which induces psychosis and the term of its use depend on individual susceptibility. The typical clinical picture of a psychosis due to amphetamine abuse presents paranoid delusions, visual and auditory hallucinations, restlessness and anxiety, insomnia and confusional states. The syndrome closely resembles a schizophrenic picture, but differs in

---

* Enlarged version of a lecture delivered at the 11th National Convention of the Israel Neuropsychiatric Society, in Haifa, May 1969.

20

so far as it fades out in the course of several days after the drug administration has been discontinued [5]. At times, however, the psychosis persists even after the cessation of the amphetamine treatment, assuming a chronic character[16]. In such cases it can be supposed that the drug was merely a precipitating factor for the onset of a psychosis, or else the result of irreversible organic changes in the brain caused by the drug intoxication. In the course of World War II, the use of amphetamine as an energizer in the Army, was started by the German Luftwaffe (Air Force). After the war, its consumption spread like an epidemic in many countries throughout the world. For instance, in the years 1940–1950 nearly a million people in Japan became dependent on amphetamine and Japanese authors were among the first to show the psychological and social dangers of the spreading abuse [17]. In the U.S.A. about 10 million people take amphetamine in various preparations [22]. A monograph by Kalant [12] which appeared in 1966, dealt with problems of amphetamine intoxication and addiction, based on observations in England and elsewhere, and in 1968 Robinson and Winnik [21] described similar experiences in Israel.

As to the personality of the addict and the motivation behind his addiction we should like to mention S. Radó (1933) [20] who explained the addiction as a need of persons under stress to alleviate their emotional states. These individuals are characterized by their tendency to depressions and states of frustration. However, by one simple movement of the hand and the consumption of the magic substance the addict is able to end these painful sensations and his suffering. This simple gesture brings back to the Ego the feeling of omnipotence experienced in childhood and makes him return to the narcissistic phase. Thus, Radó calls the addiction a narcissistic disease. There is no need of a love object outside oneself, the addict acts in accordance with the pleasure principle.

Similar statements are found in the literature (Robert Felix, Kolb, Glover) [6, 15, 8]. In the opinion of Franz Alexander [1] the drug-taking facilitates a regressive flight from difficulties and conflicts. The narcotic effect of alcohol or drugs gives physiological support to the regressive tendency to re-create a state of infantile nirvana, when the infant's needs are satisfied by the mother's breast. According to Fenichel [7] the drug action has a deep meaning for the addict. Unable to suffer tension, frustration and pain, his principal outlook is narcissistic, bent only on achieving self-satisfaction. Glover [9] illustrates the poor interpersonal relationship of the addict, for whom the drug provides enough satisfaction to replace human contact. Knight [14] compares addicts to infants who anticipate liberation from their suffering by oral incorporation and if they do not obtain satisfaction, they react by rage and disappointment.

Regarding the specificity of addiction there are different views. Some researchers speak generally of drug addiction, others consider that there may be a specific type of personality who adheres to a specific drug or group of drugs. For instance, in the view of Redlich and Friedmann, the morphine addict wishes mainly to achieve peace, serenity, to escape from tension and anxiety. The cocaine and marijuana addict tries to liberate himself from inhibitions and those who take amphetamine wish—in the opinion of these authors—to reduce their instinctual drives [19].

On hand of two clinical cases we shall now try to analyze the motivation behind amphetamine addiction.

CASE PRESENTATION

Case 1.—The patient, 25 years old, born in Israel, of Ashkenazi origin, a divorcee, was directed to this hospital because of a long-term (7 years) addiction to reducing drugs. Her use of Phenmetrazine-Hydrochloride (MARZIN) was followed by sleep disturbance, headaches, considerable loss of weight, tense restlessness. She became suspicious, quarrelsome, developed a mental dependence on the drug without which she felt depressed and defenceless. To achieve a feeling of security she increased the initial dose to over 10 pills of 25 mg. each, daily. At this hospital she received intensive psychotherapy.

In the first interview she told us that she was the youngest of 7 siblings. The parents divorced when she was 2 years old and she never saw her father since and does not remember him. (It is interesting to note in this context that initially she said that her father died when she was 2 years of age). The mother died of a chronic kidney disease when the patient was 12 years old.

In the absence of the father and mother, who was often hospitalized, a sister 17 years older than the patient and a brother 14 years her elder, became her parental images. The brother did not marry till quite recently and so was be able to support her. He fulfilled all her wishes, was tender to her, supplied her with quite an amount of money. The patient described him in a most positive manner, as a well-balanced, kind person who takes life easy. The sister, who took care of her during the long periods of her mother's illness and after her death, was described as a rigid and dominant woman.

The patient disliked the puritanical, strict rulings of her sister who was married but childless and in whose house she grew up. She was not permitted to play with her peers, was permanently told to learn and to stay at home. In this behaviour, the patient identified her with the mother, who equally insisted on her learning and receiving good marks at school. As an expression of rebellion against this strict upbringing, the patient became intimate with a boy of Oriental descent and at the age of 16 became pregnant by him. They married only towards the end of her pregnancy when she was delivered of a daughter. After a couple of years she divorced her husband.

The patient reported that she started taking anorectic drugs at the period of her conflict connected with her relations to the boy. Her use of "MARZIN" increased while she was pregnant, in her own words "she felt herself getting too fat." Consequently she ate less, partly due to loss of appetite, and partly because the thought that she was getting obese never left her. In the course of the last month before hospitalization, she lost 10 kgs. of weight.

The impression was obtained that the patient had an infantile, neurotic personality with an inclination to use defence mechanisms of denial, projection and escape.

In the course of her treatment, her ties with the mother were clarified. The patient recalls her as a strong, brave woman who made her life without her husband and alone brought up 7 children. She remains extremely attached to her mother, even now in her depressive moments, she often wishes her mother would be near her.—At later interviews, feelings of some inhibited aggressivity towards her mother became apparent. This inhibition expressed itself in such instances as when angry with the mother, the patient used to tie a kerchief around her neck and draw hard almost to choking, that is to say she turned her aggressivity towards herself or more exactly towards the image of her mother in herself. There were feelings of fear that she might contribute to the death of her ill mother. The addiction to drugs she considered a form of slow suicide, a repetition of the suicide attempt of her childhood. When the mother died, the patient felt that there was nobody for whom she should try to get on and to succeed. She stopped her music, she neglected her studies at the school where formerly she used to excel. This state came to an end when she became pregnant, she felt happy and quiet despite the fact that she was socially in an unpleasant situation, not being married. Here she identified with her mother, she felt that the child belongs to her alone, she was prepared to bring the child up by herself, just like mother who also alone brought up her 7 children.

During the treatment it became evident that in her childhood she felt herself to be the only daughter as there was a 19 years difference between her oldest brother and herself, and a 17 years difference between her and her sister. Her relations towards the siblings who brought her up were like towards parents, implicating feelings generally prevalent in an Oedipal situation. She transferred sentiments to her brother as towards a father; against the sister her attitude was negative. She competed with her, antagonized her by refusing to study at the university and by maintaining relations with the boy. She blamed her sister for being a failure in life. While under treatment, she wrote a letter threatening to commit suicide so as to show the sister "the results of her upbringing."

The feeling of loneliness in her childhood brought the patient the fantasy that she had a younger sister with whom she played in her imagination. From the time when she was 5–6 years old, she recalls that she used to cover her eyes and her ears with cotton wool and so she fell asleep with a "sweet taste in her mouth." That seems to indicate a regression to early infancy, a primitive mechanism to deny external reality.

Motivation behind the addiction to reducing drugs:

The patient started taking these when she felt that she was losing the love of her sibling-parents. She changed her dependence on these for the dependence on drugs. The new object, the pills, provided a feeling of security and courage. In the course of the treatment, the unconscious connection between food, obesity and pregnancy came to light. She recalled that when she was 6–7 years of age, she used to pick out every piece of fat from her food, out of fear that she will grow fat. She heard from children the fantasy about oral conception.—Later on, when her daughter asked her whether she was pregnant because she was so obese, she could connect her rejection of obesity

23

with the one-time infantile fantasy. This fantasy was latent in the period before treatment and came to expression only by the symptoms of revulsion against obesity.— In the same manner she also recoiled from sexual relations, was tense during intercourse and did not enjoy these relations. She was ridden with guilt feelings, a fact which she connects with her puritanical upbringing.

The reducing pills satisfy a number of desires: (a) Marzin reduces the sexual drive and helps her to control the desire which frightens her. (b) The pills act as a substitute for the dependence on the sibling-parents by whom she feels abandoned. (c) They help her to reduce in weight, to stress that she is not pergnant; they even helped her to deny her pregnancy at the time when this was really a fact. (d) When she is slim, she denies her femininity. (e) Marzin evokes her aggressive drive, she feels more secure and strong in her fight against the surrounding world, which she keeps up out of a feeling of loneliness. (f) She feels that this is slow suicide and self-destruction, self-punishment. She is afraid of her inclination to infantile and regressive dependence and here the conflict appears again. On one hand she derives satisfaction from eating, especially sweet things, but when she starts gaining weight, the anxiety connected with obesity-pregnancy returns and with it the need for reducing pills and self-starvation.

Later in her treatment the lack of oral satisfaction in her childhood was revealed and hence the fixation in the oral phase, which found its expression in the need to reduce, in fantasies of oral conception, in the fear of obesity that persistently returned during her treatment.—The mother was sick and did not nurse her, she was bottle-fed, in the first week of her life she suffered from severe diarrhea with dehydration and her life was in danger. In place of her mother, her sister took care of her since the early childhood, and the sister was not adequately trained. So she was also neglected in later years and went on lacking satisfaction of her oral needs.

The transference in treatment:

In her relation to the therapist, the inclination to dependence is strongly expressed, as is also a fear of disappointment and that she will be left in the near future. Apparently, she transferred to the therapist the feelings of frustration and anxiety that she will be left alone, as at the time her mother abandoned her during the long terms of illness and finally when she died.—Therefore, it would be better to return to her dependence on the drug. To rely on human beings is wrought with uncertainty and anxiety, the drug—on the other hand—will not disappoint her. It is easy to get it.—The only human object she is tied to is a narcissistic object—her daughter.

Subsequently, in the course of treatment, her positive feelings towards her brother came up in the transference situation. She compared him to the therapist, started to show an increased interest in the latter's personal affairs and in his family. After some months, when the negative transference was resolved, the symptoms of Erythema emotivum she was suffering from, disappeared. These formerly used to come up as an expression of inhibited aggressivity, especially when she had to face authority or public.

While under clinical treatment, which continued for over 3 years, weight fluctuations could be observed. There were periods in which she reduced very much due to her taking the MARZIN pills as a manifestation of transference-resistance to the therapist. She wished to bring shame on him, as at the time she also did to her brother. At other times when she gained weight folloiwng her inclination to eat sweets, cakes etc. she became depressed, the association between obesity and pregnancy returned and increased. At such times, she suffered from emesis as an expression of revulsion against obesity which in her fantasy was connected with pregnancy.

It appears that the patient has difficulties in giving up the symptoms of her addiction, as then she might be considered healthy and would lose her treatment and her therapist. Once she stated that the drug was a thing stronger then herself to which she was helplessly subject. This could be understood as the relation of an infant to its mother on whom it depended.

With the continuation of her treatment, her need for the drug decreased, her relations with the surrounding world improved and she was active in her work. The expression of her masochistic drives diminished. So also did the ambivalence towards her daughter. She was discharged from the hospital and continued to come for ambulatory treatment once weekly, as she expressed it "so as not to fail her daughter as her own mother failed her."

Case 2. — Adolescent, 17 years old, obese, admitted to this hospital to be treated for withdrawal from Novydrine* addiction. At admission he was found tense, restless, depressed. Orientation unimpaired, no thought disorders. Conspicuous hand tremor, dilated pupillae, accelerated pulse, all resulting from Novydrine.

Case history reveals normal pregnancy and birth. Weight at birth 5 kgs. Early development normal. At the age of two, during the War of Liberation, he was taken away from his mother for about half a year. He was then cared for by various women. When his mother returned, he hardly recognized her, mistaking her for his sister.—At this period his behaviour was peculiar.—The patient was enuretic till the age of 12, subsequently enuresis occurred sporadically till the age of 15, increasing in times of stress and frustration.

With the start of school attendance, the behavioural disorders increased. He had no patience to stay in class, could not concentrate on his studies. Nonetheless, due to an innate intelligence and quick grasp, his achievements at school were fairly good.

About this time he started gorging himself with sweets and became fat. He stole various articles from his classmates, in particular colour pencils, and he used to set fire to things. For these reasons he was directed to a pediatric psychiatric clinic where he was under treatment for a period of two years and as a result he was able to overcome his impulses to stealing and causing fires.

He became acquainted with Novydrine when 10 years of age, receiving the drug first against enuresis. The real dependence on the drug started, however, at the age

---

* Amphetamine Sulphate

of 14, when he underwent treatment against obesity. His mother, a neurotic person, sensitive to the problem of obesity, herself in the habit of taking Novydrine, very much favoured this treatment and supplied him with the drug. He felt the necessity to increase the dosage and in order to obtain Novydrine used to steal money at home as well as outside. Without the drug he felt a "nobody," empty, inferior, insecure. Taking the drug provided energy, a feeling of security, only then was he able to make contact with his friends.

In the period before hospitalization at this institute, when he reached the excessive dosage of 500 mg per diem, he suffered from insomnia and from fleeting auditory hallucinations. It seemed to him that his mother was calling him.—His sexual drive was weak and there was no interest in heterosexual relations. Under the influence of Novydrine, the sexual drive still decreased. He was very suspicious. The impression gained was of an infantile, passive personality with difficulties to create a stable object relation. As a result of treatment a slight improvement set in, the tension decreased, and the patient could be discharged from the hospital.—He returned after a lapse of two years approximately, this time for clinical treatment owing to a legal contravention, the theft of Novydrine.

The patient claimed that he could not overcome his feelings of frustration, his inability to act and his emptiness. This suffering was so intense that he felt an irresistible impulse to obtain the drug at any cost. He, therefore, broke into a pharmacy and stole a considerable quantity of Novydrine. Under the influence of the drug he felt the return of his energy, saw himself in a different light and felt himself more appreciated and better in the eyes of other people. Simultaneously, however, psychotic symptoms came up, illusions that people are talking of him behind his back, accompanied by a tremor of the hands and by tachycardia.

During psychotherapeutic interviews it became obvious that the patient was dissatisfied with his appearance. His friends always called him "Fatty," his ideal—conforming also to the longings of his mother—was to be slim.

In the course of the treatment the patient did not develop any stable therapeutic relationship with the psychiatrist, he continued to take Novydrine, a fact which he first denied and subsequently admitted. In reality he hoped to obtain from the hospital authorities a certificate of clearance stating that his drug dependence was not a manifestation of a psychological illness. When he realized that his request cannot and will not be complied with, he left the hospital.

As far as information concerning the further development of the patient could be obtained, he was able to continue satisfactorily his work in the settlement, he even married, but his interrelationships still remained superficial and unstable. The drug, however, which he apparently continues to take, represents the essential object of his affective life.

DISCUSSION

Both cases dealt with could serve as examples of the development of psychic dependence on drugs and the need of increased dosage to obtain the desired effect. While in the first case the drug intake caused insomnia and brought out character traits such as suspicion and aggressivity; in the second case, where the dose reached the excessive amount of 500 mg. daily, a psychosis ensued.

Glover and Simmel [9, 23] pointed to the close connection between depression, psychosis and drug addiction. It is stated that the drug serves in cases of dependence as a partial object with sadistic features. Its incorporation enables the addict to absorb the sadistic qualities and to externalize them in the form of aggressive tendencies. In this manner, the patient is relieved from his inward directed aggression and the resultant tension.

In our cases too the drug was used as an energizer and a means to encourage the aggressive drive against the surrounding world.—In both cases a great attachment was found to the early mother image and an oral fixation [13]; both cases suffered a severe disappointment in the wake of separation from the mother at an early age, leaving a pervading feeling of insecurity and a search for a means to relieve it. To summarize the situation in the words of one patient: "On the drug I can always rely. The pill is an object which I can always reach and which does not disappoint."

In our first case this problem-burdened relationship to the mother figure comes to the fore in an ambivalent attitude towards her pregnancy. On one hand the pregnancy is feared and connected with anxieties, on the other hand, the patient wants to become pregnant and connects this wish with the fantasy of oral conception. The latter recalls Glover's assumption of the addicts' fantasies that the drug may have an impregnative significance, but may also cause abortion [9]. The latter quality appears obvious in the Amphetamine which reduces obesity symbolic with pregnancy in the feelings of our patient. Furthermore, she considered obesity as a bad, repulsive, even dirty state which ought to be cleared up by taking the drug. Eqqually, she recoiled from sexual intercourse and therefore wished to suppress the sexual drive which she felt to be dangerous. [2].

The study of the case discloses further that the drug was unconsciously experienced as destructive and that the patient developed guilt feelings connected with its intake because in this manner she satisfied her unconscious desire for self-destruction. To expiate for these guilt feelings, later ensuing suicidal tendencies representing self-punishment, led her to a further increase in the drug dosage.

A vicious circle was thus created by the taking of Amphetamine which in the early stages brought elation and energy, and later on contributed to fatigue, depression and guilt feelings.

A similar mechanism is also one of the outstanding features in anorexia nervosa [3, 24, 25] where there is a definite rejection of obesity leading to self-starvation and loss of weight almost to the point of emaciation. Like in anorexia nervosa an incessant emesis in times when weight is on the increase, periods of constipation, a strange attitude towards food, were also found in our patient. The elevation of mood, characteristic for anorexia nervosa, was seen in our case following the intake of the drug. Further, the often encountered pattern to wit periods of starvation alternating with greedy overeating and consequent extreme oscillations in weight, were equaly observed in the case under consideration.

It goes without saying that the self-imposed starvation served also the purpose of self-punishment and alleviation of guilt in the wake of aggressive drives.

It should be pointed out finally that the patient's inner conflicts connected with the resistance against growing up, explain her rejection of femininity and pregnancy.

In some background aspects the *second case* presented here resembles the foregoing. Here too, we encounter the strong ties to the mother image [13] and the early separation which left its trace in a lack of basic trust, a constant insecurity and a lowered self-esteem, the basis for the fixation of a state of helplessness and the development of a depressive attitude. To combat this state, the patient took refuge in addiction to Novydrine which, moreover, was supplied to him at an early age by his mother. It thus becomes clear that not only does the drug constitute his stable object, but unconsciously it also replaces and represents the mother object. Simultaneously it serves to combat obesity and contributes to the realisation of the patient's ideal to be slim, which is also in line with the mother's longing to fulfil her aesthetic desires.

CONCLUSION

(1) It seems that in many cases selection of the drug on which the patient is dependent, is not accidental, but pre-determined by his specific psychic develo-ment and his personality structure, and the reaction to the specifie qualities of the drug, a fact which we tried to demonstrate in the two cases presented here.

(2) In as far as the complete liberation from drug dependency is concerned, the psychotherapeutic treatment was only partly successful. However, the fact that the suicidal tendencies were diminished, the interpersonal relations im-proved and stabilized and especially that the appearance of severe mental even psychotic symptoms connected with this sort of illness could be prevented, should not be overlooked. These rather favourable results have been attained despite the decrease in drug dependency in the course of treatment.

REFERENCES

1. F. ALEXANDER AND D. ROSS, *Dynamic Psychiatry*; pp. 134-135 University of Chicago Press, 1935.
2. D. S. BELL AND W. H. THRETOWAN, Amphetamine addiction and disturbed sexuality *Arch. Gen. Psych.* **4** (1961) 74.
3. E. L. BLISS AND C. H. BRANCH, *Anorexia Nervosa, its History, Psychology and Biology* Paul B. Hoeber Inc. 1960.

4. Committee on Alcoholism and Addiction & The Council on Mental Health: Dependence on Amphetamines and Other Stimulant Drugs.—*J.A.M.A.* **197** (1966) 1023.
5. P. H. CONNEL, *Amphetamine Psychosis.* Maudsley Monograph No.5; pp. 79–84 Chapman and Hall, London, 1958.
6. R. H. FELIX, An appraisal of the personality types of the addict. *Amer. J. Psychiatr.* **100** (1944) 62.
7. O. FENICHEL, *The Psychoanalytic Theory of Neurosis*; pp. 375–380 Routledge and Kegan Paul, London, 1955.
8. E. GLOVER, The Aetiology of Alcoholism *Proc. Royal Soc. Med.* **21** (1928) 1351.
9. E. GLOVER, On the aetiology of drug addiction *Int. J. Psychoanal.* **13** (1932) 298.
10. L. S. GOODMAN AND A. GILMAN, The Pharmacological Basis of Therapeutics; pp. 500–503 Macmillan, New York, 3rd edition, 1966.
11. E. GUTMAN AND W SARGENTH, Observations on benzedrine *Brit. Med. J.* **1** (1937) 1013.
12. O. J. KALANT, *The Amphetamines.* University of Toronto Press, 1966.
13. P. H. KNAPP, Amphetamine and addiction. *J. Ner. Ment. Dis.* **115** (1952) 406.
14. R. P. KNIGHT, The Psychodynamics of chronic alcoholism. *J. Nerv. Ment. Dis.* **86** (1937) 538.
15. L. KOLB, The Personality of Drug Addicts.—Paper presented before the Third Annual Meeting of Medical Society of the St. Elizabeth's Hosp. pp. 1–5, 1940 (cited by Felix, R.H.—see above).
16. F. LEMERE, The danger of amphetamine dependency. *Amer. J. Psychiat.*, **123** (1966) 569.
17. T. MASAKI, The amphetamine problem in Japan, *W.H.O. Technical Rep. Ser.* **102** (1956) 14–21.
18. W. MAYER-GROSS, E. S. SLATER AND M. ROTH, *Clinical Psychiatry*, p. 351 Williams and Wilkins, Baltimore, 1955.
19. F. C REDLICH AND D. X. FREEDMAN, *The Theory and Practice of Psychiatry*, p. 740 Basic Books Inc. New York/London, 1966.
20. S. RADO, The psychoanalysis of pharmacothymia (Drug Addiction) *Psychoanal. Quart.*, **2** (1933) 1.
21. S. ROBINSON AND H. Z. WINNIK, Amphetamine psychoses *Harefuah*, **75** (1968) 11.
22. A. D ROCKWELL AND P. OSTWALD, Amphetamine use and abuse in psychiatric patients, *Arch. Gen. Psych.*, **18** (1968) 612.
23. E. SIMMEL, Zum Problem von Zwang und Sucht. Report of the 5th Gen. Med. Congress for Psychotherapy, 1930 (cited by Glover).
24. H. THOMA, *Anorexia Nervosa.* Intern. Universities Press. Inc. New York, 1967.
25. M. WULFF, Ueber einen interessanten oralen Symptomcomplex und seine Beziehung zur Sucht. *Int. Z. aerztl. Psychoanal.*, **18** (1932) 28–302.
26. D. YOUNG AND W. B. SCOVILLE, Paranoid psychosis in narcolepsy and the possible danger of benzedrine treatment. *Med. Clin. N. Amer.*, **22** (1938) 637.

ILLICIT LSD USERS:

THEIR PERSONALITY CHARACTERISTICS AND PSYCHOPATHOLOGY

REGINALD G. SMART AND DIANNE JONES

One hundred LSD users and 46 nonuser controls were administered the MMPI and participated in a structured interview concerning contact with mental health agencies and social and demographic characteristics and drug use. There was a much higher incidence of psychopathology among LSD users than nonusers, with "conduct disorder" and psychosis being the most frequent profile diagnoses. Special MMPI scales provided a picture of alienation and emotional disturbances for users. Interview data suggested that these disturbances might have predated LSD use. A desire for self-change and rejection of present social values were suggested as possible explanations for the use of hallucinogens.

In the literature on LSD, much attention has been paid to its psychological effects, both short- and long-term (i.e., Katz & Waskow, 1968; McGlothlin, Cohen, & McClothlin, 1967; and Smart & Bateman, 1967). However, little attempt has been made to assess the personality characteristics and psychopathology of illicit LSD users, where adverse reactions or chronic use have not been criteria for S selection. The present paper reports a study of these variables, as assessed by MMPI responses and interview information on previous contact with mental health agencies, for a sample of illicit LSD users, varying in the number of times they have taken LSD. Comparisons are made with a matched sample of nonuser controls.

In an early study, Blum (1965) found no serious personality pathology among a group of "informal" LSD users who had taken the drug in a "party setting." But this group was very small, including only 12 Ss. Also, the study was conducted before the possession of LSD became illegal. The other groups in the study had taken LSD under special circumstances, as part of psychotherapy or in research projects and, therefore, would not be comparable to illicit users.

Twenty-one "acidheads" were studied by Blacker, Jones, Stone, and Pfefferbaum (1968), who concluded that these chronic LSD users were "passive, frustrated, angry with their parents and own life situation," and began to use LSD "often in a conscious attempt to alter their unpleasant emotions [p. 351]." These conclusions were drawn from interview material only and the study itself was more concerned with abnormal neurological findings.

Ungerleider, Fisher, Fuller, and Caldwell (1968) employed the MMPI in their study which compared 25 illicit LSD users with adverse reactions to 25 users without adverse reactions. Much more severe psychopathology was found among adverse reactions; however, those without adverse reactions were described as more defensive to the testing. No nonuser controls were used to assess the level of psychopathology in those without adverse reactions. These Ss without adverse reactions comprised a special select group composed of members of the same club devoted to drug taking and who characterized themselves as former drug addicts and ex-criminals. Such a group could not be considered representative of illicit LSD users in general.

The major aims of the present study were to determine the personality characteristics and frequency and type of psychopathology for a sample of illicit LSD users, varying in the number of times they have taken LSD, and to compare them to a matched sample of nonuser controls. MMPI responses, scored for the 8 clinical scales, the 2 nonclinical scales, and 8 special scales (Escapism, Ego Strength, Familial Discord, Authority Problems, Self-Alienation, Social-Alienation, Psychotic Tendencies, and Underachievement), and interview information on previous contact with mental health agencies, were used for this purpose. It was expected that LSD users would show more psychopathology and more family problems, feelings of alienation, and emotional difficulties (as measured by the special MMPI scales) than the nonuser group.

METHOD

Subjects. Two groups of Ss were selected for study, 100 LSD users who had bought the drug on the illicit market and 46 nonuser controls. All were paid volunteers. The illicit users were obtained through contacts with informants who knew the users prior to initiation of the project. Since pertinent characteristics of the LSD user population were not known, it was impossible to determine whether a random sample was obtained. However, special effort was made to include Ss who were older (i.e., above 25 yr.), younger (i.e., below 16 yr.), and from a variety of occupational categories. No attempt was made to select Ss who had used only LSD, and a majority had sampled a variety of other hallucinogenic and psychoactive drugs. The Ss varied in the number of times they had used LSD, some having tried it only once and a few using it more than 100 times.

In order to recruit nonusers, the interviewer gave introductory presentations about drug-related research at high schools and universities and asked for volunteers. Other nonusers were obtained through job placement agencies. Of those willing to participate, 46, similar in age, sex, and social class background, were selected. A small number of them had tried hallucinogenic and psychoactive drugs; however, none had tried LSD. Detailed information was available on social and demographic characteristics including age, sex, marital status, social class background, occupational status, education level, IQ, and drug use for both groups.

Procedure. The Minnesota Multiphasic Personality Inventory (MMPI, card form) was administered to both groups of Ss. Scores on the eight clinical and two nonclinical scales were converted to T scores and placed on profiles for comparison with normative populations. Profiles of LSD users and nonusers were first compared for the number and type invalid. A profile was designated invalid if the L (lie) score was above 7 (raw score) and/or the F (false) score above 21 (raw score) and/or the $?$ (cannot say) score above 50 (raw score). The mean T scores for both groups on the clinical and nonclinical scales were compared excluding invalid profiles. Profiles were also classified according to two-digit code groupings (5, Mf and 0, Si omitted), in which the two highest points on the individual profiles were selected (see Dahlstrom & Welsh, 1960).

The MMPI profiles were analyzed using a system of differential diagnosis, suggested and clinically validated by Meehl (see Welsh & Dahlstrom, 1956). His system involved a rapid inspectional diagnosis

which first divided the profiles into normal and abnormal. A second inspection provided a differential diagnosis of abnormal profiles into three categories: (a) psychosis, (b) psychoneurosis, and (c) "conduct disorder." MMPI responses were next scored for eight special scales. These were the Ec, Escapism scale, devised by Beall and Panton (1956); the Es, Ego-Strength scale, devised by Barron (1953); Pd_1, Familial Discord; Pd_2, Authority Problems; Pd_{4A}, Social-Alienation; and Pd_{4B}, Self-Alienation, devised by Harris and Lingoes (1955); Pq, Psychotic Tendencies factor, devised by Comrey and Marggraff (1958); and the Un, Underachievement scale, devised by McQuary and Truax (1955). Comparisons were made, excluding invalid profiles. Finally, mean T scores for Scales Ma, Hypomania; Pd, Psychopathic Deviate; and Sc, Schizophrenia; and mean raw scores on the eight special scales were compared for groups of LSD users differing in the number of times they had taken LSD.

The Ss participated in a structured interview containing questions on demographic and social characteristics and their drug use. Of special concern here was the final section of the interview which contained questions on previous contact with mental health agencies. Questions were asked about the frequency of consultations with psychiatrists, psychologists, mental health clinics, and mental hospitals and about the reasons for these consultations.

All tests and interviews were conducted by the same person.[2] In addition to the MMPI, Ss were given the Otis Quick-Scoring Mental Ability Test, Gamma Form AM.

RESULTS

Social and Demographic Characteristics

There was no significant difference between LSD users and nonusers in age, sex, marital status, place of birth, religion, education and occupation of mother and father, and IQ.

Both groups were predominantly male (above 80%), and the mean age for the groups was between 20 and 21. The age range for the LSD users was 15–37 yr., and the modal age was 19. For the nonusers, the age range was 15–30 yr., and the modal age was 20. Most were unmarried, born in Canada, and Protestant. Over one-third of their fathers were professionals or held managerial positions. The majority of fathers had completed at least 4 yr. of high school, and a one-fourth of them had attended a university. For both groups of Ss, the mean IQ was between 115 and 117. Using Wechsler's system (see Muller, 1966), over 70% of both groups fell into the

[2] All interviews and psychological testing were conducted by Karen Bateman.

31

TABLE 1
PREVALENCE OF USE OF OTHER DRUGS

Type of drug	LSD users (% of group)	Nonusers (% of group)
Marihuana	100.00	28.26
Barbiturates	33.00	15.22
Antidepressants	28.00	0.00
Stimulants	70.00	19.57
Tranquilizers	49.00	13.04

categories of Bright Normal, Superior, and Very Superior, indicating that Ss were well above average in intelligence.

Significant differences were found between LSD users and nonusers in education and occupation. LSD users had significantly less education than the nonusers; 54% of the users had completed 4 yr. of high school as compared to 73.9% of the nonusers. Also, all but three of the nonusers were students, while only 30% of the users were students, the remainder being mainly unemployed or working part-time.

Drug Use

The majority of both groups drank alcoholic beverages, but few drank excessively. However, almost twice as many nonusers as users drank as frequently as three times a week. About 85% of the LSD users, but only 39% of the nonusers, had taken psychoactive drugs, tranquilizers, barbiturates, antidepressants, and stimulants. Stimulants were the most popular, with over 70% of the users and about 20% of the nonusers having tried them (Table 1). All of the LSD users had also tried marihuana and the majority many times (61% had used marihuana over 100 times). While 28.26% of the nonusers had tried marihuana, most of them had used it only a few times.

The range in the number of times Ss in the LSD user group had taken LSD was very large, 1–400 times. However, most users had taken it fewer than 100 times (median = 7.27 occasions), while 11% had tried it only once. Most (63%) had at some time experienced adverse reactions to LSD. The most common complaint was an overwhelming state of panic, sometimes involving terrifying hallucinations. About half (56%) of the LSD users felt that

they had initially used LSD out of curiosity. A smaller number (15%) said they began to use it because their friends did. About half received their first LSD from friends and the remainder from other illicit sources.

MMPI: Validity Scales

According to the standards for judging validity, 10% of the LSD users' profiles and 6.5% of the nonusers' profiles were invalid. The profiles of the LSD users were usually invalid because of elevation on the F scale (7/10). The invalid profiles of the nonusers all had L scores above 7, but none had elevated F scores.

Elevation on F (above 17) coincided with high scores on the clinical scales, in particular the Sc (Schizophrenia) scale. The mean T score on the Sc scale for those users with F scores above 17 was 97. This tendency for a rise in Sc as the F score increases was noted by Dahlstrom and Welsh (1960). They stated that this "shows that the F score is sensitive to some of the personality mechanisms that operate in the scale for schizophrenia [p. 138]." Highly elevated F scores (16–20 raw score), according to Dahlstrom and Welsh, "(were) also obtained from test Ss who (were) resistive to the test and to the assessment process [p. 142]."

MMPI: Clinical and Nonclinical Scales

The LSD users had significantly higher scores than the nonusers (see Table 2), not including invalid profiles, on scales Sc, Schizo-

TABLE 2

MEAN T SCORES ON MMPI CLINICAL AND NONCLINICAL SCALES

Scale	LSD users	Nonusers
Hs	55.07	52.30
D	60.38	56.67
Hy	61.60*	57.19
Pd	71.92**	57.00
Mf (M)	73.66**	65.15
MF (F)	42.71	48.00
Pa	60.44	56.58
Pt	63.73	58.65
Sc	73.17**	61.65
Ma	73.14**	62.09
Si	52.00	51.40

* $p < .01$.
** $p < .001$.

phrenia; *Ma,* hypomania; *Pd,* Psychopathic Deviate; *Mf* (for males only), Masculinity-Femininity ($p < .001$); and *Hy,* Hypochondriasis ($p < .01$). The LSD user group had higher mean *T* scores on all scales with the exceptions of *Si,* Social Interest, and *Mf* (for females). On four of the scales, the mean *T* score (not including invalid profiles) for the LSD users fell above the "normal" range of variance, 30–70. These were the *Pd* scale, mean *T* score of 71.92; *Mf* scale (for males only), *T* score of 73.66; *Sc* scale, mean *T* score of 73.17; and *Ma* scale, mean *T* score of 73.14.

MMPI: Two-Digit Code

The most frequent two-digit code groupings for both groups (valid profiles only) were high *98*'s (*Ma, Sc*) or *89*'s. Twenty-one percent of the LSD users' profiles and 15.2% of the nonusers' profiles displayed these high points. This pattern has usually been restricted to the psychiatric population and has implied a rather severe hypomanic picture (see Dahlstrom & Welsh, 1960). The *94* (*Ma, Pd*) or *49* grouping occurred much more frequently in the LSD users' profiles (17%) than in the nonusers' profiles (6.5%). Those with peaks on *Pd* and *Ma* were described by Dahlstrom and Welsh (1960) as "overactive, impulsive, irresponsible, untrustworthy, shallow and superficial in their relationships" with "easy morals, readily circumvented consciences, and fluctuating ethical values [p. 192]."

There were a number of other less frequent but notable groupings. Nine per cent of the LSD users had high *84*'s (*Sc, Pd*) or *48*'s, while only 2.2% of the nonusers displayed this pattern. Dahlstrom and Welsh (1960) described people with this pattern as "unpredictable, compulsive, and nonconforming," with educational and occupational histories characterized by "underachievement, marginal adjustment, and uneven performance [p. 191]."

A small number of both groups (8% of the LSD users and 8.7% of the nonusers) had high *87*'s or *78*'s. A combination of *948* (two or more scales with the same *T* score) was common to 7% of the LSD users but none of the nonusers' profiles.

TABLE 3
FREQUENT TWO-DIGIT CODES ON THE MMPI

Code	LSD users (% of group)	Nonusers (% of group)
98 (*89*)	21.0 (9)[a]	15.2 (4.4)
94 (*49*)	17.0 (7.0)	6.5 (2.2)
87 (*78*)	8.0 (3.0)	8.7 (2.2)
84 (*48*)	9.0 (2.0)	2.2 (2.2)
96 (*69*)	2.0 (0.0)	6.5 (2.2)
984 (*498*)	7.0 (1.0)	0.0 (0.0)
93 (*39*)	0.0 (0.0)	6.5 (0.0)
83 (*38*)	2.0 (1.0)	4.4 (0.0)
43 (*34*)	4.0 (0.0)	2.2 (0.0)
82 (*28*)	4.0 (0.0)	2.2 (2.2)
64 (*46*)	6.0 (2.0)	0.0 (0.0)
Other or invalid	20.0	45.6
Total	100.0	100.0

[a] Percentage of group with code reversed.

It was clear, then, that peaks on *4, 8,* and *9,* in various combinations were most frequent among the users. The importance of these patterns was further magnified by the mean *T* scores on these scales, all of which were "abnormally" high (above 70). Except for a high frequency of the *89* or *98* code among nonusers, the frequencies of other combinations were low, and there was a very large variety of high-point pairs.

MMPI: Profile Analysis: Differential Diagnosis

From first inspection of the MMPI profiles, 96% of those for the LSD users were judged to be abnormal, that is, having a *T* score of 70 or above on one or more of the eight clinical scales. Invalid profiles were omitted from further classification. A large number of the abnormal profiles did not fit Meehl's (see Welsh & Dahlstrom, 1956) suggested criteria for any of the three diagnostic categories (see Table 3). However, 23% of the LSD users clearly followed the criteria for "conduct disorder." This category was mainly defined by a peak on *Pd,* the Psychopathic Deviate scale, a pattern thought to provide "evidence of lack of social conformity or social control and a persistent tendency to get into scrapes [Dahlstrom & Welsh, 1960, p. 188]." Another 13% of the LSD users' profiles displayed a psychotic pattern with an elevated right-hand of the profile curve and, in particular, a peak at *Sc.* An

TABLE 4

Mean Raw Scores on Selected Special Scales for the MMPI

Scale	LSD users	Nonusers
Ec	20.06**	16.53
Es	43.62**	47.40
Pd_1	5.12**	3.05
Pd_2	6.26**	4.02
Pd_{4A}	6.86*	5.53
Pd_{4B}	5.60**	3.84
Pq	3.60**	1.79
Un	11.84	11.63

Note.—Ec = Escapism; Es = Ego-Strength; Pd_1 = Familial Discord; Pd_2 = Authority Problems; Pd_{4A} = Social-Alienation; Pd_{4B} = Self-Alienation; Pq = Psychotic Tendencies factor; UN = Underachievement.
* $p < .05$.
** $p < .001$.

elevated F score was also a criterion for the psychosis category. Psychoneurosis was suggested primarily by a less elevated profile, an elevated neurotic triad, and a Pt score higher than Sc. This diagnostic category was almost nonexistent in the LSD user group. Only 1% of the profile clearly displayed this pattern.

The profiles of the nonusers were very different. Only 46% of their profiles were judged abnormal. Again, a large number were unclassifiable. However, 11% were categorized as psychosis. Psychoneurosis was also very low in this group. In contrast to the LSD users, only 2% (1 person) of the nonusers' profiles displayed the "conduct disorder" pattern.

Selected Special Scales for the MMPI

The mean difference (not including invalid profiles) between LSD users and nonusers was highly significant ($p < .001$) on six of these special scales, Ec, Es, Pd_1, Pd_2 Pd_{4B}, and Pq. There was also a significant difference between the groups at a lower confidence level ($p < .05$) on the Pd_{4A}, Social-Alienation, scale. From these subscales, it would appear that LSD users show a greater tendency or desire to escape from restrictions, have a higher incidence of familial discord, more authority problems, and feel more socially alienated and self-alienated than the nonusers. In agreement with their scores on the clinical scales, the LSD users showed more of a tendency toward psychoticism (Pq scale) than did the nonusers. The LSD users had lower scores

than the nonusers on the Ego-Strength scale, which may be interpreted as a measure of self-control. No significant difference was found on the Underachievement scale.

MMPI Scales and Frequency of LSD Use (LSD Users Only)

No significant differences were found among groups of users, differing in the number of times they had taken LSD, on scales Pd, Sc, Ma, and seven of the eight special scales. The exception was the Ec (Escapism) scale, on which the group having taken LSD only once had the highest scores and Ss who had taken it over 31 times had the lowest ($p < .05$).

Treatment for Mental Health Problems

The majority of LSD users (51%) had undergone treatment or consultation for mental health problems, compared to only 17.4% of the nonusers. The most frequent type of aid sought was from a psychiatrist, and often a number of visits were made. Twenty-two percent of the LSD users had extensive periods of therapy involving more than 10 visits to a psychiatrist, psychologist, or mental health clinic. Five percent of the users had been inpatients in a mental hospital. Few of the nonusers (6.5%) had made as many as 10 visits.

The reasons for consultation varied widely; however, there were noticeable differences between the user and nonuser groups. LSD users were frequently seen for behavioral disorders and treated for excessive anxiety, depression, hallucinations, paranoia, suicidal tendencies, and homosexuality. Family problems were also frequently stated as reasons for consultation. In most cases, Ss did not elaborate; however, it appeared that family relationships were not harmonious, and parents usually instigated consultation for the user. In contrast, the most frequent reasons given by the nonusers fell into the category of school problems: they had difficulty in their school work, were excessively tense over exams, unable to concentrate, or unable to complete assignments. Only two of the LSD users reported visiting a mental health facility because of their LSD experiences.

34

DISCUSSION

The majority of LSD users in this study were from middle- and upper-class families, but were underachievers. Their ages and IQ's were similar to the nonusers, but they had achieved several years less education. This observation was not confirmed by the scores on the special Underachievement scale, *Un*, but there are several possible explanations for this. The LSD users frequently expressed their desire or intention of returning to school, in response to questions about education. This suggested that they placed a high value on education, and that this underachievement might eventually be overcome. However, for the present, they heavy use of hallucinogenic drugs may be incompatible with regular school attendance, or school performance could be hampered by the high incidence of psychopathology among the users.

Within the user group, multihabituation was much more common than devotion to one or a few drugs. The variety of drugs taken suggests that LSD users were not seeking any particular perceptual or emotional change. Amphetamines, LSD, and marihuana differ so widely in their particular effects that the multihabituated user must be seeking a general change in perception and feeling. Perhaps this pattern of multihabituation is related to psychopathology within the group. It may be that LSD users feel themselves to be aversive and through the use of drugs aim to change, but not to change in any special way.

That there was a high incidence of psychopathology among the LSD users is clearly evident from the MMPI data. There was an extremely large number (96%) of abnormal records in the LSD user group. Their mean *T* scores on four of the clinical scales, *Pd, Ma, Sc,* and *Hy*, were significantly higher than for the nonuser group, and the first three were above the normal range of variance.

While fewer than 50% of the abnormal profiles could be accurately categorized, using Meehl's (see Welsh & Dahlstrom, 1956) system of differential diagnosis, a trend toward two types of psychopathology was indicated. These types were: "conduct disorder," characterized mainly by an elevated psychopathic deviate (*Pd*) score, and psychosis. There were almost no psychoneurotic patterns in the records.

In addition to MMPI data, psychological disturbances among a large number of the users were shown by the high incidence of previous psychiatric treatment. Half of the LSD users had been treated, many extensively, for psychological disturbances. It might be thought that this treatment was related to drug use, but most of the psychiatric consultations predated LSD use, and only a few were concerned with drug-induced problems. Also, no relationship was found, on the clinical scales of the MMPI, between pathology and number of LSD ingestions. That is, the least-frequent LSD user showed no less psychological disturbance than the chronic user. The conclusion seems to be, then, that the LSD users showed far greater psychological disturbances than the nonusers, and that much of this psychopathology predated drug use.

In light of the substantial number of LSD users' profiles characterized as "conduct disorder" (23%), another proposition could also be put forward as an explanation for drug use among these *Ss*. This type of pattern configuration suggests a tendency toward social nonconformity and a rejection of traditional values and restrictions. To some, then, drug-taking may be their chosen pattern of expressing their rejection of and deviance from the present social system. If this were the case, then the type of drug would be unimportant, as long as it was unacceptable to the larger society. For example, alcohol may not be popular, simply because it is acceptable.

The nonclinical scales of the MMPI also provided a picture of alienation and emotional difficulty. These scales showed that LSD users were more escapist, and that they felt more socially alienated and self-alienated than did controls. Also, they had experienced more family discord, more authority problems, and had less ego-strength to deal with the emotional and social difficulties created by their disturbances. Their lower ego-strength and higher tendency toward psychoticism suggests that their emotional difficulties may be of long duration. Some of these differences may have developed or increased after their drug use began, but, in any case, they would seem to present major barriers to rapid change.

REFERENCES

BARRON, F. An ego-strength scale which predicts response to psychotherapy. *Journal of Consulting Psychology,* 1953, **17**, 327–333.

BEALL, H. S., & PANTON, J. H. Use of the MMPI as an index of "escapism." *Journal of Clinical Psychology,* 1956, **12**, 392–394.

BLACKER, K. H., JONES, R. T., STONE, G. C., & PFEFFERBAUM, D. Chronic users of LSD: The acidheads. *American Journal of Psychiatry,* 1968, **125**, 341–351.

BLUM, R. (Ed.) *Utopiates.* New York: Atherton Press, 1965.

COMREY, A. L., & MARGGRAFF, W. M. A factor analysis of items on the MMPI schizophrenia scale. *Educational and Psychological Measurement,* 1958, **18**, 301–311.

DAHLSTROM, W. G., & WELSH, G. S. *An MMPI handbook (a guide to use in clinical practice and research.* Minneapolis: University of Minnesota Press, 1960.

HARRIS, R. E., & LINGOES, J. C. Subscales for the MMPI: An aid to profile interpretation. San Francisco: University of California, Department of Psychiatry, 1955. (Mimeo)

KATZ, M. M., & WASKOW, I. E. Characterizing the psychological state produced by LSD. *Journal of Abnormal Psychology,* 1968, **73**, 1–14.

McGLOTHLIN, W., COHEN, S., & McGLOTHLIN, M. S. Long-lasting effects of LSD on normals. *Archives of General Psychiatry,* 1967, **17**, 521–532.

McQUARY, J. P., & TRUAX, W. E. An underachievement scale. *Journal of Educational Research,* 1955, **48**, 393–399.

MULLER, J. (Ed.) *The clinical interpretation of psychological tests.* Boston: Little, Brown, 1966.

SMART, R. G., & BATEMAN, K. Unfavourable reactions to LSD: A review and analysis of the available case reports. *Canadian Medical Association Journal,* 1967, **97**, 1214–1221.

UNGERLEIDER, J. T., FISHER, D. D., FULLER, M., & CALDWELL, A. The "bad trip"—the etiology of the adverse LSD reaction. *American Journal of Psychiatry,* 1968, **124**, 1483–1490.

WELSH, G. S., & DAHLSTROM, W. G. (Ed.) *Basic readings on the MMPI in psychology and medicine.* Minneapolis: University of Minnesota Press, 1956.

Factors in Recognition and Management of Sociopathy and the Addictions

LEON WURMSER, M.D., and HERZL R. SPIRO, M.D.

BOTH DRUG ABUSERS AND SOCIOPATHIC PATIENTS present the physician with a plethora of seemingly somatic complaints, manipulative maneuvers, impulsive behavior, and antisocial acts. This constellation of behavior patterns all too often leaves the physician feeling unskilled, exploited, and angry. These reactions may precipitate misjudgment and mistakes. The key to managing sociopathy and drug abuse is accurate recognition followed by a calm, objective approach. While treatment of sociopaths is by and large unsatisfactory, treatment of the conditions which are often misdiagnosed as sociopathy or malingering may be highly effective. Thus, misdiagnosis and failure to implement specific treatments may lead to tragic consequences. This article will focus on recognition of sociopathy, factitious illness and malingering; differentiation of these conditions from more readily treated neuroses and psychoses; and available management techniques. Drug addiction, a specific condition classified with the sociopathic disorders, will be dealt with in much greater detail as an example of a character disorder where progress in practical treatment has occurred.

Before discussing the specific illnesses it may be well to consider the common presentations of these patients to the internist and family physician. Sociopaths, drugs addicts, patients with factitious disease, and malingerers, rarely announce their true disorder on entry to the physician's office! Their admission ticket consists of the statement: "I am ill; I suffer from . . . ." The physician then must launch into the full history, physical and laboratory examinations, which constitute an adequate work-up for a complaint which the patient knows is spurious from the outset. The doctor's feelings of annoyance alluded to above are readily understandable but rarely helpful.

When the complete battery of examinations fails to elicit evidence of a genuine organic lesion physicians are all too prone to assume that malingering, sociopathy, factitious disease, or addiction lie behind the ailment. When one considers that from 40–60 per cent of undiagnosed patients presenting for the first time to an internist will have no organic illness, the prevalence of sociopathic disorders would have to be overwhelming if most of the patients consciously "faked" the symptoms. In reality a preponderant number of patients with "spurious" complaints have *no conscious* knowledge that these complaints represent lack of organic illness. These unconsciously produced complaints are symptomatic of one of several common remediable neuroses: depressive reaction, conversion reaction, anxiety reaction, etc. Labelling these complaints with diagnoses such as sociopathy, malingering, or factitious disease results in failure to render specific effective treatment, leads to complications such as suicide, or creates chronic somatic complainers. Diagnoses imputing conscious production of symptoms should be offered on the basis of specific and clearcut diagnostic criteria rather than the physician's sense of irritation and puzzlement with the "spurious" complaint.

SOCIOPATHY

Definition and Presenting Symptoms

The American Psychiatric Association's *Diagnostic and Statistical Manual* defines sociopathic personality disturbance as follows: "Chronically antisocial individuals who are always in trouble, profiting neither from experience nor punishment, and maintaining no real loyalties to any person, group, or code. They are frequently callous and hedonistic, showing marked emotional immaturity, lack of judgment, and an ability to rationalize their behavior so that it appears warranted, reasonable and justified."

Of course, the sociopath in the nonpsychiatric physician's office hardly presents this definition as his chief complaint. Occasionally families pained by the consequences of the patient's behavior do ask for the doctor's help, and present a tale which makes the diagnosis. More often the sociopath himself will appear with a series of physical complaints. The physical complaints: (1) may be produced consciously to secure some immediate gain (malingering), i.e. escape from responsibility and punishment, obtaining medications, generating sympathy and care, etc.; (2) may be produced consciously as part of a chronic factitious illness ("Munchausen's Syndrome") (16) representing a severe psychologic disorder; or (3) most commonly represent unconsciously produced symptoms stemming from the sociopath's disordered life style.

This latter point should be emphasized in view of the often repeated generality that sociopaths inflict their discomforts on others and experience none themselves. Robins' careful research shows severe somatic distress, often disabling in degree, in 31 per cent of 94 definitely diagnosed sociopaths. Complaints such as backpain, headache, nausea, dizzy spells, dyspnea, palpitation, insomnia, chest pain, bowel trouble, abdominal pain, menstrual problems, vomiting, weight loss, and weakness are commonplace. Robins' work also indicates that psychologic distress is far more common than previously was thought. Now it should seem readily apparent that physical and psychologic distress, in the absence of any clear-cut organic lesion, occurs commonly and does not differentiate sociopathy from other disorders. So how does one go about making a diagnosis?

Recognition

The diagnosis is made on the basis of the pattern of the patient's life history, the pattern of interpersonal relationships which the patient has experienced, and the presence of certain psychologic traits. We will begin by describing the psychologic traits, which one can observe in the course of the interview and mental status examination.

The use of sociopathy as a "garbage pail" diagnosis for unpleasant patients is due at least partly to the lack of specificity of signs noted on mental status examination. In contrast, the brain syndromes, neuroses and psychoses often can be diagnosed on the basis of specific findings on mental status examination. The history of life pattern and interpersonal behavior are necessary to the positive diagnosis of sociopathy. Individuals with this condition hardly are noted for any excess of truthfulness. Thus, it is very important to speak with family members whenever possible. In attempting to pin down factitious ailments we consider this to be essential.

Mental Status Examination

On mental status examination, one usually finds a good-natured, agreeable, and even congenial patient, who may exude superficial charm and give an appearance of intelligence beyond his educational level. McCord describes this as a disease of "guiltlessness and lovelessness," while Jenkins adds that the syndrome essentially involves a lack of "the capacity for loyalty." Love, loyalty, and an ability to experience normal guilt are not qualities one can readily gain access to in a routine mental status examination. What usually impresses one is the general lack of anxiety, outward nervousness, or any deep affect. The sensitive examiner may note a certain arrogance and coldness behind the affability. There is a phony superficial "confidence man" quality. We are impressed with the global absence of such human traits as kindness and gentleness. Affect shifts in pursuit of short-term goals and may seem theatrical. There may be a rapid emergence of irritability when the sociopath is thwarted. Some of these patients can be dangerous when really blocked in their hedonistic flight. Thus, there may be the residua of frequent barroom brawls.

In the cognitive sphere the sociopath shows none of the gross irrationality or delusions of the psychotic patient. On the other hand, these patients show a profound tendency to operate from false premises and failure to learn from experience or predict obvious consequences of actions. Their inordinate capacity to rationalize past behavior nicely complements their lack of remorse or shame. Judgment is faulty and there is a tragic lack of insight into the disastrous life pattern which exploits others but destroys the self. Deceit and fraud are employed to fill immediate needs without regard to long-term effects. Thus, while the sociopath successfully victimizes many, he is his own ultimate victim. Trapped in a world of theatrical imitation his superficial grasp of reality is a thin cover for the total maladaptiveness and unreality of his existence. Cleckley has pointed out perceptively the similarities between this disorder and the true psychoses.

The psychologic traits we have just described are subtle and in and of themselves do not establish the diagnosis. It is a life history and pattern of interpersonal relationships which truly identify the sociopath.

Interpersonal Patterns

Interpersonal relationships are characterized by surface camaraderie, but no deep warmth. Robins has demonstrated that the sociopath has very few friends and few contacts with the "friends" that he has. Relationships tend to be exploitative, manipulative, and self-serving. The absence of kindly, gentle sentiments leaves a callousness and emotional bluntness. Sociopaths lack the capacity for accurate empathy, and thus are unresponsive and unheeding to the needs or feelings of others. They are perceived as untruthful, insincere, and self-centered. It should come as no surprise that such pathologic narcissism and egocentricity render the intense object cathexes requisite to happy marriage impossible. The marital history of the sociopath will usually show frequent desertions, separations, and divorces. The sex life is varigated, but impersonal, trivial, and poorly integrated. On interview there may be claims of promiscuity which would do Don Juan justice. There are often reports of deviant sexual behavior, homosexuality, and arrests pertaining to sexual offenses. The rapid change of partners does not hide the fundamental aloneness of the sociopath. Jenkins summarizes the interpersonal relationships clearly: "The psychopath lacks the capacity for loyalty and is distinguished from others by this lack. Through this lack he never attains the identification of homo domesticus. The psychopath is a basically unsocialized animal who nevertheless lives in a society."

To be in the world without loyalty or love is truly to be alone in the world. This may help one understand the childish attempt of the sociopath to relate to others through bodily symptoms and illness; to seek care as a substitute for love and warmth.

Life Pattern

On the basis of this description of psychologic traits and interpersonal behavior it is not difficult to conceptualize the life pattern led by the sociopath. According to Robins, there is often a history of wild adolescence and signs of this disorder generally appear in the early teen years (9). The over-all pattern shows a failure to follow any life plan. Education usually halts too early. The work history is terrible and there is financial dependency on others. The antisocial behavior follows no clear pattern but leads the patient to the fringes of society with repeated scrapes with the law. He often assumes alias names. The unreliability and impulsiveness lead to unprovoked desertions of home, elopements, sudden army enlistments, pointless peregrination from city to city and vagrancy.

Practical Issues in Establishing Diagnosis

Alcoholism

Alcoholism may be difficult to differentiate from sociopathy because sociopaths drink heavily and many alcoholics engage in antisocial acts. From a practical standpoint the physician should treat the alcoholism as the primary disorder (see the article on alcoholism) because the group pressure methods used with alcoholics are probably among the most effective methods in dealing with sociopathy. For the physician determined to solve the "which came first" issue a careful history of early adolescence may be helpful. Among diagnosed sociopaths

41

it has been found that the pattern of antisocial activity generally begins in early adolescence.

Hysterical Character and Conversion Symptoms

Conversion symptoms in a hysterical patient may produce the same type of mental status examination as described for the sociopath. We suspect that many an attractive young female sociopath is misdiagnosed as hysterical while many impoverished males with conversion reactions are mistakenly labelled sociopaths. We would emphasize the following differential points: (1) the early onset of sociopathy, and (2) the startling variety and severity of antisocial acts in the sociopath investing many different areas of his life and showing great chronicity and repetitiveness. Because conversion reactions may be highly responsive to psychotherapy, we recommend their specific treatment even if the conversion symptom coexists with sociopathic features. Again, when in doubt diagnose and treat the more remediable psychiatric disorder instead of dwelling on the sociopathy.

Depressions and Neurotic Disorders

Disorders such as depression should be diagnosed without difficulty on the basis of specific findings on mental status examination (see the article on depression). The life pattern and interpersonal relationships are almost the opposite of sociopathy. The fact that chronically depressed patients are labelled "crooks" and treated as though they were sociopaths is not related to any real problem in differentiating the conditions. In view of the high remission rates of treated depressives it would seem appropriate for even the busiest physician to interview his patient with sufficient thoroughness to establish the diagnosis with accuracy and institute specific treatment. This is true also of the other neuroses. Specific mental status examination findings concerning anxiety, phobias, obsessional thoughts, true dissociative episodes contrast with the usual mental status examination found in sociopaths (see above). Furthermore, the life pattern is strikingly different. Treat the symptom neurosis and hope that symptomatic remission will alleviate the more resistant character problems.

Psychotic Disorders

The unrealistic and disrupted life pattern of sociopaths may seem similar to that of peregrinating "burnt out" chronic schizophrenics.

In this form of schizophrenia mental status findings of florid cognitive disorder are less prominent than usual. The concrete thinking, autism, loosened associations, flattened inappropriate affect and "cognitive slippage" of chronic schizophrenia can be demonstrated with careful examination. Some believe that an intermediate state between sociopathic and schizophrenic disorders, "schizo-pathic disorder," exists. Certainly, some schizophrenic patients act in a highly antisocial manner. Where schizophrenia is suspected we strongly advise a trial of phenothiazine medication. (See the article on recognition and management of the ambulatory psychotic patient.)

DRUG ABUSE AND DRUG ADDICTION

Diagnosis and treatment of drug abuse have to be based on:

1. Precise knowledge of the consequences of drug use and an honest representation of this information—as contrasted by the vague mythology and thrillingly stark scare propaganda, and by the equally unscientific move towards full legalization of a number of toxic substances, and

2. The recognition that drug abuse and drug addiction are merely symptoms of severe underlying problems, mostly of a compound psychological and social nature; this implies that treatment of drug abuse alone is like treatment of a fever without considering the underlying illness.

Terminology

The terminology is at present in flux but the term "drug abuse" refers usually to the use of any drug in a manner that deviates from the approved medical or social patterns within a given culture (6). Usually psychologic dependence is part and parcel of drug abuse—the conviction of the user that his emotional well-being depends on the occasional or frequent intake of the drug. "Drug addiction" is much more specific. To qualify drug abuse as "drug addiction" two additional criteria have to be added to that of psychologic dependence: tolerance and physical dependence. "Tolerance" means that the dose of the addicting drug has to be slowly increased in order to provide for the same effect desired by the user; in turn he is resistant against higher doses: usually lethal amounts of a drug may be without *any* (desired or untoward) effect. This implies also that an effective blockage against any other drug intake of the same pharmacologic type has been established. The third criterion of drug addiction (besides tolerance and psychologic dependence) is physical dependence, a strictly physiologic need to continue the intake of the drug in order to avoid withdrawal symptoms.

We can divide the following considerations into a first part dealing with true addiction and a second part about mere abuse. The main substances of the first category are: narcotics, barbiturates, phenacetine, alcohol and nicotine; nonaddictive substances encompass amphetamines, marihuana, cocaine, and LSD.

THE ADDICTIONS

Narcotic Addiction

Most of the opiates [heroin, morphine, hydromorphone (Dilaudid), dihydrocodeinone (Dicodid)] and several non-opiate narcotics [meperidine (Demerol) and methadone] have a number of aspects in common which are of interest to the physician.

1. Contrary to widespread belief, chronic use of narcotics, including addiction, produces no known somatically or intellectually serious adverse effect. Stable addiction is compatible with a long productive life, social adjustment and physical health (11). Whether or not the patient functions somewhat below his full potential of creativity and activity, however, is neither proven nor disproven.

2. Unstable intake of narcotics (typical when the dose is not known) entails a vacillation between overdose and withdrawal; both states are incompatible with psychosocial adjustment and physical health. Overdose, in particular, very often leads to death (via respiratory arrest).

3. Other untoward side-effects and complications of the illegal use of narcotics are infections caused by unclean injections: phlebitis, subacute bacterial endocarditis (with a high mortality rate, since it is often caused by staphylococci), hepatitis, and effects of adulterations of the drug with quinine or digitalis.

4. Withdrawal without substitution is not dangerous, but uncomfortable (comparable to flu). Withdrawal becomes life threatening only in cases of congestive heart failure and other serious diseases and if carried out very abruptly by injecting an antagonist such as nalorphine.

5. In regard to its effect upon criminality, one has to distinguish the direct from the indirect effect: directly the use of narcotics is very calming and tranquilizing and thus soothes the propensities for violence. Also, during the withdrawal state the addict's possible ag-

gressiveness is dampened by the high degree of discomfort. It is the truly abstinent addict who may become violent (17).

Indirectly, however, the illegal status of all narcotics coupled with the high cost of maintaining any habit, forces the user into criminality of exorbitant dimensions. It has been estimated that in some of the larger cities up to 50 per cent of all crimes are committed in order to get drugs or the property needed to finance the drugs. Typically, the crimes are directed towards property, not life.

6. Physical signs of narcotics use are narrow pupils, lowered respiratory rate, slight hypotension, decrease of urinary output, constipation and sometimes nausea. Very important are old and new needle marks on the forearm, and traces of previous phlebitis; less important are signs of liver damage.

Treatment

The treatment of narcotics use depends upon whether one deals with: (1) acute overdose, (2) a state of addiction, or (3) a state resulting from pharmacologic withdrawal.

1. *Overdose* is a medical emergency of utmost gravity. The typical signs are: stupor or profound coma, low respiratory rate, cyanosis, progressive fall of blood pressure, and pinpoint pupils. Emergency treatment consists in prompt restoration of respiration by such means as oxygen therapy and artificial ventilation and injection of narcotic antagonists (nalorphine or levallorphan), 3–5 mg. intravenously, judiciously repeated over the course of 20–30 minutes (5).

2. *Addiction* is treated best by gradual withdrawal from all narcotics with decreasing amounts of methadone; the amount of methadone is gauged so that only mild withdrawal symptoms appear. Abstinence is reached within 7–10 days. Usually withdrawal is carried out on an inpatient basis. Novel attempts at protracted withdrawal with methadone on an outpatient basis combined with rehabilitative measures are still in an experimental state. In this connection, one has to keep in mind the fact that addicts tend to exaggerate vastly the extent of their habit.

3. As easy as the *pharmacologic withdrawal* is, as difficult it is to treat the psychologic dependence and the underlying emotional and social problems. At present it seems most rational to start out: (a) with strict surveillance in form of regular urine controls (thin-layer chromatography), counseling or psychotherapy and a measure of constraint in the form of civil commitment, in order to maintain the motivation for treatment. Many addicts will fail with such an approach (8).

45

A number of alternative or sequential methods have been used with varied success: (b) the use of narcotic antagonists (nalorphine, cyclazocine, naloxone): side-effects or shortness of duration or physical dependence limit their usefulness; (c) Methadone maintenance (4): the social benefits are unquestionable, but the psychologic consequences have not yet been studied sufficiently; furthermore, one has to be aware that one engages with this method in a partial legalization of narcotics addiction, usually for a lifetime; (d) therapeutic community (like Daytop, Phoenix House, Synanon) with strong emphasis on group pressure and solidarity, shaming of the deviant, and long-term re-education of the individual. At present, a sequential and parallel combination of several methods appears most promising (2,19).

Barbiturate Addiction

Most of the points made in regard to narcotics addiction pertain to barbiturates and glutethimide (Doriden) as well. What is different, however, is: (1) the drug is usually taken by mouth so that the complications of injection in the form of infection are missing; (2) since they are legally available their dosage is usually well known so that accidental overdose is less likely and the vacillation between overdose and withdrawal less frequent; (3) sudden withdrawal is very dangerous, since it leads to convulsions and a delirious state and, unless appropriately treated, to death. Once delirium develops even administration of large doses may not suppress it.

Treatment

Since treatment of barbiturate use varies, the physician must distinguish between acute intoxication, withdrawal, and psychologic dependence.

1. *Acute intoxication.* Treatment includes maintenance of respiration (including oxygen therapy), and treatment of shock and renal failure (e.g., blood transfusion, hemodialysis). The use of analeptic agents is controversial. No specific antagonists are known; bemegride (50 mg. intravenously, in 3–5 minute intervals) has been recommended (15).

2. *Withdrawal treatment.* Pentobarbital is a suitable substitute for barbiturates as well as for glutethimide (Doriden), paraldehyde, chloral hydrate, meprobamate and even alcohol (there exists cross-tolerance between these types of addictions). Most patients require 0.2–0.4 grams every 6 hours. Withdrawal may take 10–20 days (7).

3. *Psychologic dependence.* Very little is known about the long-term treatment of barbiturate users and their psychologic dependence. Urine surveillance, strict supervision (including parole), psychotherapy, therapeutic community living would appear to be rational measures, but nothing is known about the success rate of any type of therapy.

Phenacetine, Alcohol and Nicotine Addiction

Phenacetine forms part of most analgesics and is often combined with barbiturates (e.g., Empirin, Fiorinal). Reports from Europe indicate that true addiction with physical dependence and massive tolerance occurs. Kielholz and Battegay write: "Since World War II this addiction has become almost a national disease, particularly in the German speaking part of Switzerland." The consequence of long-term use of these analgesics consists in: (a) interstitial nephritis and pyelonephritis with subsequent death due to uremia, and (b) blood damage (anemia, sulf- and methemoglobin), also often leading to death. Of course, this addiction is frequently complicated with barbiturate addiction.

We cannot dismiss the suspicion that this form of addiction and the ensuing renal and hematologic complications may be much more widespread in the United States than it appears on the surface because most physicians are not aware of this possibility. The typical patient with this addiction is a woman taxing herself beyond her capacity, suffering from headaches, sensitive, touchy, and showing in the late stages of the addiction a characteristic ashen, even leaden discoloring of her skin, intractable headaches, exhaustion, and irritability.

A discussion of alcohol and nicotine addiction, perhaps socially, physically, and emotionally, the most devastating forms of addiction, has to be omitted in this context.

ABUSE WITHOUT ADDICTION

Amphetamines and Cocaine

Recognition of amphetamine and cocaine users is not too difficult: the agitation and restlessness, the driven, flighty, uncontrolled, irritable behavior, the tangential, jumpy, often fragmented way of talking, the straw-fire type of rage are typical. Tremulousness, insomnia, and loss of appetite are well known. Most important is the inclination to paranoid reactions: suspiciousness and rage based on delusional misconceptions can lead to senseless outbursts of violence and murder. Hallucinations may occur with high usage, and often the picture cannot be distinguished from that of an acute schizophrenia.

The combined use of barbiturates and amphetamines, e.g., in the form of Dexamyl, is very frequent because of the synergistic quality of their euphorizing effects and the mutually antagonistic quality in regard to sedation and stimulation. It is our opinion that the use of such combinations should be discouraged in every situation including depressions and obesity.

Therapy for amphetamine users consists in treating the underlying personality disorder. Paranoid symptoms precipitated by the abuse can be treated with phenothiazines. Of course, even high doses can be withdrawn abruptly.

Marihuana

Marihuana smoking has the following direct effects:

1. It produces a mild sense of euphoria and relaxation and some sensory distortion; it interferes with work and driving ability, though probably less so than alcohol.

2. Sporadic use can precipitate in susceptible individuals prolonged and severe emotional disorders: depressive and paranoid developments, reactions of strong anxiety and rage (18).

3. Chronic users show a general decline of purposiveness in their life, are apathetic, decrease in their scholastic achievements, and most typically, are rambling and tangential, fragmented and disorganized in their thinking and talking, shifting and drifting in their dealing with a topic. Particularly characteristic are the long, empty silences, the unfinished sentences, the loss of the thread of the conversation or of the "point" of a question or discussion.

4. Physical signs include: reddening of the eyes, coughing, rapid heartbeat and some unsteadiness.

Again therapy consists in treating the underlying neurotic or psychopathic problems. It is noteworthy that the symptoms described under 2 (above) respond excellently to brief, intensive, focally oriented psychotherapy. The other symptoms disappear with the discontinuation of the habit.

Other substances, as mescaline, nutmeg, STP (DOM) have generally the same effects. Lysergic acid diethylamide (LSD) has the same, only more, intense results. Suicide and homicide may ensue (again just an increase of the reaction described under 2). Chromosomal damage has been widely publicized. Glue sniffing—another psychodelic—can be lethal since it produces brain and kidney damage.

PSYCHOTHERAPY OF THE DRUG ABUSER
AND DRUG ADDICT

The problem of treating the drug abuser and addict is similar to that described for the therapy of other sociopathic conditions and personalities. It can be summarized in three principles:

1. The patient seeks, in a pervasive fashion, external solutions for internal conflicts. Limitations, restrictions, warning and punishment as well as rewards and gratifications are accepted exclusively in the form of external actions. Instead of dealing with matters of conscience, anxiety, purpose of one's life, and mastery of one's infantile wishes, every problem is projected into a pill, into the threat by a punitive authority or into conning other people and agencies into providing him with an unending, limitless gratification. This leads to the second principle, the supreme and unmitigated power of the pleasure principle.

2. The patient manifests an inability to renounce gratification in the here and now, an unwillingness to accept delays, detours and refinements of pleasures, rage and despair if he does not get immediate satisfaction, and hungry greediness and compulsive insatiability of pleasures.

3. Infantile self-centeredness and magical expectations, and demanding and helpless behavior rule the relationships of the drug abuser and drug addict with their parents, spouses, friends and children. Disregard for the needs of others, exploitation of others for their own demands, vacillation between admiration for the other person as long as he is seen as vested with magical power and as a well of plenty, and rage and disregard for the other as soon as he fails to remain a source of omnipotent support—all this leaves the people around the drug abuser and addict enraged and embittered unless it does not out-exploit the exploiter himself. The latter indeed is often the hallmark of the families whose offspring turn to drugs. These relatives may not allow themselves the easy escape with drugs, but rather typically, though not always, we observe an unpredictable shifting back and forth between overpermissiveness and self-indulgence in certain regards and harshest, most inconsiderate severity and sadistic punitiveness, the giving in to temper tantrums of their

own where no holds are barred. Very often the drug user comes from a broken family.

In the treatment of these personalities one can chose between two paths: one may either try to educate the patient with measures of reward and punishment or one may attempt to help him to mature by renouncing his infantile demands with the help of such measures as being a guiding model and ideal, through insight or through group inspiration.

Role of the Family Physician

The role of the nonpsychiatric physician in the treatment of drug abusers and addicts is of crucial importance.

1. As a family physician one may start out with preventive efforts. His role is to make parents aware of that peculiar mixture of seductive permissiveness and indulgence with angry and demanding punitiveness which sets the stage for later sociopathic and drug abusing behavior. In particular, he may point to the incongruence of self-indulgence with alcohol, smoking and limitless abundance and the vindictive prohibition and restriction of some of the wishes and customs of their teenage children. The adolescent is extremely sensitive to that kind of hypocrisy and shows his contempt by his actions toward his parents and doctors.

2. Skillful treatment of the drug-using adolescent and young adult lies mainly in the hands of the family physician and internist. A nonvindictive non-moralistic approach calmly describes without exaggeration the effects and risks with certain drugs, focuses not on the symptom (the drug use), but quickly moves on to some of the more important psychologic difficulties such as the problems of living in an overly complex and overwhelmingly stimulating culture, the hypocrisies and strains in our social fabric, the tensions in their families, the conflicts between peer group and the "establishment" (schools, parents, and community-at-large), and the difficulty in mastering the onslaught of sexual, aggressive, and narcissistic urges. One need not be a psychiatrist to deal with such problems of maturation and self-discipline and to help others to live a more rational and harmonious life.

3. If more severe neurotic or character disorders appears, the physician is well advised to refer the patient early enough to an experienced, well-trained psychiatrist for evaluation.

4. The criteria of various forms of drug abuse should be kept in

mind. If there is suspicion of use of narcotics, hypnotics and amphetamines, one may send the urine to the laboratory where reliable thin-layer chromatography tests are carried out for a modest fee. At this time only a few laboratories are experienced enough to do this test with a high degree of trustworthiness.

5. If the physician knows of a chronic narcotics user, he may contact the United States District Attorney and inquire as to which provisions of the Narcotic Addict Rehabilitation Act of 1966 may be applicable to his case. Also he may request information from the United States Department of Health, Education and Welfare, Public Health Service. The three titles of this act relevant for the physician provide for court commitment of eligible drug addicts who have been convicted, or charged with an offense, or who voluntarily request treatment to inpatient care (primarily in Lexington) and to an outpatient rehabilitation service. Such a procedure may be initiated by the court, by the addict himself or by a related individual. Eligibility depends upon an examination indicating that the patient is likely to be rehabilitated through treatment.

Comparable laws may be enacted shortly for the other drugs described in this article.

6. It is of cardinal importance that every physician is aware of the signs of an overdose with any of the drugs mentioned and that he begins immediately the necessary countermeasures as described above.

7. Nowhere is the attitude of godlike superiority, of the unquestioned right for authority, and of dogmatic self-righteousness assumed by many physicians tested as severely as by drug users. They may seduce him either into the stance of benevolent Savior with magical potency, or if he fails, into a punitive, vindictive attitude of a spurned parent. There are few places where the physician may be taught as much to be humble and to scrutinize carefully his own unreasonable expectations and self-glorifications.

References

1. American Psychiatric Association *Diagnostic and Statistical Manual on Mental Disorders*. A. P. A., Washington, 1952.
2. BRILL, L., and JAFFE, J. H. Relevancy of some new American treatment approaches for England. *Brit. J. Addict.* 62:375, 1967.
3. CLECKLEY, H. *The Mask of Sanity*. Ed. 4. Mosby, St. Louis, 1964.
4. DOLE, V. P., NYSWANDER, M. E., and WARNER, A. Successful treatment of 750 criminal addicts. *J. Amer. med. Ass.* 206:2708, 1968.

5. JAFFE, J. J. "Narcotic Analgesics." In *The Pharmacological Basis of Therapeutics*, Ed. 3, L. S. Goodman and A. Gilman (Eds.), Macmillan, New York, 1965, Ch. 15, p. 262.
6. JAFFE, J. H. "Drug Addiction and Drug Abuse." In *The Pharmacological Basis of Therapeutics*, Ed. 3, L. S. Goodman and A. Gilman (Eds.), Macmillan, New York, 1965, Ch. 16, p. 285.
7. *Ibid.*, p. 303.
8. JENKINS, R. L. Psychopathic or antisocial personality. *J. nerv. ment. Dis., 131:*318, 1960.
9. JOHNSON, A., and SZUREK, S. Etiology of sociopathic behavior in delinquents and psychopaths. *J. Amer. med. Ass. 154:*814, 1954.
10. KIELHOLZ, P., and BATTEGAY, R. Treatment of drug addicts in Switzerland. *Comprehens. Psychiat. 4:*229, 1963.
11. KOLB, L. *Drug Addiction, A Medical Problem.* Thomas, Springfield, 1962, p. 117.
12. KURLAND, A. A., WURMSER, L., KERMAN, F., and KOKOSKI, R. Deterrent effect of daily urine analysis for opiates in a narcotic out-patient facility: A two and a half year study. Reported at the 29th Annual Meeting of The Committee on Problems of Drug Dependence, National Research Council, Feb. 16, 1967.
13. McCORD, W., and McCORD, J. *Psychopathy and Delinquency.* Grune, New York, 1956.
14. ROBINS, L. M. *Deviant Children Grown Up: A Sociological and Psychiatric Study of Sociopathic Personalities.* Williams and Wilkins, Baltimore, 1966.
15. SHARPLESS, S. K. "Hypnotics and Sedatives." In *The Pharmacological Basis of Therapeutics*, Ed. 3, L. S. Goodman and A. Gilman (Eds.), Macmillan, New York, 1965, Ch. 9, p. 123.
16. SPIRO, H. R. Chronic facitious illness: Munchausen's syndrome. *Arch. gen. Psychiat. 18:*569, 1968.
17. WURMSER, L. Drug addiction and drug abuse—A synopsis. *Maryland med. J. 17:*68, 1968.
18. WURMSER, L., LEVIN, L., and LEWIS, A. Chronic paranoid symptoms in users of marihuana and LSD as observed in psychotherapy. Presented at the 31st Annual Meeting, Committee on Problems of Drug Dependence, National Research Council, Feb. 26, 1969.
19. WURMSER, L. Four-phased outpatient treatment program for narcotic addicts. (Unpublished.)

DRUG DEALING PARANOIA

MICHAEL SERBER

Summary.—Drug dealing paranoia is a recently observed clinical entity which has been successfully treated in 2 of 3 youthful cases. Onset of paranoid symptomatology was the direct result of selling drugs in a "drug scene." The paranoid symptoms observed ranged from moderate to severe, and complete remission of symptoms in all cases reported occurred within 1 wk. after cessation of drug dealing and temporary physical removal from the drug environment. In areas where drug use is extensive this syndrome is likely to be exhibited by patients who seek attention and thrills by becoming "amateur" drug dealers. The psychotherapy consisted of firm counseling to give up the drug dealing and a temporary change of environment. Minor tranquilizers were prescribed in 2 of the 3 cases.

Paranoid states are a common condition in our society. The onset of paranoid symptomatology has been reported with the use of hallucinogenic and other drugs. Recently, with the advent of amateurs dealing in or selling drugs, a new occupational hazard, drug dealers' paranoia, has made its appearance. The cases described were all in their late teens or early twenties. They used the drugs in moderation and entered the "business" for thrills or attention from their peer group. One of the three cases I have seen began dealing in drugs because he wanted some money quickly but later said he really enjoyed, for a limited time, being the recipient of a great deal of attention. The cases I have seen would, when not dealing in drugs, be diagnosed as schizoid personalities. Their interpersonal relations were poor. They were loners, frequently depressed and lacking the techniques necessary for successful interpersonal relations.

The paranoid state became manifest usually after 3 to 6 wk. of drug dealing when it appeared that they could no longer handle both the attention and the high stress levels necessary to sell drugs. The clinical manifestations ranged from paranoid personality to a state which without a careful history has been diagnosed as paranoid schizophrenia. The paranoid condition in all three cases cleared within 1 wk. after the cessation of drug dealing and the actual physical withdrawal from the drug scene. The use of major tranquilizers was unnecessary even though the acute clinical appearance might have warranted their use. The increased traffic in drugs and the subsequent involvement of young people might make the syndrome relatively common where drug traffic is particularly heavy. It is interesting to note how quickly the symptomatology cleared after cessation of the anxiety-producing activity. Psychotherapy consisted in all three cases of forceful advice as to the necessity of giving up drug dealing and temporary environmental change. Minor tranquilizers, such as chlordiazepoxide or diazepam were prescribed to two of the patients during this period.

Case I

L.M., a 19-yr.-old female college sophomore, was a product of a broken home. She lived with her mother, a successful executive, who had poorly fulfilled her parental responsibilities. The patient had made two suicide attempts at 17 after she had complained of being unhappy at school and having few friends. At 18 she began using LSD and marijuana which she described as a "groove." At 19 she moved away from home and began dealing in drugs, enjoying the surge of attention which accompanied her new endeavor. After 4 wk. of dealing she called for an appointment. When she was seen, she appeared disheveled and confused saying that the FBI was after her and she had been afraid to leave the apartment she shared with two other girls. She told of her drug dealing, and it was strongly suggested that she return home temporarily and cease dealing in drugs immediately. She was given diazepam (10 mg. T.I.D.). One week later, when seen again, she was no longer paranoid and a 2-yr. follow-up has indicated no exacerbation of paranoid symptoms even though she continued having major problems in her interpersonal relations and used marijuana sporadically.

Case II

An 18-yr.-old male with a history of being a loner graduated from high school and entered a large state university. He began living in a dorm and was introduced to the use of LSD and marijuana which he would use on weekends. Six mo. after he arrived on campus he began dealing in drugs because he wanted to make $500 quickly. Within 3 wk. after he began selling, he felt that people were after him, his teachers were out to get him, and his roommate was going to turn him in to the authorities. He became frightened and left campus to go home for 1 wk. His symptoms completely cleared during that time and he decided to drop out of school.

He sought out treatment 6 mo. after his paranoid attack complaining of his loneliness and his inability to return to school. He has been free of any paranoid episodes and has ceased the use of marijuana and LSD.

Case III

A lonely 22-yr.-old girl has been in psychotherapy for 2 yr. Finally she was able to leave her parents and complete college but still felt herself as inadequate in most situations. She had used marijuana occasionally since she was 18. During a trip to Mexico with a boyfriend she managed to buy six kilos of marijuana which she sent home stuffed in armadillos. When she returned, she began selling the marijuana "for kicks." Within 3 wk. she became extremely suspicious, broke up with her boyfriend, could not trust anyone, and sat around her home afraid to leave. She asked for professional help at this time. She was advised to stop drug dealing and go home to her parents for 1 wk. She was given chlordiazepoxide (10 mg. Q.I.D.). When seen 5 days later, her paranoid symptoms were gone, and she was able to resume her regular job and social relations.

SURVEY OF OPIATE ADDICTION AMONG FEMALES IN THE UNITED STATES BETWEEN 1850 AND 1970

Walter R. Cuskey, T. Premkumar and Lois Sigel

SUMMARY

This survey paper represents the result of an exhaustive review of several journals and many books. The primary focus has been on the changing pattern of opiate abuse among females. The survey covers a period spanning more than a century, beginning in 1850.

An historical overview is presented of drug abuse among females, the magnitude of the problem and society's view of addiction in the major periods of American drug history. These periods are separated by landmark events that have influenced the drug scene profoundly. They include the period before 1914 when the Harrison Act was passed; the period between the passing of the Act and the establishment of Federal Drug Treatment Hospitals at Lexington and Fort Worth; the interim period till the outbreak of World War II; and the post World War drug scene.

The review traces the behavioral and social changes characterizing the different periods. These include mean age of addicts, geographic distribution of addicted females, race, and religious persuasion. Other personality factors examined include deviancy and personality disorders. Family circumstances, addicted couples, marriage and problems of divorce and separation are also analyzed. Problems associated with pregnant addicts and the effect of addiction on new-born babies are discussed. The harmful effects on babies of non-opiate abuse by mothers is also presented.

Reference is made to special sub-groups of female addicts and a brief prognosis of future drug patterns is presented.

INTRODUCTION

Any discussion of, or survey on, female addiction must start from the rather apparent fact that females are different from males, and that the interaction of addiction with these differences must have characteristic social, psychological and physiological results and implications. The differences are not only physical; they are also related to the roles, functions and freedoms of females in our society, and to their abilities to cope with, or be defeated by, the problems that addiction raises. For instance, the effects of the addiction of a pregnant woman or a mother are generally a good deal more serious, both to society and to the child, than the addiction of the father, who may have disappeared immediately after conception.

Further, just as there are substantial addiction differences between males and females, there are very probably substantial differences between different kinds of females, and between individuals. Would standard demographic breakdowns, such as age, race, socio-economic level and the like, reveal the patterns best, or would it be better to use the material we have to set up typologies? Obviously, the black prostitute who is kept subservient to her pimp through addiction to heroin represents a different kind of person and problem from a white suburban girl looking for relief from discomfort and boredom. Would considering both as variations on a common scale of "addiction" really describe them or outline the influence of drugs in our society?

Severe drug abuse, especially narcotic addiction, tends to impose its own personality on that of the addict, particularly in America, where the cost usually imposes a criminal life style. Many addicts, despite original differences, take to acting as though they came from a common bin. But the patterns of women are still distinct from those of men. They differ from one another, too, but they do express their femininity in common ways. There are fewer female addicts, and their forms of use and abuse are somewhat different. They are, by nature or social role, more law-abiding, and when narcotics became illegal in the United States, when their use in patent medicine was curtailed and most sources became illicit, the female addict population fell much more rapidly than that of the male. Women do not have the equipment for, nor are they as temperamentally given to, violence; they (again whether by nature or role) tend to be more passive, so the forms of criminal or moneyraising activities they use to keep going are seldom violent. A very large proportion become prostitutes. Addiction has devasting effects on pregnancy, childbirth and infancy: babies are smaller and they suffer withdrawal pains and other maladies; more are still-born or die soon after. Families and the future of the race depend more on women. Women are treated differently in courts and jails, go to prison on different charges, and adjust differently and more unhappily to prison life.

SURVEY LIMITATIONS AND ISSUES

A paper of this type generally starts the body of its presentation with a form of defensive apologetics: the material was more recalcitrant than anyone could have expected, and sources were scarce. The facts are that relatively little hard, useable data about female addicts exist, and much of those use varying frames of reference, selection-criteria, time spans, or fragments of the population. As a result, findings often do not provide much more than scattered pieces from different jig-saw puzzles. Over time, the definitions of "addiction" themselves have changed. Many voices have spoken, some of them clearly and profoundly; but still, too many have spoken with parochial accents, or even in different languages.

This paper, therefore, found it necessary to impose its own, we hope unifying, frames of reference and criteria. These frames of reference will be historically-comparative, typological, and will emphasize patterns and trends instead of statistics. It is easy to point out, and true enough, that drug addiction today is different from previous periods, and from country to country, and that looking backward can be very misleading. Women are not only different from men but from their grandmothers, and so are their patterns of response and addiction. Patterns of drug addiction and procurement have also changed. We have, in short, a whole new "bag", both of narcotics and behavior. This being so, what good is history?

But these facts and questions themselves are based on the assumptions that change occurs and is important; and that change will continue. More than in any other western nation, drug addiction in the United States tends to reflect its past and foreshadow its future.

Finally, this paper cannot presume to cover the literature on all drugs of abuse, nor even all "dangerous drugs". Therefore we have concentrated on the narcotic drugs, primarily the opiates. They are the most addictive, and have had the greatest social impact in the United States up to and including the present. Fuller treatment of the growing impact of exotic combinations, the hallucinogens, hypnotics and stimulants will be deferred to other articles.

HISTORICAL OVERVIEW

America had more addicts during the last half of the nineteenth century than it has today, despite the tremendous and frightening increases since World War II, and the skyrocketing rises in the past few years. This is true even though the total population before World War I was less than half of that today, and despite the even more significant fact that the U.S. was much less urbanized then, and drug addiction has a high correlation with urbanization. No other western nation has such a history of drug abuse.

Female Addiction, 1850–1921

In Britain, until 1926 at least, a drug addict was "a rather rare and even exotic creature, confined almost entirely to medical professionals with a fringe of bohemians"[1]. Not so in America. Since 1850 at least, the use of opiates in America has been greater than our officials could cope with, understand, or record accurately. At the beginning of the century, as today, authorities assumed that they had not approached the true figure by half. This history has had a great and often determining influence on the control methods and philosophy our nation has employed against drugs; and the differences in histories between America and such countries as Britain and France have made it difficult to exchange information, or to profit from the solutions they put forth.

In 1867 a writer could say:

The habit is gaining fearful ground among our professional men, the operatives in our mills, our weary serving women, our fagged clerks, our former liquor drunkards, our everyday laborers, who a generation ago took gin. All our classes from the highest to the lowest are yearly increasing their consumption of the drug.[2]

A druggist in 1870, describing the increased use in his New England town of 10,000 said that, though the population had not increased in 20 years, his sales of opium had gone up from 50 pounds to 300, and sales of laudanum, a solution of opium in alcohol, had quadrupled. His experience was typical.

All authorities who collected data on addiction, or observed it, remarked on the large number of women addicts. *The fact is that during this entire period, from before the Civil War until immediately following the First World War, female drug addicts outnumbered male addicts two to one!* In view of our present situation and our present illusions, this fact is so astonishing that it should be repeated: from about 1850 until 1920, when the restrictions of the Harrison Act of 1914 became firmly established, twice as many women as men were addicted to narcotics. (The Harrison Act did make some technical provision for medical control and treatment of addicts, but the overall effect, from the way it was enforced and interpreted by the Federal Bureau of Narcotics, was to make narcotics illegal, and to shift the control of addiction from a medical to a law enforcement problem and responsibility[3].)

During the Civil War the widespread use of morphine as a pain-killer for the wounded administered with the newly-developed hypodermic syringe created a mass of opiate-addicts greater than at any time in our history.

There was a parallel development among women. In 1868 Horace Day spoke sympathetically, if perhaps too romantically, of the "anguished and hopeless wives and mothers, made so by the slaughter of those who were dearest to them, [who] have found, many of them, temporary relief from their sufferings in opium".[2]

In 1913 Tennessee passed an Anti-Narcotic Law which included provisions for providing maintenance dosages to the addicted, and for the filing of data. Reporting on the operation of this law in 1915, L.P. Brown, State Food and Drugs Commissioner, said that there had been 2370 persons registered during the preceding year — 784 men and 1586 women. (He projected these figures to indicate a total of about 270,000 addicts for the entire United States "by no means so many as sensational writers appear to want us to believe [but]. . .bad enough".[2])

Throughout the studies and surveys made of addicts from pre-Civil War days to about 1920, the high ratio of women to men is constantly emphasized. In 1877, Marshall presented a study to the Michigan State Board of Health. He found that "the total number of opium eaters reported in the places given is 1313; of these 803 are females and 510 are males."[2] In a survey of druggists in 1885, Hull reported that he found 215 users of opium in various forms, including multiple use (morphine 129, gum opium 73, laudanum 12, paregoric 6, McMunn's Elixir 4 and Dover's Powder 3). Of these, 86 were men, and 129 women.[2] In 1913 Jacksonville, Florida had a law requiring druggists to report sizeable sales of opiates (three grains of morphine or equivalent) to the health office; sales were recorded to 228 men and 313 women. Projecting the same percentages for the entire nation (estimated population in 1913 of 97,163,330), Terry and Pellens gave the incidence as 782,118.[2] Current estimates (1972), on addiction with a national population well over twice as large, are 250,000.[4]

In many ways the period from pre-Civil War to immediate post World War I was like a film negative of the present. In 1913 Negroes made up a small majority of the population of Jacksonville — 34,200 blacks to about 33,000 whites; yet male addicts were 133 white to 40 black, and females 219 white to 94 black.[2] We do not have comparable figures from Jacksonville today but authorities agree that the racial percentages have shifted radically towards the darker minority groups.

According to figures from the hospital at Lexington, Kentucky, in the last thirty-odd years we have moved from the 11.6% of non-white admissions reported by Pescor[5] in 1936 to the 56% non-white reported by Ball and Chambers[80] in 1966, with the trend continuing. A study of female addicts between 1961 and 1967 by Cuskey *et al* shows similar effects[6].

In other respects also the old pictures were reversed. Different kinds of addicts came on the scene. In the post Civil War years a number of druggists pointed to the high incidence of use among physicians themselves; and most authorities blamed much addiction, even the "vast majority", on "the unpardonable carelessness of physicians, who are often too fond. . .of relieving every ache and pain by the administration of an opiate".[2]

In short, most of the addicted (and this must include the wounded of the Civil War who became hooked), were helped and recruited to this condition by the medical profession. They were either medical personnel themselves, or were addicted during treatment by prescription. The highest percentage of female addicts started by taking opiates to relieve pain, rather than for euphoria or escape. They were started by ignorant, frightened or harassed physicians taking the easy way, or through opium-laden home-remedies and patent medicines. (In Eugene O'Neill's autobiographical, *Long Day's Journey Into Night,* the mother's addiction to morphine is blamed on an incompetent doctor[7].)

Before regulation, the availability of opium (then widely grown in the United States) must have seemed a godsend to patent-medicine makers. How else could they so confidently predict and secure pleasurable relief for so many complaints and ensure a continuing and growing demand? It appeared widely (as did alcohol) in such commonplace remedies as cough medicines, liniments, and the various cure-alls sold from the wagons of the medicine-shows. Terry and Pellens report that there was even a good deal of opium in "the dangerous so-called 'cures' of relief for opium-eaters' preparations designed to stop addiction".[2]

So, finally, most of those addicted were a good cross-section of respectable and health-conscious America, particularly among women. According to Hull's[2] report from Iowa, "the majority of them [addicts] are to be found among the educated and most honored and useful members of society; and as to sex, we may count out the prostitutes so much given to this vice, and still find females far ahead so far as numbers are concerned".[2] How can we account for this apparent wide acceptance of opium? But why not? Opium was legal; it did kill pain; it did provide intoxication. And, strangely enough by present concepts, it was generally viewed as a relatively respectable substitute for alcohol. Opium was common among those "who crave the effect of a stimulant, but will not risk their reputation for temperance by taking alcoholic beverages".[2]

The descriptions in popular legend of "average" women during the Victorian and post-Victorian periods tend to be somewhat contradictory. On one hand they are often depicted as warm, strong, omnipresent and long-suffering earth mothers, enduring frequent births with little anesthetic, working hard with little help, caring for and feeding large broods. On the other hand they may be portrayed as delicate, ignorant and rather unworldly, given to frequent and mysterious female distempers and "vapours". Both kinds of women would need frequent relief from pain, tedium, and nervous tension. Our grandmothers used many home remedies and patent medicines whose ingredients would shock us today. Nor is that picture of frequent recourse by women to drugs really so alien to us today — they simply substituted the use of various pain killers, barbiturates and amphetamines for opium.

The Harrison Act of 1914

In 1914 the Harrison Act was passed. From 1919 to 1923 there were clinics dispensing low-cost narcotics in over 40 cities.[3] They are generally believed to have failed. What was more important, the federal narcotics officials felt they were bad, and moved to discredit and end them. This decision has since caused some controversy, renewed, since the opening in 1968, of clinics in Britain.[1]

However, passage of the Harrison Act was the watershed event that started the change that was to affect the entire complexion of American drug control and the pattern and extent of female drug abuse. The closing of American clinics within the decade or so effectively put an end to legal distribution of drugs to addicts, and pretty well destroyed medical influence over control. The strong decline of female addiction from two-thirds of the total before 1920 to the present one-fifth represents a radical change, however gradually it came about.

"In 1915" Terry and Pellens report "two things occurred simultaneously — the importations decreased, and the illicit traffic began to develop. This doubtless was due chiefly to the fact that chronic users, because of the restrictions placed upon physicians and pharmacists in the handling of these drugs, sought their supplies from underworld sources."[2]

The typical female addicts before 1920 had bought most opiates openly across the drug counter. When opium became illegal and disreputable, they were not likely to follow the prostitutes into that dark and expensive world of the pusher and the black marketeer, if they could avoid it. Certainly they were not likely to supply many new recruits.

The period between the world wars saw a general decline in opiate addiction, slight among men, significant among women. Heroin was the primary drug of addiction for both males and females. As Ball points out, the Harrison Act not only put strictures on the almost unlimited licit and legal distribution of narcotics, but made the illicit market profitable, so that a new pattern of illegal, black-market drug distribution came to be superimposed on the older, legal one.[2]

Establishment of Federal Drug Addiction Hospitals : 1935

Major bench marks in the drug history of the United States occurred in 1935, when the federal drug hospitals at Lexington and Fort Worth were established. These were important events, because they more firmly estab-

lished the federal government's predominant role in drug control and treatment efforts. They also reflected the prevailing law-enforcement emphasis —
prevention and control through custodial and punitive means rather than
treatment. The hospitals became centers for the study of drug problems in
the United States, and the primary sources for reliable statistics. Much of
what we know of the demographic characteristics, personalities and histories
of American opiate abuse comes from Lexington and Fort Worth records.

Female addiction, like female alcoholism, tends to be either hidden or
tied in with male addiction. Robinson listed a number of representative
reasons why the female addicts in Lexington had started on drugs. Of the
seven sources listed five were male; one was a peer group which might have
included males; and only one (older women friends) was female.[8] In each
case, male or female, the source was someone already addicted. Modern drug
abuse has been called the new plague.[9] Certainly it spreads by contagion.

The first female opiate addicts were accepted for treatment at Lexington
in July, 1941, and are still being accepted there. Females of all races, registered at Lexington, admitted voluntarily or not, constitute about 18% of
the total, coming close to the best estimates of the ratio of female to male
addicts in the nation at large.

Post World War II Developments

Another major event in the history of American drug addiction occurred
during and immediately after World War II. In wartime it is the males who,
in cohorts, suffer the pain and wounds, and who are willing to pay the price
to continue the good times they had learned abroad, or to kill the pain and
achieve the euphoria they first found in the hospital. The increase in addiction was not as profound in women. Women did achieve a form of emanci-
pation — war work, and more going around without husbands or boyfriends.
But they were not as directly affected. Nevertheless, the greatest predispos-
ing factor for female addiction — at least in an illicit opiate market — was the
addicted male associate.

Addiction Defined: World Health Organization (WHO) 1952

A major reason why the figures on drug abuse and addiction before World
War II had been so unsatisfactory was simply because there had been so few
precise and generally accepted definitions. Subjects that stir up as much
emotion as the use and abuse of drugs need to be defined more precisely
than most, or the definitions will become whatever the sensation seekers
and headline writers say they are. When the control agencies themselves

seek to promote their own viewpoints and concepts, each will use those definitions that best suit its purposes.

Internationally, it was not until 1952 that the World Health Organization (WHO) itself finally got around to making a formal distinction between addiction and habituation, spurred by the fact that it had been impossible for years to discuss or even define the subject with any medical precision, without such distinction.

Accordingly, they drew distinctions between two wide groups of drugs: those truly addictive, and those that do not produce compulsive physiological craving, but are so desirable to their devotees that they would miss them if forced to do without them, and so become "habituated" to them.

The resulting definitions, however, like all those that had preceded them, were still inadequate, and in 1964 the WHO committee threw out both "addiction" and "habituation" as meaningless terms and adopted instead the catchall term of "drug dependence". Moreover, the Committee insisted that definitions and concepts must be reviewed regularly because of rapidly changing scientific knowledge, and the proliferating forms of drug use and dependence.

In October 1968 the Committee adopted the following definitions:

DRUG: Any substance that, when taken into the living organism, may modify one or more of its functions.

DRUG ABUSE: Persistent or sporadic excessive drug use inconsistent with or unrelated to acceptable medical practice.

DRUG DEPENDENCE: A state, psychic but sometimes also physical, resulting from the interaction between a living organism and a drug, characterized by behavioral and other responses that always include a compulsion to take the drug on a continuous or periodic basis in order to experience its psychic effects, and sometimes to avoid the discomfort of its absence. Tolerance may or may not be present. A person may be dependent on more than one drug.

An important aspect of these definitions is that they point out and emphasize the variability of dependence from one drug to another, and for that matter, from one person to another. Drug dependence includes many variations.

We can, using the example of Willis, develop a table which classifies the varieties of physical and psychological dependence associated with the various drugs of abuse.[10] It must be noted that this cannot be a rigid classification since the forms of dependency are themselves not rigidly defined.

DRUG	PHYSICAL DEPENDENCE	PSYCHOLOGICAL DEPENDENCE
Opiates	always	always
Barbiturates	only develops if dosage maintained well above usual therapeutic levels	varies enormously, tends to be intermittent
Amphetamines	none	variable
Cocaine	none	marked
Cannabis	none	variable

As for the drugs used by women, they do not differ from those used by males, except in degree and percentages. The various drugs commonly abused by women include relaxants (tranquilizers), anti-depressants (mood elevators), amphetamines, diet pills, barbiturates (sedatives), and opiates.[11]

Cockett thought it "fruitful to attempt a first classification of individuals, which disregards the actual drugs used and is primarily quantitative".[12]

I. Those who have taken drugs on one occasion (or a very few occasions) only.

II. Those who take or have taken drugs intermittently (example, over weekends for at least six months).

III. Those who take or have taken drugs regularly (daily or several times a week for several months or longer).

IV. Those who are diagnosed as addicted (regular users who display withdrawal symptoms on reception into custody).

Cockett analyzed at great length, and with considerable insight, the development of drug abuse behavior. He found that it can be measured in terms of two primary variables and a secondary variable. The two major variables are (1) the degree of drug involvement, and (2) the length of time the abuser had been taking drugs. "Not surprisingly, these two factors correlate quite highly. The longer people go on taking drugs, the more heavily involved they are likely to become." In other words, drug-taking behavior is not something determined primarily by the addictive characteristics of the drugs themselves, but by the characteristics of the abuser (though addictive properties will, of course, affect behavior once addiction has set in.)People given to drug involvement will go on from marihuana to opiates and/or barbiturates not primarily because there is a cause and effect relationship, but because there is a cause and effect relationship between the kind of person deeply involved in drug abuse and in the use of a variety of drugs.

TABLE I

Estimated Number of Addicts in the United States between 1877 and 1971

Year	Author	Estimated Number of Addicts in the U.S.	Ratio of Females to Males in Sample
1877	Marshall	251,936	1.58
1884	Hull	182,215	1.15
1913	Terry	782,118	1.38
1915	Brown	269,000	2.02
1918	Treasury Dept.	237,655	
1919	Hubbard	140,554	
1920	Butler	264,276	
1965	Pres.'s Comm. on Law Enforcement	55,700	
1968	Special Sub-Comm. on Alcoholism and Narcotics	110,000	
1971	Special Study Mission of the House of Representatives	250,000	0.20

BEHAVIOR AND SOCIAL CHARACTERISTICS

Who is the female addict, and what is she, that so many people with so little knowledge so widely condemn her?

Investigators do not speak of "typical" addicts. There are many different types. Some may be defined by the kinds of drugs used, by the kinds of life styles they have, by region, by special circumstances; some are also daughters of female addicts of the past.

When, in this article, we describe a "typical" or even "representative" addict, we are in fact considering the average of the largest, or most widely detected, sub-group today — the female opiate abuser. Even within this group there are varieties. Undoubtedly, in time, as more data on other sub-groups of women become available, they will be categorized; and they may contrast sharply with the heroin addict.

General Characteristics

Age In a study of 120 women addicts published in 1929, Magid found that the preponderance of them (102) were between 20 and 40 years of age, with slightly more than half over 30.[13] Pescor found the average age of the first 100 female admissions into Lexington to be 43.[5] In a study of female addicts in the Illinois Reformatory for Women in 1960, Robinson found that the average addict age was 27.5 years, the average inmate age 30 years, and the average of all females in Illinois at the time almost 33 years.[8] This is skimpy evidence, but it seems to support the general impression that female addicts are becoming slightly younger. Black female addicts have consistently been younger than their white cohorts, and their life styles and other factors also show distinctive differences.

During the 1960's the situation described in the literature becomes cloudy. In a study of 168 subjects at Lexington in 1965, Chambers found a mean of 30.4 years for black women and 37 years for white (overall average, 33.5).[14] But those populations outside Lexington seem to run fairly consistently younger averages according to Wiesen[15], Blum[16], Weiland[17], and Hall[18]. However, Lexington always includes a sizeable percentage of repeaters (almost 60% of Chambers' sample), previously treated and released in the fond hope of remission or cure; so the expectation that the Lexington population should be older than that on the street (which includes some who have never been caught or treated at all) seems justified, and the data support this conclusion of Williams[19] and Cuskey.[6] In most respects the admissions to Ft. Worth and Lexington are good indicators of admissions throughout the nation, as Ball notes, but not for age. The female addicts are not only older than those in the street, but are older than the men admitted, 31.9 years.[20] Officers are more reluctant to arrest women, perhaps women are engaged in less serious crimes, or they avoid capture and detection. When admitted, they are older.

As noted, black female addicts are generally younger than whites; all studies reviewed confirm this. Between 1961 and 1967 Cuskey found that the median ages for white females dropped from 35-39 to 30-34; but black median ages remained the same, at a considerably lower level — 25-29.[6] In 1965 Cuskey and Williams found the average age for white women to be 37.1 years, and for blacks 30.3. Mexican-American female admissions to Lexington were even younger — 19-20.[21] One factor might be, of course, the greater willingness of police to arrest blacks; but it cannot be the determining factor.

On the basis of admissions records, the "typical" female addict is not much younger in the 1960's than her sister in 1929, and she may be older than her other sister of 1944. But blacks and other minority groups are much younger — and with more data, this trend should be confirmed.

Region The south and southwest, the more conservative parts of the country, are still strongly influenced by the old pre-Harrison Act pattern (except for what might be called a heroin band along the Mexican border). Writing in 1965, Ball could still define *Two Patterns of Opiate Addiction*. The more modern, illicit pattern centers around the use of heroin, alone or in combination; it is characteristically urban, slum, male and minority. It is the typical pattern in the large cities and in New York, Puerto Rico, the District of Columbia, Illinois, New Jersey, Arizona and New Mexico. The older pattern might, "for want of a better name. . . be termed a southern pattern. . .exemplified by Alabama, Georgia and Kentucky". Less than 5% of addicts admitted to federal drug hospitals from these states use heroin; they still follow the older prescriptions of paregoric, morphine, codeine and dilaudid. Many (or most) were semi-legally or legally acquired through physicians or drug stores, for relief of pain and tension. The typical "southern" addicts are white, generally from small towns; addiction started at a later age, marihuana use is uncommon, and less than 20% earned their living by illegal means, with over 50% employed.[22]

Pescor reported in 1944 that the pre-war female addict probably came from small towns or rural areas, very likely from the South, at most from a small city of less than 50,000 people.[5] Since then the drug problem has concentrated in the big cities, particularly New York, Chicago and Los Angeles. Half of all the approximate 50,000 female addicts live in New York. By 1966 83% of female addicts came from large metropolitan areas, and only 17% from the south.[23]

Race It is impossible to discuss regional distribution or religion − or for that matter patterns and delinquency − without running into the question of race. Race is in many ways the prime variable for analysis − intimately associated with differences in region, life styles and patterns of use. Association, of course, is not the same thing as cause. America's drug history, social problems and law-enforcement philosophy are as much "causes" as individual weaknesses, or genetic differences.

The study of Chambers *et al* noted many race-associated differences between white and black addicts. Over 91% of the female addicts they studied came from the South, North Central, and Middle Atlantic regions. But that bare statistic told only a small part of the tale. The South contributed 50% of whites, but only 14% of blacks; the North Central region (predominantly the urban areas of Chicago, Detroit, and other cities) contributed almost 51% of the black addicts but only about 21% of the white; and the Middle Atlantic provided about 17% of the white and close to 32% of the black addicts. The rest of the blacks came from the Pacific coast (3.5%), while the rest of the whites were scattered, including 3.6% from Puerto Rico. In short, the white women came typically from the South, while the blacks came mainly from the North Central regions. Further, while 78.4% of the white women reported that they came from urban areas, all of the black women did.[14]

All researchers agree that there has been a large shift in racial composition and geographical origin among addicts starting from before World War II. In 1929 Magid reported that the typical female addict was white and Protestant.[13] In 1935 and 1936 about 11% of all admissions to Lexington were non-white. By 1964 the Federal Bureau of Narcotics estimated that only about 28% of the narcotic addicts were minority group members, and in 1966 it was found that this applied to 56% of those in Lexington.[5] Nevertheless, examining only the 168 female addicts admitted to Lexington in the last half of 1965, Chambers found that white women outnumbered blacks by about two to one.[14] In other words, though minority group members made up the majority of all addicts, whites still predominated among women. Cuskey reported somewhat similar findings in a continuing trend, comparing female admissions during 1961 with those of 1967. However, though there were still more white women, the gap was rapidly narrowing. In 1961, 150 white women compared to 134 black were admitted voluntarily and in 1967 the count was 89 to 84. In 1967 Cuskey reported that almost half, 48.7%, of his female population was black. What may be significant is that a higher percentage of black admissions were of repeaters: 6.5% more white women were admitted for the first time in 1967 than in 1961; but black female first-timers decreased by 1.4%. Facilities that serve urban areas exclusively, or prisons, report even higher percentages of blacks and other non-whites, according to studies by Royfe,[24] Jaffe,[25] and Bates.[26]

Religion   In Ellinwood's study 47% of the women were found to be Protestant, 30% Catholic, and 17% had no clear religious preference.[23] Investigators reporting on exclusively urban population find fewer Protestants. About 55% of Willis' sample from New York were Catholic, reflecting the huge Puerto Rican barrio population.[10] As time passes, and the increased shift to urban patterns continues, along with an increased rate of addiction, it is safe to predict that the female addicts will become increasingly, Negro, Puerto Rican and Mexican-American, with a higher national percentage of Catholics and non-believers.

The Patterns

Many of the disabilities that blacks or other urban poor or minority groups suffer are specific to their situations, and cannot be simply and directly applied to middle-class whites, even after a time lag. Ghettoization of cities is a social and economic phenomenon more than a racial one, though it affects blacks and other minorities more profoundly than it does whites. And the involvement of big money and organized crime in drugs is not directly related to race or sex either. Nevertheless, in a rough way, it is correct to say that the developing patterns of opiate addiction, particularly heroin, become manifest and intense in blacks before whites, in the poor before the well-to-do, and in males before females. It is also true that, in addition to other new developments in drug use, the whites and females have been catching up more rapidly in the past decade than ever before.

Cuskey reported that by 1967, more than three-fourths of his black subjects lived either in the North Central (52.4%), or Middle Atlantic states (26.2%) — mostly urban areas.[6] Nearly 64% of all Negro women patients in Williams' sample came from New York, Washington and Chicago, while less than 30% of white patients came from these cities.[19] On the other hand, Cuskey found that 42.7% of his whites came from the South in 1961, and 52.4% in 1967[6]. Chambers found that about 30% of Mexican-Americans have migrated to the cities in recent years[21]. All these figures confirm the change toward the urban, minority, non-Protestant, heroin pattern.

The progression from marihuana to heroin or other hard drugs, deemed invariable by some law-enforcement people, is also race and region related, being associated predominantly with the urban pattern. In Chambers' study, 68.4% of the black female addicts had used marihuana.[14] But Mizener, in a study of college drug abusers, found that three-fourths of the medium to heavy marihuana smokers not only had not moved on to heavy drugs, but had discontinued all drugs by their senior years.[27] It might be noted that many of these reformed pot smokers had come from metropolitan areas, but few were ghetto blacks. Most inner-city populations, especially deviants, do have a high rate of progression from pot to heroin. Glaser et al comparing drug-using offenders in New York with drug-free offenders, found that about 40% of the marihuana-smoking offenders had heroin records five to ten years later.[28]

Recent studies indicate to what extent the white women of the Southern pattern still follow the pre-war tradition. Of the white women in Chambers' 1965 study, almost half (45.4%) got their drugs from medical sources, and even at the time of treatment got them from physicians (one-third) or druggists (about one-fifth). Only about 37% preferred heroin, the drugs of choice remaining the legal or quasi-legal codeine, morphine and paregoric.[14]

Almost 90% of Negroes, on the other hand, were introduced to drugs by their peers, who do not include physicians. Invariably they chose heroin (93%), and listed pushers (91.2%) as their source. Williams reports that in his study only one patient from the entire Chicago, Washington and New York grouping had a legal source of drugs — while two-thirds of the Southern patients got their drugs from physicians or pharmacies.

Chambers *et al* also found rather surprising differences between the races in the drug they chose, preferred, and were primarily addicted to. "Among the Negroes, heroin was overwhelmingly the first opiate used, the opiate which was currently being used, the drug the addicts preferred to use, the drug which they used most frequently." About 81% preferred heroin, 93% used it most frequently. By contrast, only one-third of the white women used heroin most frequently, and only 36.9% preferred it. The whites most frequently gave medical or quasi-medical reasons for beginning their addictions; the black women (who averaged six years younger) spoke of "kicks" or "curiosity" and addiction through the pressure of peers, or in social situations.[29]

One of the better studies of the sources of female addiction is that conducted in Wisconsin. They found that in the reasons cited for initial drug abuse, curiosity (43%) was highest, with social pressure and pleasure also cited frequently. Why did they keep on? Most claim they did so for gratification or kicks, though almost as many admitted that they were hooked and could not quit. In the case histories quoted in *Drug-Trip Abroad,* it was generally agreed that long-time addicts got little positive kick out of opiates. They became necessities, "like insulin for diabetics", to achieve relief and ward off the pain of withdrawal. Those case histories were predominantly of men; but the physical response of women to opiates seems little different. To the long-time female addict, as to the male, "curiosity" and "kicks" are part of a legendary golden age of the past.[1]

Deviancy and Personality

Deviancy "The practical effect of American narcotics laws is to define the addict as a criminal offender", Schur[3] states in *Crimes Without Victims.* Further, as noted, in the United States, most addicts have to take to crime to pay for their drugs. Strictly speaking, therefore, to speak of deviancy of addicts is in a large part to speak of addiction itself.

But even without the legal aspects, who can say that addiction is not a deviant method of behavior and social adjustment? There is a great deal of evidence of deviance among addicts, and much of it precedes drug use. There is some evidence, in addition, that we are dealing with a psychological and social maladjustment that expresses itself in a form considered deviant.

TABLE II

Female Addict Demographic Characteristics

Year	Author	Type of Sample If Other Than General Population	Mean Age of Sample	Predominant Race in Sample	Predominant Influence on Initiation into Drug Use
1929	Magid		30	*	Medical Treatment
1936	Pescor		43	Mostly White	Medical Treatment
1961	Cuskey		82% over 25	*	*
1961	Chambers	Mexican-Americans	26.4	*	*
1961	Robinson	Prison	27.5	Mostly Negroes	*
1966	Ellinwood		31	60% White 40% Negroes	* *
1967	Cuskey		69% over 25	*	*
1967	Chambers	Mexican-Americans	26.2	*	*
1968	Hall	Prison	33	Mostly White	Peer Group
1968	Glaser		32.8	50% White 40% Negroes 10% Other	
1969	Poplar	Nurses	41.7	Mostly White	Medical Treatment
1970	Chambers	Negroes	*	*	Peer Group
1970	Chambers		33.7	67% White 33% Negroes	Peer Group

*Information Not Reported

Addiction may be a form of adjustment to intolerable stress for maladjusted people. And in a pathological environment it may seem desirable compared to alternatives. Chein notes that addiction often serves, for the addict, "a humanizing function, by offering an identity, a place in society where one belongs, and a vocation around which to build one's life".[30] Descriptions of the addicts who stay in treatment in Britain according to Schur[3] and Cuskey[1] seem to show inadequate persons who have trouble relating or finding communion, except through drugs.

Some views of the personalities of addicts conflict. Most agree, however, that the majority of addicts are of average intelligence, and many are higher.

Schuster says: "He [the addict] generally is an insecure, easily bored, unstable individual who, too often, is above average intelligence and unable to follow long-term goals".[31] In contrast, Preble and Casey find the adolescent addict involved in a meaningful existence pursuing challenging and demanding jobs and other interests.[32] But Ausubel states that his subjects appeared to have lost interest in life and are not motivated to achieve.[33] Analyzing teen-age abuse, Levy states that during the turbulent teenage years certain individuals turn to narcotics and other drugs for "magical solutions" to problems.[34] Rado[35] and Fencichel[36] also point out the naive willingness of many users to accept drugs as "magical" instruments. Merton, in his "anomie" theory, hypothesizes that the addict is a "retreatist" from society, withdrawing from all aspects of competitive life.[37]. Cloward[38] and Chein et al[30] have, in a sense, all elaborated upon Merton's findings, suggesting that the adolescent addict cannot find a legitimate role in society, and often not even a successful criminal one.

As addiction becomes more widespread, and the ghettos worse, much of the blame for deviancy must be shifted from the imperfections in the addicts to the imperfections in the environments. To some children, addiction may be a reasonable option to a seriously abnormal environment. All these considerations indicate that the kinds of personalities who do or can become addicted may be becoming almost as numerous as the authorities who have opinions on the subject. Kolb describes five different types of addict personalities, and stresses that the borderlines between them are vague, with possible borrowing of traits back and forth.[39]

Deviant behavior cited in female sample populations are certainly broad and inclusive enough. Magid, in 1929, said that the female addict was much like other women, which was certainly true then.[13] Now, heroin addicts do have a high incidence of personality disorders. Addiction may be becoming a catch-all for misfits.

The theory that addiction is caused by, or is aided by, a pre-existing character or personality defect has existed for over a century.[40] Many modern investigators agree [41], [42], [43]. In a comparative study of adult and adolescent addicts, Willis finds that deviancy must be present early in life, before drug abuse, or at least that it must develop very soon after onset.[10] This character defect need not necessarily be genetic, but could develop from the interaction with poverty and ghetto conditions in early childhood.[44]

Some authorities criticize this theory of predisposition, pointing out that these conclusions are reached concerning persons already deviant; that the emotional problems are described at the time of admission to prison or treatment, usually a time of maximum disturbance.[45] O'Donnell points out that we cannot know the condition of addicts before or apart from addiction, unless we can somehow separate the effects of the deviancy and addiction.[46]

Personality   No doubt great deviancy is consistently found in heroin addicts. In the sample at Lexington, Chambers *et al* found that all of the 91 women who remained in treatment for seven or more weeks had some kind of mental problem or deficiency: over 32% had personality trait disorders, 21% were sociopaths, about 32% had personality pattern disorders, 8.8% psychiatric disorders, 2.2% were neurotics, and 1% had brain damage.[14] Compared to other studies, Chambers' findings of disorders were rather high, but all findings were higher than the general population. All but one of Hall's addict-prisoners were found to be disturbed[18], and Ellinwood's study finds about 80% disturbed.[23] How much is independent of the addiction itself, of course, is impossible to determine.

Willis found that about one-half of his female subjects exhibited psychological disturbances even during childbirth. Another one-third had had severe tantrums in childhood, and about 45% were persistent truants from school. Most had been picked up as delinquents during adolescence.[10]

Committing crimes to get money for opiates is an almost inevitable concomittant of addiction. But the crimes female addicts commit tell a good deal about their particular problems.

In a study of female addict-prisoners by Ellinwood, 13 had been jailed for stealing, 37 for sexual offenses (prostitution), and only 7 for assault. Thirty-three were jailed for narcotic offenses.[23]

Female addicts commit fewer crimes of violence than male addicts, and are convicted and jailed less often and for shorter sentences; yet they also are employed less frequently and for shorter periods, and undergo fewer voluntary withdrawals. Prostitution and dependency give them surer, and perhaps safer forms of getting money when legal methods fail.

Chambers *et al* also found that over 90% of female Mexican-American addicts were unemployed, or involved in crime.[21] The two areas of crime in which women exceed men are prostitution and shoplifting — a form of non-violent theft. Of a sample of 89 female addicts in Wisconsin in 1969, 11 depended on prostitution to support their opiate habits, 25 depended on theft, while only 16 worked or borrowed the money.[15]

In studies of women's prisons such researchers as Ward and Kassabaum have demonstrated that lesbianism is a common female adjustment to prison.[48] But the amount of this homosexuality and frigidity, particularly their increase, along with the increase in attempts at marriage, must also involve other factors. Authorities claim a direct link between drug abuse and sexual deviancy. It is taken for granted by most addicts and those who work with them, that opiates have a definitely inhibiting effect on the sex drive. (See *Drug-Trip Abroad* for first person accounts.[1]) Some addicts find little difference, but most do.

Burke says that adolescent addicts of both sexes have real fear of homosexuality.[48] (This is a common factor, of course, in many weak personalities who have trouble establishing strong identities.) Hague points out that adolescent homosexuals turn to drugs because of their rejection by society.[49] Almost one-half of Willis' sample admitted to homosexual orientation.[10] Ellinwood found that 34% of his female subjects, many of whom were married, admitted to occasional or heavy homosexual activity. In fact, only 33% said that they had not experienced frigidity with men.[23] Isbell established that narcotics suppress the libido, and thus reduce the frequency of intercourse.[50]

Burke concluded, too, that the understanding of love is generally distorted among adolescent addicts. There is little question of their need, but it "has a very infantile quality to it". For instance, their idea of true love often calls for no limit to giving by the other person. "Any imposition of limits upon behavior, however slight that imposition may be, is reacted to as a negation of love or as a proof that the love in question never existed."[48]

FAMILY LIFE

Youth and Early Sorrow

There is a great deal of evidence that female addicts, like males, come from "malignant familial environments". Since urban ghettos are concentrations of poverty, minority groups, broken families, psychopathology and lawlessness, who really knows what causes what? If an addict doesn't come from a broken home he can certainly create one.

Still, the associations are there. In 1944 Pescor reported that the female addicts at Lexington would typically have some family history of alcoholism, and that the parents would be in "marginal economic circumstances".[5] The poor lived in a state of permanent crises, often only a step from disaster.

74

TABLE III

Female Addict Abuse Characterists

Year	Author	Predominant Drug of Choice	Mean Age at Onset of Addiction	Source of Drugs	Proportion Legally Employed %	Proportion with Criminal Record %
1929	Magid	Morphine	25	legal	*	*
1936	Pescor	Morphine	29	legal	*	0
1961	Cuskey	*		*	39.4%	22.5%
1961	Chambers	*		legal	*	
1961	Robinson	*	25	*	*	100.0%
1966	Ellinwood	Heroin	18		30.0%	70.0%
1967	Ball	Heroin	25.8	illegal		
1967	Cuskey	Heroin		illegal	15.0%	48.6%
1967	Chambers	Heroin	19.9	illegal	10.0%	100.0%
1968	Hall	Heroin	24.8			100.0%
1968	Glaser	Heroin	25.4	illegal	30.0%	80.0%
1069	Willis	Morphine			40.0%	60.0%
1969	Poplar	Demerol		legal		
1970	Chambers	Heroin		illegal	15.8%	91.2%
1970	Chambers	*	25.9	illegal	20.5%	69.6%

*Information Not Reported

The home life of the typical addict of 1944 would therefore be disturbed, and sometimes abruptly shattered by death, separation and divorce. Chambers *et al* found that the majority of their 1965 addicts had been reared in homes broken before they were 16. Race differences could be summarized by adding, "with the blacks, more so".[14]

Chein *et al* report that the parents of female addicts have more discord than most parents, that fathers are gone for long periods of time or are generally ineffectual, and that mothers are dominant in the homes and in their children's lives.[30] This is practically the definition — at least a dominant description — of the slum family. Female addicts' childhoods are often tormented and bad; they are usually either denied the gratification they need or are overindulged and given excessive mothering.

While most female addicts came from disturbed homes, with parents who worked with their hands, this was by no means true of all. All sections of society were represented among female addicts. Chambers *et al* for instance, found that about 21% of the addicts had fathers in professional or managerial occupations, and 5% in clerical sales. All told, about 26% were white collar, 74% blue collar.[14] The real pinch seems to come not from poverty, but from unstable homes, and from emotional thwarting and deprivation.[30] They found that the differences between races in this matter, too, was significant. Two-thirds of the fathers of white female addicts were blue collar, compared to 86.4% of black.[14]

There seems to be a significant relationship between mental disturbance, alcoholism, and drug dependence within families, for at least the last three decades. Pescor reported that female addicts almost always had some history of alcoholism in the family (if not parents, then a close relative).[5] This confluence of problems, problem families and drug dependency, has increased. About 40% of Ellinwood's sample had a close relative who had abused drugs, usually a parent or sibling. Nearly 30% had a parent who had served time in prison.[23] Willis reported that in his sample 30% had one or two alcoholic parents, about 13% had a parent who had been hospitalized for mental disorder, and half had one or both parents who were known to be mentally disturbed.[10] Guze *et al* could definitely link social pathology, alcoholism and emotional disorder within the family[51, 52, 53, 54].

In such malignant family structures the contagion within the family can rule: the non-addicts are frequently introduced to drugs and alcohol by other members of the family, and encouraged in abuse by them. Chambers found that 11% of his patients at Lexington reported that they were introduced to narcotics by an addicted family member. Moreover, the infected family usually is part of an infected environment.[14] Robinson says, "Junk is pushed where the population is least protected and where

76

people are most avidly seeking a way out."[8] Cuskey *et al* speak of "the sick environments" with their "psychological forces and environmental reinforcements that condition addicts to return to habits even when they receive so little heroin that psychological forces must be minimal."[1] In such environments physical health and proper nourishment have low priorities, and mental health is under constant siege. From childhood on it is very likely that the addict will have poor physical and mental health. Hall[18] and Stoffer[55] note that upon admission to treatment or prison, addicts are usually underweight and suffering from a number of physical and nutritional troubles of long standing. Ellinwood found, in his sample, that 13% had a history of asthma, 10% of thyroid disease, 13% of hypertension, and 10% of hepatitis. Even before they began using drugs 43% reported suffering painful menstruation and 23% miscarriages.[23]

The Addict Couple

It is scarcely surprising therefore that female addicts have great marital difficulties. They almost seem to seek out trouble. Like seeks out like: addicts (and potential addicts) marry one another. This is not only because they are thrown together and are hardly attractive to persons who do not take drugs, but also through a sort of magnetism of like traits and characteristics, inborn and acquired. Perhaps losers must seek solace where they can find it. Kraus[56] and Stein[57] have established this preference of like for like, and Guze *et al* in a series of studies[51, 52, 53, 54], demonstrated that children from multi-problem families marry more frequently than chance can account for. Eisenstein[58], O'Donnell[59], and Cuskey *et al*[60] have shown, more specifically, that alcoholics and addicts quite often find spouses with the same addiction. A good place to start the study of marriage problems among female addicts, therefore, is to study addict couples. Almost all of the addiction-associated problems appear among addict couples. In 1966-67, 85 couples from all parts of the United States were treated at Lexington for addiction. Three-quarters were on heroin, the rest on diverse opiates; about three-fifths white (principally WASP), 28% black, 5% Puerto Rican, and the rest racially mixed. Of those reporting, 20% of the men and 23% of the women had had no previous marriage, and the majority of the rest had had no more than one. Present marriage had lasted four years among the heroin addicts, nine years among the others.

At time of hospitalization, the husbands averaged 35 years, the wives 31; both had been on drugs since about 20. Two-thirds of all had dropped out before finishing high school. Almost half the women had started using drugs only within the present marriages.[60]

Deviance, apart from and usually preceding addiction, had been strong in both husbands and wives while still adolescents. About half the boys had been arrested before 18, and before drug involvement; about half the girls had been married before 18, with four out of five marriages failing.

Early school dropout and arrest for the boys, and early pregnancy and marriage for the girls, indicate poor family lives and poor training in social and sexual control.

These patterns persisted throughout adulthood, marriage and hospitalization. Few of the adults were able to pursue reasonably normal personal and work lives. Most found partners in their own subculture: 54% of men and 60% of women married partners already addicted. Almost half of both men and women were married to partners diagnosed at Lexington as psychotic. Findings by Chein *et al*[30] and Vaillant[61] were similar. O'Donnell[59], in like fashion, found that his subjects tended to marry partners already deviant, and to become deviant themselves, if they had not already been so.

Marriage and the Female Addict

In spite of marital difficulties, female addicts do get married, and at a higher rate than formerly. To match, an increasing number per year fail. In Cuskey's comparative study, 25% of the 1961 sample were single when they entered Lexington, but only 17.3% of the 1967 patients were. In 1961 there were more intact than broken marriages – 41.2% to 33.4%; in 1967 the reverse was true – 36.4% to 46.2%.[6] Ellinwood found that only 30% of his female addicts, compared to 41% of his males, were single.[23] O'Donnell, too, has noted the trend toward more marriages among female addicts.

Divorce and Separation

More marriages accompanied by more divorces must result in a kind of revolving-door situation. Back in 1944 Pescor[5] had predicted that many women addicts would ultimately be divorced or separated. The trend is confirmed not only by Cuskey's figures[6], but also by Weiland.[17] Chambers *et al* found even higher rates of increase of divorce and separation for Mexican-American female addicts, despite their Catholic background – from 35.7 in 1961 to 50% in 1967. Some studies, particularly of Negro addicts, do show a higher percentage of intact marriages than these figures might indicate.[14] But these "intact" marriages include many common-law relationships of one year duration or more that are not considered marriages at all in many reckonings.

A more persuasive objection to making much of increased rates of marriage, separation and divorce among female addicts comes from the fact that there are similar, if not necessarily parallel, increases in all separations and divorces.[62] Interestingly, the divorce rate for male addicts is still significantly lower than for females, though it did rise from 10% in 1961 to 25.2% in 1967.[6] Female addicts tend to be more sympathetic to their addicted spouses than the reverse. It often works out to their disadvantage. (O'Donnell[59] and Eisenstein[58] document a similar phenomenon among alcoholics, indicating that this tendency lies in the nature of women, rather than of the drug.) Women will wait, often until they and their children have become social outcasts and they have suffered considerable damage, before they divorce, and then they are quite apt to go out and marry another addict or alcoholic.[58] Men are generally apt to shake loose much more quickly.

In sum, addicted women tend to marry addicted men, or at least men with severe problems. Into these homes children are born, often in poverty, in disturbance, in pathology, seldom with adequate care and food, and must then learn to live and build up adequate personality structures and identities. Hereditary factors, seriously disturbed parents, a malignant social environment, and all the distorted learning and conditioning experiences of such a background, interact in ways we cannot foresee. We do know some of the results. And what about the long-term consequences of successive generations of such matings?

COMPLICATIONS IN PREGNANCY

Maternity

What happens to pregnancies and babies? In 1944 the typical female addict had one child. Ellinwood reports that female opiate addicts with families had, on the average, three children.[23] Figures are now more reliable because the increase of pregnant addicts coming into hospitals in the last decade has spurred research. In 1960, only one out of 164 admissions to the New York College-Metropolitan Hospital Center was a female addict. By 1969 the ratio was 1 to 47. Moreover, physicians have come to realize that many of the symptoms that they had ascribed to other causes were actually caused by, or associated with, the effects of drugs and addiction.

Maintaining good health in order to have healthy babies is, in most cases, low in the order of priorities for addict mothers. Blinick[63] and Perlmutter[64] note that hepatitis and some liver diseases are frequent among pregnant addicts. Howard found that 27% of the hepatitic subjects in his sample shared needles despite firm knowledge, or belief, that the needlesharer had hepatitis.[65]

Since prostitution is common, there is much VD — little of it treated or reported until the victim comes in for medical care. Stone *et al*[66] report 17% positive serologies in their sample; in Perlmutter's[64], 40%, previously untreated. Stern[68] found that the average patient had made less than one visit to the clinic prior to delivery. A great number appeared already in active labor.

Stone *et al*[66] found that 30% of the sample was anemic; at least 90% of Stoffer's population had some abnormality in menstural function[55]. Stone[66] found from a study of over 300 patients that more than 90% had had little or no prenatal care; 41% had some complication. There are high percentages of breech birth, pre-eclamptic toxemia and of hemorrhaging. Ignorance, poor health habits, unsterile needles, malnutrition and prostitution take their toll among babies as well as mothers[66].

Obviously the typical addict, being unable to concentrate on anything beyond the necessity of the next fix, would have great difficulty being a good mother. Many are saved the trouble, because the rates of prematurity, of still-births, and of other neonatal deaths are a good deal higher than in the non-addict population.

Precipitate Labor

Reviewing histories from a number of admission groups over the past decade, Stone found that 62% of addicts went into labor before completing the 38th week.[66] Zelson found that 60% did not go to full term.[67] Of course in these matters, the memories and reported physical symptoms (like time of last menstrual period) of addicts are untrustworthy, so precise figures are difficult. Still, in 1967 only 6.2% of all live births in the United States were born prior to 37 weeks (Trends in Prematurity, United States, 1950, 1967); and ten times the normal rate of prematurity is significant. Addicts also suffer long labor both in total length and in the length of various stages.[64, 68]

The Babies

Prematurity and Low Birth Weight   The babies from addicted mothers are not only born earlier, but weigh less[68, 69, 70, 71]. In a study of 22 heroin-addicted women in the Obstetrics Service of the Brooklyn-Cumberland Medical Center, Perlmutter found that almost 57% of infants weighed less than 2,500 grams and averaged 2,296 grams.[64] Cobrink,[72] Semoff,[73] and others found a somewhat higher mean rate of 2,600 grams in the general population. Many experts have assumed that the rate of prematurity explained the light weights; but others have pointed out that they are light even for their own stage of development, and even full-term babies average lighter weights, indicating the possibility, as suggested by Snyder,[74] of retarded intrauterine growth. Undoubtedly the poor living and nutritional habits contribute to this.

The high incidence of breech presentations is related, apparently, to the light weight. Stern found 12% breeches in his addict sample, compared to 4.8% in the general admissions to the Metropolitan Obstetrical Service.[68] About 10% of Perlmutter's sample were breeches.[64]

Hooked Babies   Sussman says that between 1875 and 1963, 286 cases of neonatal addiction were recorded. Since then there has been a sharp rise; the New York Hospital Committee found 300 cases in 1966 alone.[70] Several other studies since 1960 reported that from 60% to 90% of infants born to female addicts show symptoms. Nevertheless, many babies still pass through the system undiagnosed. Mothers often deny addiction. Some do not show obvious symptoms.[55] Sussman states that physicians need to be attuned to addiction signs in the babies themselves and that urine and blood studies must be made within 24 hours of delivery, since narcotic metabolites disappear rapidly.[70]

Most addict babies show symptoms severe enough to justify medication. Zelson found almost 78% of his baby sample needed treatment[67]; Cobrink found 60% in his.[72] If the mother took a fix a week or less before delivery, the baby would generally show symptoms; if more than a week, generally not.[75] Other investigators report that dosages of 12 milligrams or more daily would probably bring moderate to severe disturbances in newborns.[76]

Babies usually show symptoms within 24 hours, and they may last from a few days to two months. These may include rapid respiration, grunting, rib retraction, intermittent cyanosis, apnea, excess activity and trembling, twitching, convulsions, shrill crying, suckling of fingers as though hungry, vomiting, diarrhea, excess weight loss, sneezing and sweating. Since many newborns have one or more of these symptoms anyway, it is hardly surprising that before 1960 many of the withdrawal symptoms went undetected. Infants generally require no special treatment beyond swaddling, demand feeding schedules and limited handling. Paregoric and chlorpromazine have proven to be quite effective in treatment.

Dead Babies   Fitting in with the rest of the pattern of complication and pathology, many addict babies are miscarried, born dead or die soon after birth. In a study of 66 addict mothers, Stern reported that about 7% of infants were stillborn.[68] In his study Perlmutter found a rate of 17.4% of perinatal deaths, compared to 2.2% among non-addicted mothers.[64] Stoffer found that of the 40 infants in his sample who survived pregnancy, about 10% died soon after, and about one quarter were critically ill but survived after therapy.[55] In the past, the death rate for infants with symptoms who were untreated ran as high as 93%. But Hill reports that as of 1963 the death rate for those who showed symptoms and were treated was 9%.[77] Other reports show a total mortality rate in the infant addict population of 7% - 20%. Life or death may depend on quickness of diagnosis and treatment.

Most authorities place much or most of the blame on prematurity.[69] But a few are finding evidence of toxicity from the drugs themselves. Courville found distinct evidence of the feasibility of the direct action of narcotics on the nerve cell, or from indirect vasomotor action through the blood vessels.[78] Obviously such babies are extremely vulnerable, and need diagnosis and immediate and thorough help.

SPECIAL SUB-GROUPS

There are some sub-groups of female addicts that have distinct identities and characteristics. Perhaps most distinct are the female medical professionals, primarily nurses, who, like physicians, have access to opiates in their work, use legal and medical sources, and whose age, motivation and distribution are generally different from the rest of the addicts. From 1962 to 1967, 90 registered nurses were admitted to the Lexington Hospital for treatment of opiate addiction. Two-thirds had obtained drugs from physicians' or hospital supplies, while the remainder got theirs from drugstores, family, fraudulent prescription (which they were in a good position to forge) and, only lastly, pushers. At time of hospitalization they averaged 42 years of age and came from 30 states. By far, the most common drug used was Demerol, followed in turn by morphine, paregoric, codein, Darvon and the barbiturates — the medicine cabinet choices. Far down the list was heroin. The average age of these ladies was 41.7 — much older than the female addicts at Lexington.[79]

THE FUTURE

The history of female drug involvement and treatment is, therefore, closely associated with society's attitudes towards drug use as reflected in the laws and law-enforcement practices. When opiates were provided legally by physicians and druggists, female addicts were created and treated accordingly. When drug control fell into the hands of law-enforcement agencies, addiction fell, and treatment was administered in reformatories. However, since the early 1960's, important changes in patterns of female drug abuse and addiction have been taking place. These are concurrent changes, not all related.

TABLE IV

Female Addict Maternity Characteristics

Year	Author	Mean Age of Mother	Proportion of Pre-mature Birth	Proportion with Breech Presentations	Proportion with Obstetrical Complications	Proportion of Cases with V.D. at Admission	Proportion of Perinatal Mortality	Proportion of Neonatal Addiction	Proportion of Congenital Anomalies
1956	Cobrink		45.0%				0	91.0%	0
1963	Sussman		53.0%	21%			10.0%	79.0%	5%
1966	Stern		18.5%	12%	40.9%	20%	7.1%		
1967	Perlmutter	27.3	56.5%	10%		24%	17.4%	54.5%	13%
1968	Stoffer	28.9				68%	17.5%	57.5%	
1969	Blinick		34.0%	9%	11.0%	18%	3.0%		
1971	Stone	26.7	50.0%	9%	26.0%	17%	3.6%	67.4%	1%

First, many new self-help and drug-free treatment facilities have sprung into being and into popularity, including Synanon and Daytop Village. Increasing numbers of women are accepting help from these sources and from similar therapeutic groups.

Second, synthetic narcotics have been developed, notably methadone, which has provided addicts with maintenance support that allows them to give up opiates and lead relatively crime-free and trouble-free lives, without prostitution or theft. Clinics and treatment centers, many attached to hospitals, most admitting female patients, have risen in most major cities and enjoy widespread community support. They use methadone, psychotherapy, or other treatments in various combinations. The general public, alarmed by rising drug-crime statistics, has changed old attitudes towards addiction and addicts. All these developments presage a turning toward medical and social forms of control.

Other developments in the last decade have not been so encouraging. The gaps between men and women, whites and blacks, are narrowing. More women are getting involved in violence. The prostitute and her pimp, operating as a team of muggers, are reported to be significant in Times Square if not yet in the statistics. The increase in the number of addicts seems out of control. Writing in 1969, Ball and Chambers could compute that there were 108,424 known addicts in the United States of whom almost 31,000 had just been reported that year[80]. Since then, addiction has more than doubled and 50,000 or more are women.

A matter of great concern is the emerging pattern of sedative-hypnotic and stimulant abuse among middle-class women. Many of these are synthetics and are abused in combination. As Chambers and Moldestad have observed, "among contemporary opiate abusers, concurrent sedative abuse is the prevalent drug pattern regardless of which opiates are being abused".[14] It is impossible to watch this ominous development and not be stirred by the inevitable echoes of an old and sad song, becoming a trifle scratchy from the years but all too recognizable: legal drugs and respectable people, a majority of whom are housewives and working women, searching for something to combat the stress, pain and fatigue of life — something that is not illegal, or widely condemned, or even very noticeable. Little pills in little packages, with little attention paid to the addiction or psychosis that might come with that package. Predominantly middle-class, predominantly white . . .

History may not repeat itself in detail, but events do tend to respond in similar fashion to similar pressures, similar needs, and similar mistakes.

REFERENCES

1. Cuskey, W.R., A.W. Klein and W. Krasner (1972) *Drug-Trip Abroad.* The University of Pennsylvania Press, Philadelphia.
2. Terry and Pellens (1970) The extent of chronic opiate use in the United States prior to 1921. In: *The Epidemiology of Opiate Addiction in the United States.* Ball, J.C. and C.D. Chambers, eds. C. Thomas, Springfield.
3. Schur, E. (1965) *Crimes Without Victims.* Prentice-Hall, Inc., Englewood Cliffs.
4. Meyerstein, A.N. (1964) Drug addiction: A review. *J. of Sch. Health.* 34:77.
5. Pescor, M.J. (1944) A comparative statistical study of male and female drug addicts. *Amer. J. of Psych.* 100:771.
6. Cuskey, W.R., H. Clifford and A. Moffett (1971) A comparison of female opiate addicts admitted to Lexington Hospital in 1961 and 1967. *HSMHA Rep.* 86:332.
7. O'Neil, E. (1956) *Long Day's Journey into Night.* Yale University Press, New Haven.
8. Robinson, B.F. (1961) Criminality among narcotic addicts in the Illinois State Reformatory for Women. *Ill. Med. J.* 119:320.
9. de Alarcon, R. (1969) The spread of heroin abuse in a community. *Bull. on Narc.* 21.
10. Willis, J.H. (1970) Drug dependence: some demographic and psychological characteristics in United Kingdom and United States subjects. *Br. J. Add.* 64:135.
11. Chambers, C. and D. Schultz (1971) *Ladies Home Journal,* Nov. p. 190.
12. Cockett, R. (1971) *Drug Abuse and Personality in Young Offenders.* Appleton Century Crofts, New York.
13. Magid, M.D. (1971) Narcotic addiction in the female. *Med. J. and Rec.* 129:306.
14. Chambers, C., L. Hinesley and M. Moldestad (1970) Narcotic addiction in females: a race comparison *Int. J. of the Add.*
15. Weisen, R.L., R. Wang and T.J. Stemper. The drug abuse program at Milwaukee County Institutions — a six month report. *Wisc. Med. J.* 69:141.
16. Blum, R.H. *et al.* (1970) *Society and Drugs.* Jossey-Bass, Inc. San Francisco.
17. Weiland, W. and C. Chambers (1970) Two methods of utilizing methadone in the outpatient treatment of narcotic addicts. *Int. J. of Add.* 5:332.
18. Hall, M.E. (1968) Mental and physical efficiency of women drug addicts. *J. Ab. Soc. Psych.* 5.
19. Williams, J.E. and W.M. Bates (1970) Some characteristics of female narcotic addicts. *Int. J. of Add.* 5:245.
20. Ball, J.C., W.M. Bates and J.A. O'Donnell (1966) Characteristics of hospitalized narcotic addicts. *Health Education Welfare Indicators.* March
21. Chambers, C., W.R. Cuskey and A.D. Moffett (1970) Mexican opiate addicts. In: *The Epidemiology of Opiate Addiction in the United States.* Ball, J.C. and C.D. Chambers, eds. C.C. Thomas, Springfield, Illinois.
22. Ball, J.C. (1965) Two patterns of narcotic addiction in the U.S. *J. Criminal Law, Criminology and Police Science.* 56:210.
23. Ellinwood, E.H., W.A. Smith and G.E. Vaillant (1966) Narcotic addiction in males and females: a comparison. *Int. J. of Add.* 1:33.
24. Royfe, E.H. (1966) Social and psychological characteristics of 100 patient drug addicts. *Penn. Psych. Quart.* 5:38.

25. Jaffe, J.H., M.S. Zaks and E.N. Washington. Experience with the use of methadone in a multi-modality program for the treatment of narcotic users. *Int. J. of Add.*

26. Bates, W. (1968) Occupational characteristics of Negro addicts. *Int. J. of Add.* 1:2.

27. Mizener, G.L., J.F. Barter and P.H. Werme (1970) Patterns of drug use among college students: a preliminary report. *Amer. J. Psych.* 127:15.

28. Glaser, D., J.T. Incardi and D.V. Babst (1969) Later heroin use by marihuana-using and non-drug adolescent offenders in N.Y.C. *Int. J. of Add.* 4:1.

29. Chambers, C. and A.D. Moffett (1970) Negro opiate addiction. *The Epidemiology of Opiate Addiction in the United States.* Ball, J.C. and C.D. Chambers, eds. C.C. Thomas. Springfield, Illinois.

30. Chein, I., D.L. Gerald, R.S. Lee and E. Rosenfeld (1964) *The Road to H: Narcotics, Delinquency and Social Policy.* Basic Books, Inc., New York.

31. Schuster, D.U. (1971) Drug treatment: avenues open to physicians. *Ind. J. State Med. Assn.* May, p. 417.

32. Preble, E. and J. Casey (1969) Taking care of business. *Int. J. of Add.* 4:1.

33. Ausubel, D.P. (1958) *Drug Addiction.* Random House, New York.

34. Levy, N.J (1968) The use of drugs by teenagers for sanctuary and illusion. *Amer. J. of Psych.* 28:48.

35. Rado, S. (1963) Fighting narcotic bondage and other forms of narcotic disorders. *Comp. Psych.* 4:160.

36. Fencichel, O. (1945) *The Psychoanalytical Theory of Neurosis.* W.W. Norton Co., New York.

37. Merton, R.K. (1957) *Social Theory and Social Structure.* Free Press of Glencoe, New York.

38. Cloward, R.A. and L.E. Ohlin (1960) *Delinquency and Opportunity.* Free Press of Glencoe, New York.

39. Kolb, L. (1962) *Drug Addiction: A Medical Problem.* C.C. Thomas, Springfield, Illinois.

40. Dole, V. and M.E. Nyswander (1966) Rehabilitating heroin addicts after blockade with methadone. *N.Y. State J. Med.* August, p. 2011.

41. Hill, H.E., C.A. Haertzen and R. Glaser (1960) Personality characteristics of narcotic addicts as indicated by the MMPI. *J. Gen. Psych.* 62:127.

42. Glaser, F.B. (1970) Misinformation about drugs: a problem for drug abuse education. *Int. J. of Add.* 5:595.

43. Winick, C. and S.M. Finch (1962) The psychiatrist and juvenile delinquent. *J. Amer. Acad. Child Psych.* 1:619.

44. Robins, L., H. Gyman and P. O'Neal (1962) The interaction of social class and deviant behavior. *Amer. Soc. Rev.* 27:4.

45. Dole, V. and M.E. Nyswander (1967) Heroin addiction — a metabolic disease. *Arch. Int. Med.* 120:19.

46. O'Donnell, J.A. (1968) Social factors and follow-up studies in opio addiction. *Res. Pub. Ass. Res. Nerv. Mental Dis.* 46:333.

47. Ward, D.A. and G.G. Kassebaum (1964) Lesbian Liaisons. *Trans-Action* 1:28.

48. Burke, E.L. (1968) Patient values on an adolescent drug unit. *Amer. J. Psych.*

49. Hague, B. (1969) In San Francisco's tenderloin. *Amer. J. Nurs.* 69:2180.

50. Isbell, H. and W.M. White (1953) Clinical characteristics of addiction. *Amer. J. Med.*

51. Guze, S.B., D.W. Goodwin and J.C. Crane (1960) A psychiatric study of the wives of convicted felons: an example of assortive mating. *Amer. J. Psychiat.* 126:12.

52. Guze, S.B., E.D. Wolfgram, J.K. McKinney and D.P. Cantwell (1967) Psychiatric illness in the families of convicted criminals, a study of 519 first-degree relatives. *Dis. Nerv. Syst.* 28:651.

53. Guze, S.B., V.B. Tuason, P.D. Gatfield, Stewart and B. Picken (1972) Psychiatric illness and crime with particular reference to alcoholism: a study of 223 criminals. *J. Ner. Ment. Dis.* 134:512.

54. Guze, S.B., D.W. Goodwin and J.B. Crane (1969) Criminality and psychiatric disorders. *Arch. Gen. Psychiat.* 20:583.

55. Stoffer, S.S. (1968) A gynecological study of drug addicts. *Amer. J. Obs. and Gyn.* 101:779.

56. Kraus, A.S. and A.M. Lilienfeld (1959) Some epidemiologic aspects of the high mortality rate in the young widowed group. *J. Chron. Dis.* 10:207.

57. Stein, Z.M.A. and M. Susser (1969) Widowhood and mental illness. *Br. J. Rev. Soc. Med.* 23:106.

58. Eisenstein, V. (1956) *Neurotic Interaction in Marriage.* Basic Books, Inc. New York.

59. O'Donnell, J. (1969) Narcotic addicts in Kentucy. *Public Health Service Publication,* No. 1881.

60. Cuskey, W.R., H. Clifford, A.D. Moffett and T. Premkumar (1972) Drug addiction among married couples at the Lexington Hospital, 1966 and 1967. Unpublished manuscript.

61. Vaillant, G.E. (1966) A 12-year follow-up of N. Y. narcotic addicts. *Arch. Gen. Psychiat.* 15.

62. Divorce Statistics Analysis, United States, 1964 and 1965. *Public Health Service, Vital and Health Statistics,* Series 21, No. 17, U.S. Department of Health Education and Welfare.

63. Blinick, G., C. Wallach and E.M. Jerez (1969) Pregnancy in narcotic addicts treated by medical withdrawal. *Amer. J. Obs and Gyn.* 105:997.

64. Perlmutter, J.F. (1967) Drug addiction in pregnant women. *Am. J. Obs. and Gyn.* Oct. 15, p. 569.

65. Howard, J. and P. Borges (1970) Needle sharing. *Health Soc. Behav.* Sept. 11, p. 220.

66. Stone, M.L., L.J. Salerna, Green and C. Zeison (1971) Narcotic addiction in pregnancy. *Am. J. Obs. and Gyn.*

67. Zelson, R.E. and E. Wasserman (1971) Neonatal narcotic addiction: 10 years observation. *Ped.* 48:178.

68. Stern, R. (1966) The pregnant addict: a study of 66 case histories, 1950-1959. *Am. J. Obs. and Gyn.*

69. Rosenthal, T., S.W. Patrick and D.C. Krug (1964) Congenital neonatal narcotics addiction: a natural history. *Am. J. Pub. Health* 54:1252.

70. Sussman, S. (1963) Narcotic and methamphetamine use during pregnancy. *Am. J. Dis. of Child.* 106:325.

71. Claman, A.D. and R.I. Strong (1962) Obstetric and Gynecologic aspects of heroin addiction. *Amer. J. Obs. and Gyn.* Jan. 15.

72. Cobrink, R.W., T. Hood, Jr., E. Churid and L.B. Slobody (1956) The effects of natural narcotic addiction on the newborn infant. *Amer. J. Dis. Child.* 92:504.

73. Semoff, M.C.F. (1967) Narcotic addiction of the newborn. *Arizona Med.* 24:933.

74. Synder, F.F. (1949) *Obstetrical Analgesic and Anesthesia: Their Effects Upon Labour and the Child.* W.B. Saunders and Co., Philadelphia.

75. Neuberg, R. (1970) Drug dependence and pregnancy: a review of the problems and their management. *J. Obs. and Gyn.* 77:1117.

76. Nesbitt, R.E.L., Jr. (1957) *Perinatal Loss in Modern Obstetrics.* F.A. Davis Co., Philadelphia, p. 159.

77. Hill, R.M. and M.H. Desmond (1963) Management of narcotic withdrawal syndrome. *Ped. Clinics of N. Amer.* 10:67.

78. Courville, Cited in Nesbitt, R.E.L., Jr. (1957) *Perinatal Loss in Modern Obstetrics.* F.A. Davis Co., Philadelphia, p. 159.

79. Poplar, J.F. (1969) Characteristics of nurse addicts. *Am. J. Nur.* 69:117.

80. Ball, J.C. and C.D. Chambers (1970) Overview of the problem. In: *The Epidemiology of Opiate Addiction in the United States.* Ball, J.C. and C.D. Chambers, eds. C.C. Thomas, Springfield, Illinois.

Acknowledgments

The authors would like to acknowledge the valuable contribution of their colleagues who assisted in the preparation of this survey – Miss Gwendolyn Braxton, Miss Regina Holmes, and Mr. William Krasner; and to Mrs. Barbara Martin for her assistance in the typing of the manuscript. This manuscript could not have been completed without their assistance.

Comparison of Female Opiate Addicts Admitted to Lexington Hospital in 1961 and 1967

WALTER R. CUSKEY, Ph.D., ARTHUR D. MOFFETT, M.S.W., and HAPPA B. CLIFFORD, M.A.

THE Clinical Research Center in Lexington, Ky., formerly the Public Health Service Hospital, was established in May 1935 for the treatment of narcotic addicts. By December 1965, about 45,000 addicts had been admitted for a total of about 75,000 admissions. Female narcotic addicts were first accepted for treatment at the Lexington hospital in July 1941. With the exception of 109 women treated at Fort Worth (1947–52), all female addicts, with 14,866 admissions, received their treatment at the Lexington facility. These admissions represented 18 percent of total admissions during the period when women were being treated at the Lexington hospital.

These women voluntarily sought treatment in overcoming drug addiction. Some came from great distances. As their case histories show, some came to avoid arrest and others to avoid the torments of addiction. They possessed a knowledge of the Lexington hospital and the money to get there.

Most patients stayed at the hospital from 5 to 14 days to become detoxified and then apparently returned to their previous life situation, in which a relapse usually occurred. Approximately 40 percent of the women returned to Lexington to go through the detoxification treatment a g a i n. They became "winders," the term used at Lexington to describe patients who spend their lives in and out of the hospital.

Limited information is available on patients who do not return to the hospital. O'Donnell studied patients coming from Kentucky only, but his conclusions w e r e limited (1). Few followup studies (2–5) on Lexington patients have been undertaken, although some studies have been done on patients from other institutions (6–8). All these investigators found high relapse rates among the addicts. The relationship of race and sex to relapse w a s neither clear nor consistent.

Various empirical studies have comprehensively documented the similiarities and differences between white and Negro opiate addicts. Bates (9) and Chambers and associates (10) have provided descriptions of white and Negro addicts. Southern white addicts have been the subject of an extensive s t u d y by O'Donnell (11, 12) and O'Donnell and associates (13). Glaser (14) and Chambers and co-workers (15)

have described female addicts, while Ball and associates (16) and Ellingwood and associates (17) have compared male with female addicts. Ball and co-workers have also reported changes in the incidence and prevalence of opiate addiction among females (18), but specific changes over time within the female addict population have not been assessed, although changes have occurred within other addict populations.

In this study we sought evidence of changes within the female addict population between 1961 and 1967. Race, having already been demonstrated as a significant control variable, was incorporated with time, thereby producing a frame of reference to measure changes within the race cohorts of female addicts.

Research Design

From January through June 1961, 284 women were admitted to the clinical research center at Lexington for treatment of narcotic addiction. The racial distribution of these addicts was 52.8 percent or 150 whites and 47.2. percent or 134 Negroes. During the same period of 1967 there were 173 women admitted for treatment, with the racial distribution of the addict patients almost identical to that of 1961: 51.4 percent or 89 were whites and 48.6 percent or 84 were Negroes.

The study was designed to ascertain any significant time-race differences through three separate statistical comparisons: (a) white women admitted in 1961 and their 1967 counterparts; (*b*) Negro women admitted in 1961 and their 1967 counterparts; and (*c*) all women admitted in 1961 compared with all women admitted in 1967.

The variables selected for these comparative a n a l y s e s were grouped into three categories: (*a*) pretreatment background characteristics, (*b*) geographic distribution, and (*c*) characteristics at admission to treatment. Although comparable 1961 data were not available, selected variables specifically relevant to drug use for the 1967 patients were compared with the race control. These variables included whether the opiate abused was heroin or another drug, whether marijuana was ever used, what method was used to administer the drug, and whether the pusher was the primary source of the drug. This analysis was done to provide data for the contemporary female addicts and to replicate the findings of other studies.

Addicts' Social Characteristics

Three pretreatment background characteristics were available for this comparative analysis (table 1): (*a*) level of formal education, (*b*) marital status (civil) immediately before entering treatment, and (*c*) primary means of support.

Level of formal education. The distribution of attained formal education did not change significantly between 1961 and 1967 regardless of the addict's race. Several findings, however, required some elaboration.

1. Female addicts frequently have pursued formal education beyond high school. In 1961, of those admitted to the Lexington hospital, 15.3 percent of all white and 1.5 percent of all Negro addicts, a total of 8.8 percent of all the women, had pursued higher educations. By 1967, a total of 13.3 percent of the female addicts, 20.2 percent of the whites and 6.0 percent of the Negroes, had gone beyond high school.

2. The number of women who dropped out before completing high school significantly decreased between 1961 and 1967. While 64.8 percent of all female addicts were school dropouts in 1961, only 55.5 percent were in 1967 ($X^2=3.916$; $P=0.05$). This reduction can be attributed primarily to the fact that Negro women remained in school longer.

Marital status. Several significant changes occurred relevant to the marital status of these female addicts. Probably most important was the significant increase in the number of female addicts who had attempted a civil marriage but had failed. In 1961, 33.4 percent reported a broken marriage, a proportion not in excess of that found in their base populations for that time period. In 1967, however, 46.2 percent reported broken marriages. At least in these addict populations, the significant increase in terminations of marriage can be attributed to a disproportionate increase among white addicts.

Table 1. Pretreatment background characteristics of female addicts admitted to Clinical Research Center, Lexington, Ky., 1961 and 1967

Pretreatment characteristics	White		Negro		Total	
	Number	Percent	Number	Percent	Number	Percent
1961						
Education:						
Below high school	83	55.3	101	75.4	184	64.8
High school	44	29.3	31	23.1	75	26.4
Above high school	23	15.3	2	1.5	25	8.8
Marital status:						
Single	24	16.0	48	35.8	72	25.4
Intact marriage	77	51.3	40	29.9	117	41.2
Broken marriage	49	32.7	46	34.3	95	33.4
Primary means of support:						
Work	79	52.6	33	24.6	112	39.4
Dependent	55	36.7	53	39.6	108	38.0
Illegal	16	10.7	48	35.8	64	22.5
1967						
Education:						
Below high school	42	47.2	54	64.2	96	55.5
High school	29	32.6	25	29.8	54	31.2
Above high school	18	20.2	5	6.0	23	13.3
Marital status:						
Single	9	10.1	21	25.0	30	17.3
Intact marriage	35	39.3	28	33.3	63	36.4
Broken marriage	45	50.6	35	41.7	80	46.2
Primary means of support:						
Work	16	18.0	10	11.9	26	15.0
Dependent	45	50.6	18	21.4	63	36.4
Illegal	28	31.5	56	66.7	84	48.6

Significant differences between 1961 and 1967 (2 degrees of freedom)

Formal education.................... $X^2 = 4.448$; $P =$ not significant.
   White addicts.................. $X^2 = 1.634$; $P =$ not significant.
   Negro addicts.................. $X^2 = 4.945$; $P =$ not significant.
Marital status...................... $X^2 = 8.324$; $P = <0.02$.
   White addicts.................. $X^2 = 7.679$; $P = <0.05$.
   Negro addicts.................. $X^2 = 2.874$; $P =$ not significant.
Primary means of support........... $X^2 = 43.744$; $P = <0.001$.
   White addicts.................. $X^2 = 32.631$; $P = <0.001$.
   Negro addicts.................. $X^2 = 19.786$; $P = <0.001$.

These findings can be compared to the study by O'Donnell (1) on Kentucky women, who also had a high rate of unstable marriages. There was a marked tendency to select an addicted or otherwise deviant husband (narcotics user, alcoholic, criminal, mentally ill) and a moderate tendency to make deviants of nondeviant spouses. Forty-nine percent of the married women had at least one deviant spouse. These women were usually younger (mean age 22.7 years). Fifty percent had started using drugs for pleasure or to substitute for alcohol, and 75 percent had had contact with addicts. Ninety-two percent of these women had contact with the drug subculture, and 64 percent had a history of arrests.

In contrast, the women who did not have an addict husband tended to be older (mean age 37 years) and had not begun drug use for pleasure. These women had had no extensive contact with addicts, and only 41 percent were involved in the drug subculture. Sixty-five percent of these women obtained their drugs from one physician. Only 12 percent had a history of arrests.

While the data obtained in the current study did not include information concerning the number of children of these women, data from other studies permitted an estimate. A study of married-couple addicts by Cuskey and associates (19) indicates that in 1966 30 women patients had 59 children, and that in 1967 26 women patients had 53 children, an average of two children for each woman. This finding corresponds closely to those of O'Donnell and co-workers (13): an average of 2.2 children for the women patients he studied in 1963. It also compared with the 1960 Kentucky census data, which show an average of three children for women within the 35–39 age group and 3.5 children for women older than 59 years. Thus it might be inferred that the women in this group also would have an average of two children each.

Means of support. Of all the pretreatment background characteristics, the most significant changes occurred in how the female addicts supported themselves. Generally, both the number of those legally employed and those who were dependents decreased, and the number of those resorting to illegal activities as a primary means of support increased—from a little more than 10 percent to more than 30 percent among the white addicts and from a little more than 36 percent to almost 67 percent among the Negro addicts. Regardless of race, the number of female addicts who resorted to illegal activities as their primary means of securing money for drugs significantly increased.

Residence. The female addicts admitted during 1961 had primarily resided in three geographic regions, as defined for the U.S. census: the South, North Central, and Middle Atlantic regions. Sig-

Table 2. Geographic distribution of female addicts admitted to Clinical Research Center, Lexington, Ky., 1961 and 1967

Region	White		Negro	
	Number	Percent	Number	Percent
1961 total	150	100.0	134	100.0
New England				
Middle Atlantic	31	20.7	80	59.7
North Central	42	28.0	34	25.4
South	64	42.7	16	11.9
Mountain	4	2.7		
Pacific	9	6.0	4	3.0
1967 total	89	100.0	84	100.0
New England	4	4.5	2	2.4
Middle Atlantic	8	9.0	22	26.2
North Central	22	24.7	44	52.4
South	47	52.8	13	15.5
Mountain	5	5.6	2	2.4
Pacific	3	3.4	1	1.1

nificant differences in race existed in the number of patients contributed from these three regions (table 2).

The South contributed 42.7 percent of the 150 white female addicts but only 11.9 percent of the 134 Negro addicts. The Middle Atlantic region contributed 59.7 percent of the Negro addicts but only 20.7 percent of the white addicts. The North Central region contributed 28.0 percent of the white and 25.4 percent of the Negro addicts. The remaining 3.0 percent of Negro addicts resided in the Pacific region. The remaining 8.7 percent of white addicts were contributed as follows: 2.7 percent from the Mountain region and 6.0 percent from the Pacific region. Thus in 1961 the South contributed the largest number of white addicts, while most Negro addicts came from the Middle Atlantic region.

In 1967 the number of patients contributed from the South, North Central, and Middle Atlantic regions did not change significantly from the number reported in 1961. Three changes did occur, however, with respect to the proportion of white and Negro addicts contributed by each of these regions. The North Central region replaced the Middle Atlantic region as the largest contributor of Negro addicts, the New England and Mountain regions increased their contribution of both white and Negro addicts, and the Pacific region decreased its contribution of both white and Negro addicts.

In 1967 a total of 90.3 percent had been admitted from the South,

North Central, and Middle Atlantic regions (table 2). The South contributed 52.8 percent of all the white addicts but only 15.5 percent of the Negro addicts. The North Central region contributed 52.4 percent of the Negro addicts, replacing the Middle Atlantic region as the greatest contributor, and only 24.7 percent of the white addicts. The Middle Atlantic region contributed 26.2 percent of the Negro addicts and 9.0 percent of the white addicts. The remaining white addicts were distributed as follows: 5.6 percent from the Mountain region, 3.4 percent from the Pacific region, and 4.5 percent from the New England region. The remaining Negro addicts were distributed as follows: 2.4 percent from the Mountain region, 1.1 percent from the Pacific region, and 2.4 percent from the New England region. Thus, in 1967 the South still contributed the largest number of white addicts, while most of the Negro addicts were now being contributed by the North Central region.

Characteristics of Admissions

Three characteristics were available for comparative analysis when the addicts were admitted for treatment (table 3): (a) whether the addict was entering the hospital voluntarily or as a Federal prisoner, (b) whether entry was the first admission or a readmission, and (c) age of the addict.

Status at admission. Most addict patients in both time periods were admitted voluntarily; the proportion of female addicts voluntarily seeking hospital treatment for opiate addiction increased significantly, however, between 1961 and 1967. Although the numerical increases that occurred within each race cohort were not statistically significant, their cumulative increase was, which indicated greater knowledge and acceptance of this treatment program and the existence of the skills and resources to get there. The greatest increase occurred among Negro addicts: from 79.1 percent in 1961 to 89.3 percent in 1967.

No significant changes occurred in the proportionate representation of first and readmissions in either of the race cohorts or in the population as a whole. In general, there was a slight increase in the proportion of white and Negro addicts admitted to Lexington for treatment for the first time between 1961 and 1967. In 1961, 57.3 percent of the women were admitted to Lexington for first treatment, while in 1967 these patients were 60.1 percent of the clinic's female population. While this slight increase is not statistically significant, the racial analysis shows that the proportion of white first-admission patients increased 6.5 percent and the Negro first-admission patients decreased 1.4 percent.

Four of every 10 women had readmissions, indicating that a large number of female addicts of both races were experienced in the Lexington treatment process. Of the women admitted in 1967,

Table 3. Characteristics at admission for treatment of female addicts, Clinical Research Center, Lexington, Ky., 1961 and 1967

Characteristics of admission	1961		1967		X²	Probability
	Number	Percent	Number	Percent		
Voluntary	244	85.9	161	93.1	5.448	0.02
White	138	92.0	86	96.6	1.324	N.S.
Negro	106	79.1	75	89.3	3.798	N.S.
First treatment	163	57.3	104	60.1	.329	N.S.
White	83	55.3	55	61.8	.001	N.S.
Negro	80	59.7	49	58.3	.040	N.S.
Above age 25	233	82.0	119	68.8	10.675	.01
White	126	84.0	65	73.1	3.801	N.S.
Negro	107	79.8	54	70.2	6.478	.02

NOTE: N.S., not significant.

Table 4. Age distributions of female addicts, Clinical Research Center, Lexington, Ky., 1961 and 1967

Age group (years)	White [1]		Negro [2]	
	Number	Percent	Number	Percent
1961 total	150	100.0	134	100.0
15–19	3	2.0	2	1.5
20–24	21	14.0	25	18.7
25–29	24	16.0	46	34.3
30–34	16	10.7	36	26.9
35–39	20	13.3	16	11.9
40–44	14	9.3	5	3.7
45 and over	52	34.7	4	3.0
1967 total	89	100.0	84	100.0
15–19	5	5.6		
20–24	19	21.3	25	29.8
25–29	12	13.5	24	28.6
30–34	19	21.3	12	14.3
35–39	7	7.9	14	16.7
40–44	11	12.4	7	8.3
45 and over	16	18.0	2	2.4

[1] Median age: 1961, 35–39; 1967, 30–34.
[2] Median age: 1961 and 1967, 25–29.

15.7 percent of the white and 11.9 of the Negro were being treated for at least the fourth time. These proportions were not significantly different from 1961, when 18.7 percent of the whites and 11.9 percent of the Negroes were admitted for at least the fourth time.

Age at admission. Female addicts of both races were younger at admission in 1967 than their counterparts in 1961 (table 4). Eighty-two percent of the addicts were over age 25 at admission in 1961, while in 1967 the representation of this group had significantly decreased to 68.8 percent. Similar decreases in the proportion over age 25 were noted in each of the two racial groups, although only the decrease for Negro addicts was statistically significant.

Comparison of median ages indicated no change for Negro addicts; the median was in the 25–29 category. A decrease occurred for the white addicts, however; the median fell from 35–39 in 1961 to 30–34 in 1967. White female addicts had been and continued to be older than the Negro addicts.

Characteristics of drug abuse. Information on characteristics of drug use by female addicts was available only for 1967 (table 5); similar data were not recorded for 1961. Comparison by race was made to provide this information on the contemporary addicts. Four

Table 5. Drug abuse characteristics of female addicts admitted to Clinical Research Center, Lexington, Ky., 1967

Addiction habits	White		Negro		X^2	Probability
	Number	Percent	Number	Percent		
Opiate used:						
Heroin_____	30	33. 7	79	94. 0	67. 5019	0. 001
Other_____	59	66. 3	5	6. 0		
Marijuana ever						
used_____	40	44. 9	74	88. 1	35. 8054	. 001
Administration:						
Intravenous_____	51	57. 3	78	92. 8	38. 8034	. 001
Other_____	38	42. 7	6	7. 2		
Source of drugs:						
Pusher_____	44	49. 4	80	95. 2	44. 6505	. 001
Other_____	45	50. 6	4	4. 8		

variables pertaining to these addicts and drug abuse were available for analysis: whether the narcotic abused was heroin or another drug, whether marijuana was ever used, what method was used to administer the drug, and whether the pusher was a primary source of drugs.

Attributes associated with the abused drugs, how they were used, and from whom they were obtained were all identifiable by the addict's race. These were also predictable from the earlier studies of female addicts. T h i s study therefore replicated the earlier studies.

Negro female addicts generally had smoked marijuana and had been addicted to heroin, which they purchased from pushers and administered intravenously. White addicts had been identified significantly less often by any of these attributes and abused a variety of other drugs, including dilaudid, percodan, morphine, paregoric, laudanum, codeine, demerol, and dolophine.

Life Style

The demographic study of the f e m a l e patients of Lexington would seem to indicate the existence of three major life styles characterizing the white heroin addict, the white medical addict, and the Negro heroin addict. A forthcoming sociological study of the 1967 data is expected to give additional information on the following general types.

White heroin addict. A relatively young woman who seems to be characterized by the early use of marijuana and the present use of heroin, administered intravenously and obtained from pushers. She probably would have an addicted spouse, one or more broken marriages, and support herself by illegal means.

White medical addict. Seems to use drugs other than heroin, which she usually obtains from one physician. She seems not to have used marijuana and not to have used intravenous drug administration. She seems to be older, not to have an addicted spouse, and to work or be dependent on others for her support.

Negro heroin addicts. Seem to compose a more homogeneous group of younger persons, most of whom would have used marijuana, obtained heroin from pushers, and used it by intravenous injection. The majority of these young women earn their livelihood by illegal means, usually prostitution, and have been arrested. They have a high rate of broken marriages.

The lives of these women, and especially of those married to deviant spouses, reflect a life style deeply enmeshed with the drug culture. That this is related to a life history of problems is evidenced by the psychiatric diagnoses made at Lexington in which personality disorders and psychoneurotic disorders were found to be most frequent for the women examined. A high incidence of school dropouts, broken marriages, and illegal activity also was evidenced.

The emerging pattern of the life situation of the women included in these studies shows an involved history of social, economic, and psychological problems, with recurrent relapses requiring hospitalization. This study corresponds closely to Clifford's study (20) of the relapse patterns of mentally depressed patients in France, where the social contagion of other adults and children was noted.

These findings imply the need for a preventive mental health program directed to the addict population. Particular attention would seem to be required in child psychiatry and in meeting the socialization needs of children living in pathogenic or pathologic situations. This would be most urgent for the female children, especially Negro, whose life alternatives are generally limited to their immediate family and its social network.

These findings also imply the need to study the social support systems available to addicts returning to their former environment after hospital treatment and to develop possible alternatives.

Treatment Effectiveness, Cost

The fact that four of every 10 women patients constitute readmission cases indicates the great difficulty in finding and applying a truly effective treatment modality. Certain mounting social and economic investments in each patient as he or she returns for additional periods of treatment also are implied.

Economic costs. As yet there is insufficient research to permit an

Table 6. Modality of treatment and cost per day per drug addict, June 1, 1967–July 1, 1969

Modality	Cost per day
Medical psychiatric, Federal:	
Lexington Clinical Research Center	(¹)
Fort Worth Clinical Research Center	(¹)
Medical psychiatric, Philadelphia:	
University of Pennsylvania Hospital Psychiatric Center	$84. 00
Temple University Hospital	80. 00
General Hospital Psychiatric Service	61. 00
Psychiatric Center	34. 00
Medical psychiatric, Pennsylvania State:	
Haverford State Mental Hospital	32. 40
Byberry State Mental Hospital	14. 80
Norristown State Hospital	11. 90
Communal: Guadenzia House	12. 50
Punitive:	
Pennsylvania State Correctional Institution	9. 60
Philadelphia prisons	7. 13
Legal authority with specialized treatment:	
Goodwill (National Addiction Rehabilitation Act of 1963)	5. 55
Institute for Alcoholism and Drug Addiction	5. 20
State Board of Vocational Rehabiltation	1. 84
Religious: Teen Challenge	3. 42
Chemical substitition:	
New York Methadone	5. 48
Narcotics Addiction Rehabilitation Program of the West Philadelphia Community Mental Health Consortium	3. 28
Young Great Society	1. 43

¹ Not available.

overall view of the economic costs of drug addiction and abuse. There is some indication, however, of the direct service costs for several treatment modalities employed in 1967 (21). The cost per patient per day fluctuated greatly with the type of treatment (table 6). The chemical substitute modality, usually on an outpatient basis, had the lowest cost range. Medical-psychiatric service costs in Philadelphia had the highest cost range. They also had the added advantage of permitting the patient to retain an active economic and social role, avoiding to a great extent the

problems related to recidivism. The effectiveness and costs of the different modalities of treatment have not yet been evaluated.

Data are not available to the public on costs at the Federal addiction treatment centers in Lexington and Fort Worth. Thus it is impossible to estimate the expense of the usual 5- to 14-day treatment for the patients in this study. Moreover, as the research in treatment modalities and administrative arrangements at Lexington continues, there is little likelihood of a standard comparable cost figure becoming available.

A study of the treatment modalities, with their effectiveness and cost, is very important to communities that are planning to organize their resources for dealing with the epidemic proportions of drug abuse.

To the direct and indirect treatment costs should be added other economic costs relating to drug addiction and abuse. These figures should include the costs of law enforcement, courts and prisons, property damage and theft—more than $900 million in Philadelphia in 1969—insurance, accidents, and the lost production, income, and consumer market potential of the incapacitated addicts and their victims.

Social costs. While the social costs of drug addition and abuse have been felt by the public in a general way, as evidenced by the news media, no valid estimate has yet been made of them. Available data indicate clearly defined social costs. These include a damaged self-image; deterioration of personal health, productivity, and creativity; personal degradation from criminality and prostitution; high death rates; family disorganization with the resulting damage to the marriage partner, the children, and the extended family members; and aggression against individuals and their property, producing a climate of general insecurity (22).

These social costs produce the contagion phenomenon and the potential of a hard core pathogenic segment in the population.

Preliminary studies have shown that for each pathologic adult at least one other adult and two children are affected (23).

The social, psychological, and cultural environment of the children living in the drug subculture would seem likely to produce another generation of ever younger drug abusers or deviants. These children are culturally trapped and instructed in the drug culture and in the illegal means used to support it. This would seem to be especially true for the young Negro addicts.

REFERENCES

(1) O'Donnell, J.: Narcotic addicts in Kentucky. PHS Publication No. 1881. U.S. Government Printing Office, Washington, D.C., 1969.

(2) Pescor, M. J.: Follow-up study of treated narcotic drug addicts. Public Health Rep Supplement No. 170, pp. 1–18, 1943.

(3) Kuznesof, M.: Probation for a cure: An analysis of 84 drug addict cases committed to the United States Public Health Hospital for treatment as part of probation. U.S. Probation Office, Southern District of New York, September 1955. Mimeographed.

(4) Hunt, G. H., and Odoroff, M. E.: Followup study of narcotic drug addicts after hospitalization. Public Health Rep 77: 41–54, January 1962.

(5) Duvall, H. J.: Locke, B. Z., and Brill, L.: Followup study of narcotic drug addicts five years after hospitalization. Public Health Rep. 78: 185–193, March 1963.

(6) Vaillant, G.: A twelve year followup of New York City addicts. I. The relation of treatment to outcome. Amer J Psychiat 122: 727–737 (1966).

(7) Diskind, M., and Klonsky, G.: Recent developments in the treatment of paroled offenders addicted to narcotic drugs. New York State Division of Parole, Albany, 1964.

(8) Gerard, D., Lee, R., Rosenfield, E., and Chein, I.: Post-hospitalization adjustment: A followup study of adolescent opiate addicts. Research Center for Human Relations, New York University, 1956.

(9) Bates, W.: Occupational characteristics of Negro addicts. Int J Addictions 3: 345–350 (1968).

(10) Chambers, C., Moffett, A., and Jones, J.: Demographic factors associated with Negro opiate addiction. Int J Addictions 3: 329–343 (1968).

(11) O'Donnell, J.: Narcotic addiction and crime. Soc Prob 13: 374–385 (1966).

(12) O'Donnell, J.: The rise and decline of a subculture. Soc Prob 15: 73–84 (1967).

(13) O'Donnell, J., Besteman, K., and Jones, J.: Marital history of narcotic addicts. Int J Addictions 2: 21–38 (1967).

(14) Glaser, F.: Narcotic addiction in the pain-prone female patient. Int J Addictions 1: 47–59 (1966).

(15) Chambers, C., Hinesley, R., and Moldestad, M.: Narcotic addiction in females: A race comparison. Int J Addictions 5: 257–258 (1970).

(16) Ball, J., Bates, W., and O'Donnell, J.: Characteristics of hospitalized narcotic addicts. Health, Education, and Welfare Indicators, March 1966, pp. 1–10.

(17) Ellingwood, E., Smith, W., and Vaillant, G.: Narcotic addiction in males and females: A comparison. Int J Addictions 1: 33–45 (1966).

(18) Ball, J., and Chambers, C.: Epidemiology of opiate addiction in the U.S. C. F. Thomas, Inc., New York, 1970.

(19) Cuskey, W., Clifford, H., and Moffett, A.: Drug addiction among married couples. Int Bull Narcotics. In press.

(20) Clifford, H.: L'analyze du contenu sociologique dans dix cas psychiatriques. [Unpublished dissertation.] Institut de Psychologie, de Sociologie et de Pédagogie, Université de Lyon, 1969.

(21) Moffett, A.: Cost analysis of narcotic treatment programs. Narcotic Research Information Exchange. In press.

(22) Clifford, H.: Un modèle pour le coût social de la maladie mentale. [Unpublished dissertation.] Institut de Psychologie, de Sociologie et de Pédagogie, Université de Lyon, 1969.

(23) Clifford, H.: L'analyze des données sociologiques in psychiatrie sociale. [Unpublished dissertation.] Institut de Psychologie, de Sociologie et de Pédagogie, Université de Lyon, 1969.

Treatment of Narcotic Addiction

Current Approaches
to the Treatment of Narcotic Addiction*

JAMES F. MADDUX, M.D.

IN A book about the opium habit written 100
years ago, Day noted that the medical profession was by no means agreed as to the proper
treatment of the opium disease.[1] At that time and
well into the 20th century the literature on treatment of narcotic addiction was primarily concerned
with treatment of the acute abstinence syndrome.
Many procedures and substances were used. Pre-
occupation with treatment of acute abstinence continued until about 1938, when Kolb and Himmelsbach[2] showed that the acute abstinence syndrome
is self-limited and disappears regardless of what
treatment is given for it, provided the opiate is
taken away from the patient. Controversy about
treatment of acute abstinence has about disappeared, but disagreement still characterizes treatment of narcotic addiction. Current divergent
opinion is expressed on issues related to legal
control of opioid drugs, civil commitment, and
maintenance of opioid dependence.

After the Harrison Narcotic Act was enacted in
1914, many addicts became law violators and

* Read at the 73rd Annual Convention of the National
Medical Association, Houston, Texas, August 11-15, 1968.

found themselves incarcerated. To remedy this situation, two Public Health Service Hospitals in Lexington, Kentucky and Fort Worth, Texas were opened in 1935 and 1938, respectively. Treatment of both prisoner and voluntary addicts was authorized. The programs of these hospitals represented pioneering advances at that time. Not only the acute abstinence syndrome, but the more important mental and emotional problems were to be treated.[3] It was felt that by residence in a drug-free environment for months, the patient would become unconditioned to his habit of taking narcotics to relieve distress. Psychotherapy, work therapy, and other activities were provided. Over the years the treatment programs of these two hospitals have changed to include group therapy and group counseling, milieu therapy, remedial education, vocational training, use of patients as therapeutic agents, efforts to develop transitional and posthospital services, and evaluation research.[4] In 1967 the two hospitals were placed under the National Institute of Mental Health and were designated Clinical Research Centers. They have new missions of clinical research on drug abuse and personality disorders.

Narcotic addiction seems to occur as a continuum varying in severity from person to person and varying in time in a given person. Some persons apparently use narcotic drugs occasionally for prolonged periods without developing physical dependence or compulsive use. For others compulsive narcotic use becomes the dominant feature of their lives and they experience alternating periods of abstinence and relapse for many years. Studies at the Addiction Research Center by Himmelsbach,[5] Martin[6], and Wikler and Pescor[7] indicate that continued and recurrent opioid use may occur in part as a result of protracted abstinence and conditioning factors. Signs of protracted abstinence may last for as long as six months. Addicted persons vary in personality and social circumstances, but clinical observers report characterological difficulties in most of their addict patients. They are described as lacking internal controls, seeking immediate gratification, blaming others for their problems, easily angered and hurt, and as exploiting and manipulating others. Their life histories frequently reveal chaotic family experiences, school failure, and unstable vocational experience. Most represent formidable treatment problems.

Since 1950 many State, local, and voluntary programs for narcotic addiction has been established. In 1967 Winick and Bynder[8] identified 165 programs for treatment of drug users and addicts. Most of the treatment facilities with which I am familiar attempt to provide a flexible combination of treatment services to deal with the combination of pharmacological, psychological, and social problems presented by the addict patients. Some notable exceptions occur in a few experimental programs which emphasize a special treatment modality. From the wide range of agencies, programs, and services existing today I have identified six features of current treatment approaches which have attracted professional or public attention. Some of these are concerned with conditions related to treatment, and other represent specific components of treatment. The six features are: continuity of treatment, civil commitment, methadone maintenance, narcotic antagonists, mutual help, and religious experience.

CONTINUITY OF TREATMENT

Most modern treatment programs attempt to provide a continuity of treatment, prehospital, hospital, and posthospital. An experiment in providing a continuum of services for narcotic addicts was initiated by the Fort Worth Clinical Research Center in 1966, in collaboration with 15 community agencies in San Antonio. Posthospital adjustment of 140 control subjects who had institutional treatment alone will be compared with 124 experimental subjects who were offered the continuum of services. Our initial experience has indicated that although most voluntary patients without legal pressure make only minimal use of the services available, some learn over a period of time to use casework and other helping services.

Halfway houses for addicts have been established to ease the transition from institution to community. Reports from two experimental halfway houses in Los Angeles[9] and Houston[10] indicate that these facilities experienced some difficulty with their residents. Significant number of the residents resisted engagement in treatment activities, a stable therapeutic community could not be maintained, and recurrent disrupting events of rule-breaking, theft, and narcotic use occurred. A one-year followup of a control group and an experimental group by the Los Angeles facility showed no significant difference in outcomes as measured by return to narcotic use and criminal activity.

Although many voluntary subjects show a limited capacity for engaging in it, continuity of care represents a distinct advance in treatment. It is expected that many local services for addicts will eventually be affiliated with community mental health centers.

CIVIL COMMITMENT

For many years clinical staff at the Lexington and Fort Worth Centers have recurrently recommended civil commitment for addict patients who want treatment but demonstrate inability to use it. Over the years about three-fourths of the voluntary patients without legal pressure have left the hospitals against medical advice. Since 1960 rehabilitation programs utilizing civil commitment have been developed in California, New York, Massachusetts, and Maryland. The programs utilizing civil commitment provide continuity of treatment as well as some measure of external control.

Legislation enacted in California in 1961, and amended in 1963 and 1965, provided for civil commitment, institutional rehabilitation, and mandatory aftercare. A large facility with a capacity for 2200 subjects, the California Rehabilitation Center, was established at Corona. The period of commitment varies from two and one half years for persons voluntarily seeking commitment, to seven years for persons committed subsequent to conviction for law violation.

In 1962 New York enacted a law providing for civil commitment of addicts in lieu of prosecution. A new law in 1966 established a New York State Narcotic Addiction Commission and provided for extensive programs of treatment, research, and education. The new law provides for civil commitment initiated by self or other as well as for commitment in lieu of prosecution. At the end of 1967 care was being provided to 2251 court certified addicts in 19 residential rehabilitation centers.

A radical change in the Federal treatment programs has begun under provisions of the Narcotic Addict Rehabilitation Act of 1966. The Act provides not only for civil commitment by United States Courts, but in addition authorizes post-hospital care and supervision, permits the Surgeon General to make contracts with State and community facilities for care of committed addicts, and authorizes grants and jointly financed arrangements with governmental and private organizations for demonstrations, training, surveys, and treatment centers. The National Institute of Mental Health administers these new activities, now generally called "the NARA program." The Act provides for civil commitment under three conditions. Title I authorized civil commitment in lieu of prosecution. A narcotic addict charged with violating a Federal law may, if he elects it, submit to an examination to determine if he is a narcotic addict and is likely to be rehabilitated through treatment. He may subsequently be committed to treatment for a period of 36 months. After an initial period of treatment in a hospital he may be conditionally released for supervised aftercare.

Under Title II, an addict convicted of a Federal law violation may, following examination, be committed to treatment for a period not to exceed ten years. He may be conditionally released after six months of institutional care.

Title III authorizes commitment initiated by voluntary petition of the narcotic addict or a related individual, if State or other facilities are not available. Following examination, the person may be committed to a hospital for a period not to exceed six months. On release from the hospital, he may be committed to care and custody of the Surgeon General for three years of posthospital treatment.

Hospital care of patients committed under Title I and Title III is provided at the Lexington and Fort Worth Centers. Title II patients were initially sent to these Centers, but in the future will be treated in special facilities developed by the Bureau of Prisons. The posthospital care of NARA patients is carried out by State and community agencies under contract with the Public Health Service. To provide field supervision and assistance to agencies, the National Institute of Mental Health has established field offices in New York, Chicago, Los Angeles and San Antonio. Additional field offices will be established.

Although the new law was enacted in 1966, the NARA program was not started until June, 1967, when funds became available from a supplemental appropriation by Congress. During fiscal year 1968 the courts sent 581 patients to the Lexington and Fort Worth Centers for examination. Most of these, 59 per cent, came under Title III, that is, their commitment was initiated by voluntary petition. Seventy per cent of the patients admitted for examination were subsequently committed for treatment.

Subjects not committed for treatment were found in most instances to be narcotic addicts as defined by the law, but most showed such consistent antagonistic behavior that they were considered not likely to be rehabilitated. Both institutions have secure units in which we can hold some of these persons, but they use an inordinate amount of staff time, and they demoralize patients attempting to engage in the rehabilitation process. I think that some of these patients do want help, but the initial exposure to therapy mobilizes such intense anxiety and depression that they engage in a frantic flight from therapy. At the Fort Worth Center we have recently established a closed intensive treatment unit for a small number of these difficult patients to see if we can show them that therapeutic engagement does not signify catastrophe.

Civil commitment restricts freedom of the individual, but for temporary periods and under appropriate judicial process. Some addicted persons having legal freedom also want freedom from their psychopharmacological slavedom, but cannot mobilize sufficient inner strength to achieve it through voluntary engagement in treatment. For such persons the temporary external control of civil commitment may provide a necessary support in their struggle for abstinence.

METHADONE MAINTENANCE

In 1964 in New York City, Dole and Nyswander[19-14] began their experiment of maintaining heroin addicts on methadone. The general idea of the project consists of treating heroin addicts by first stabilizing them on a daily maintenance dosage of methadone and subsequently undertaking rehabilitation, rather than the usual sequence in other programs of first withdrawing the narcotic drug and then attempting rehabilitation.

Heroin addicts enter and remain in the program voluntarily. The general criteria for admission include heroin addiction for at least four years, no major addiction to barbiturates or other substances, absence of psychosis and serious medical illness, age range about 20 to 40, and repeated unsuccessful treatment attempts. About 60 per cent of applicants were accepted during a recent 14 month period. The project has a waiting list of several hundred applicants.

The patients are initially hospitalized for a period of six weeks. During this time they are given gradually increasing oral doses of methadone until they are stabilized on a single daily dose of about 100 milligrams. After leaving the hospital the patients return to an outpatient clinic for a regular daily dose of methadone. Since few patients are discharged from the program, the case-load constantly increases; over 300 patients have been admitted.

The program does not provide formal psychotherapy, but some counseling and social assistance are given, and much informal interaction among staff and patients occurs. I observed a high level of morale among patients and staff on a visit to the program in 1966.

The investigators have reported that former heroin users can be stabilized on methadone without escalation of dosage. The methadone blocks the euphoric effect of heroin and other opioid drugs. Patients have discontinued illicit heroin-seeking and other antisocial behavior. About three-fourths of the patients who have been in treatment for six months or longer have become productively employed.

Replication of the methadone experiment has begun in other centers. In Philadelphia, Wieland[15] has stablized about 40 patients on methadone, and has reported that 80 per cent are working or going to school. Freedman[16] stabilized 15 opiate addicts on methadone. After a period of over one year, seven had dropped out, but eight were functioning well in the community.

In its support of opioid dependence, methadone maintenance stands out in sharp contrast to other treatment approaches. Whether some of the patients can eventually be withdrawn from methadone remains a question for the future.

NARCOTIC ANTAGONISTS

The opioid antagonist, nalorphine (nalline) was initially used in California[17] for detecting opiod use, and it has subsequently been used as a monitoring and deterrent device for narcotic users under legal supervision. This drug precipitates an abstinence syndrome in persons physically dependent on opioid drugs. Nalorphine testing never received widespread use as a component of treatment. Its use for detecting opioid use is in recent years being displaced by testing of urine for opioid drugs.

Very recently some exploratory studies have begun with another narcotic antagonist, cyclazocine, not for the purpose of detecting opioid use, but for the purpose of blocking effects of opioid drugs. Cyclazocine is a long acting narcotic antagonist, effective when given orally. It has analgestic action, and it may produce undesirable side effects of sedation, dysphoria, and perceptual distortion. Tolerance to these side effects develop if small doses are given initially and the dosage is slowly increased over a period of several weeks.

In 1966 Martin and associates[18] reported an experiment in which subjects hospitalized at the Lexington Center were stabilized on a daily dosage of about four milligrams of cyclazocine and subsequently tested with single and chronically administered doses of morphine. The investigators found that chronically administered cyclazocine antagonized the euphoric effect of morphine as well as its physical dependence-producing property.

Jaffe and Brill[19] have reported their experience with 11 narcotic addicts who voluntarily accepted treatment with cyclazocine. Nine of the 11 continued taking cyclazocine as outpatients for varying periods. At the time of the report one patient had been maintained on cyclazocine for three months.

Freedman and associates[20] stabilized 58 abstinent addicts on cyclazocine. After discharge from the hospital 31 were dropped, but the remaining 27 continued on cyclazocine for at least two months.

It appears that some addicts will accept cyclazocine maintenance at least for short periods. Two kinds of benefits may accrue from cyclazocine treatment. First, since opioid drugs no longer have the desired effects, the patient may cease his chase after illicit drugs and become engaged in rehabilitation. Second, recovery from protracted abstinence and extinction of conditioned responses prompting opioid use may occur.

MUTUAL HELP

Formally organized mutual helping activity among narcotic addicts has existed for many years and has taken several forms. At the Lexington and Fort Worth Centers the staff have attempted to exploit the mutual help potential of the patients. Group therapy was started in 1950 and continues to be a major therapeutic activity. A number of self-government and other sociotherapeutic activities have been developed. In 1964 at the Fort Worth Center a special unit for 30 patients was established which not only governs itself, but in addition has regular small group therapy sessions conducted by rehabilitation oriented patient leaders.

Several programs employ former addicts as regular staff members. The Addiction Research Center in Puerto Rico employs former addicts as clinical aides and community orienters. Southmore House, the halfway house for addicts in Houston, employed a former addict patient as a counselor. The Patrician Movement—Operation CHAPS, a community agency for addicts in San Antonio, has employed two former addicts who work as field counselors. The methadone maintenance program in New York City employs former heroin addicts now maintained on methadone to provide counseling and other services to patients.

An Addicts Anonymous group patterned after Alcoholics Anonymous was started in the Lexington Center about 1948, and a similar group began in the Fort Worth Center in 1954. These groups have continued to present time. In 1949 a former addict patient from Lexington started a Narcotics Anonymous group in New York City and similar groups were reportedly established in 14 other cities.[21] A Narcotics Anonymous group began in San Antonio in 1966 and continues to the present time. Its continued survival has depended substantially on the sustained assistance of a social worker in our San Antonio continuum of services project.

A striking innovation in mutual help of narcotic addicts, the Synanon Foundation, began in 1958 in Santa Monica, California.[22-26] This program is directed almost entirely by former narcotic addicts. Beginning with some spontaneous informal group discussions of a small number of narcotic users, the movement has grown in ten years to become a large formal organization reportedly having over 800 residents. Residential facilities have been established in Santa Monica, San Diego, San Francisco, Detroit, and New York. A large new facility is being constructed at Tomales Bay, California.

The program evolved the leadership of one individual, Mr. Charles E. Dederich. Initially the organization was governed as a benevolent autocracy with Mr. Dederich in direct personal interaction with all members, but increasing size of the organization dictated the evolution of a bureaucratic structure with several levels of executives and coordinators.

The person seeking admission to Synanon does not receive a friendly welcome. The intake interviews expose him to an ordeal of challenging and often sarcastic questions about his motives and behavior. Once admitted he is withdrawn without medication, and he is assigned to menial work. For about six months the resident cannot leave the Synanon House unless accompanied by a more advanced resident. He can progress to a phase in which he works at an outside job approved by the staff, but he coninues to live at the House. Eventually some residents live outside but return regularly to participate in the program. Some residents are promoted to coordinator positions and pursue work careers inside the Synanon organization.

A central therapeutic activity consists of "synanons" or "games" conducted three or more times weekly. In these small group discussions the members provoke intense emotional interaction by aggressive mutual confronting about problem attitudes, feelings, and behavior. They verbally attack, castigate, and ridicule each other, often in gutter language. While hostile verbal attack occurs regularly in the games and in other interactions, the residents also show mutual approval in friendly and affectionate language.

Premature departure from Synanon occurs frequently. Cherkas[23] reported that of 844 admis-

116

sions from September 1, 1958 to April 1, 1964, over half, 459, left prematurely. It was felt that most of these returned to drug use. Markoff[24] reported that 25 per cent of the total admissions to Synanon from its inception to January 1962, were known to have continued their abstinence from drug use on a two year followup, but complete followup on all admissions was not available. Yablonsky and Dederich[26] reported that 80 of the 170 persons in Synanon in 1963 had been "clean," that is, abstinent, for a year or longer.

Another mutual help program managed and staffed by abstinent addicts, Daytop Village, began in Staten Island, New York, in 1963.[27] This program was sponsored by the probation department of a New York court, and was initially supported by a grant from the National Institute of Mental Health. The program is directed by a former addict and is modeled on the Synanon program. Some differences from the Synanon approach include effort to reach the addict on the street, group meetings with relatives, and a plan for evaluation using a control group.

RELIGIOUS EXPERIENCE

Institutional programs for addicts usually provide religious services and other activities; for some patients renewal of religious faith seems to serve as an important component of their rehabilitation. Several local voluntary programs have been founded and supported by religious groups. These programs provide a variable spectrum of medical, counseling, vocational and other professional services, and may not emphasize explicit religious practice. Examples are Exodus House[28] in New York City, and the Patrician Movement—Operation CHAPS in San Antonio.

The Teen Challenge movement, initiated in 1958 in New York City by the Reverend David Wilkerson,[29] provides an exception to the usual pattern of multiple professional services in church sponsored programs. This movement makes a straightforward evangelistic attempt to reach delinquent and addicted youth. The workers walk the streets to find their clients, preach on street corners, and attempt to surround them with love. A number of young heroin users have reportedly become abstinent while participating in the Teen Challenge program. Several attribute their change to the intense religious experience of baptism of the Holy Spirit.

EVALUATION OF CURRENT TREATMENT APPROACHES

Comparative studies which clearly identify one treatment method as uniformly applicable for all addicts and more successful than others have not been done. All the treatment approaches I have described can cite success cases of addicts who have remained abstinent for varying periods or who have improved their social performance while maintained on an opioid drug, but all seem to have numerous cases who were not accepted or who did not engage in treatment or who dropped out or who became readdicted. Cross comparison of results is confronted by treacherous problems in research methodology. Sources of error lie in the concepts, definitions and procedures for measuring the variability of the subjects, the circumstances of their living, paths to treatment, and posttreatment experience. Some important variables, for example, the craving for drugs, and the inner struggle for abstinence, cannot be measured directly and precisely. O'Donnell[30] has suggested that you should read followup studies of addicts with a skeptical eye and with a few grains of salt handy. They can lead to inappropriate judgments about comparative success and failure of different treatment programs. For example, Ramirez[31] contrasted a relapse rate of about 92 per cent for addicts treated at Lexington to a relapse rate of 5.6 per cent obtained in the program in Puerto Rico. He was probably referring to a followup study by Duvall and others[32] which indicated that 97 per cent of a sample of 453 subjects discharged from the Lexington Center and followed in New York City became readdicted at least once during five years following discharge. Ramirez stated that 5.6 per cent of 124 heroin addicts who completed treatment in Puerto Rico became readdicted, but he did not give the duration of the post-treatment followup. A relapse rate for a five-year period cannot be usefully compared with a relapse rate for an unknown period.

The Synanon Foundation has opposed evaluation which would count subjects who engaged in the program and subsequently relapsed to narcotic use, for this information might harm the spirit of hope and opportunity which prevails in the Synanon program. This is not a negligible consideration in evaluation studies, for faith and hope represent important ingredients of any psychosocial therapeutic process, and evaluation procedure could adversely affect the therapeutic outcomes which it attempts to measure. For this or other reasons professional workers may also resist specific evaluation procedures, but most have sufficient exposure to scientific tradition to accept empirical measures of results. Further, many professional workers having experience with narcotic addicts do not become dismayed by enumerations of relapse. They have come to view relapse not as treatment failure, but as an event which may occur in the course of treatment and which in some instances heralds a significant advance in the rehabilitation process.

I doubt that a single treatment of choice will ever be established for narcotic addiction, for the addicts represent a heterogeneous population with varied readiness and motivation and capacity to engage in one form or another of treatment. Some with sufficient personal strength can engage voluntarily in outpatient psychotherapy or counseling. Others need the external legal control of commitment. Some are drawn to mutual help programs, and some to religious experience. Methadone maintenance may become accepted for some addicts who seem intractable over long periods to other treatment efforts. This is not to say that all treatment methods are equally good for all addicts, but rather that differentiation of treatment approaches provides multiple invitations, opportunities, and paths whereby opioid-dependent persons may begin to seek gratification less from drugs and more from interpersonal experience.

LITERATURE CITED

1. DAY, H. B. The Opium Habit, with Suggestions as to Remedy. New York: Harper and Bros., 1868. (Cited by Sonnedecker, G. in Emergence and Concept of the Addiction Problem," R. B. Livingston, ed. Narcotic Drug, Addiction Problems. U. S. Govt. Printing Off., Washington, D. C., 1958.

2. KOLB, L. and C. K. HIMMELSBACH. Clinical Studies of Drug Addiction III. A Critical Review of the Withdrawal Treatments with a Method of Evaluating Abstinence Syndromes. Pub. Health Rep., Supp., 128, 1938.

3. KOLB, L. Drug Addiction as a Public Health Problem, Scientific Monthly, 48:391-400, 1939.

4. MADDUX, J. F. and S. N. KIEFFER and W. P. JURGENSEN, et al. New Developments in Federal Narcotic Treatment Hospitals, in Rehabilitating the Narcotic Addict, Sells, H. F., ed. U. S. Government Printing Office, Washington, D. C., 1966.

5. HIMMELSBACH, C. K. Clinical Studies on Drug Addiction. Physical Dependence, Withdrawal, and Recovery. Arch. Int. Med., 69:766-772, 1942.

6. MARTIN, W. R. Pharmacologic Factors in Relapse and the Possible Use of the Narcotic Antagonists in Treatment, Ill. Med. J., 130:489-494, 1966.

7. WIKLER, A. and F. T. PESCOR. Classical Conditioning of a Morphine Abstinence Phenomenon, Reinforcement of Opioid-Drinking Behavior and "Relapse" in Morphine-Addicted Rats. Psychopharmacologia (Berl.) 10:255-284, 1967.

8. WINICK, C. and H. BYNDER. Facilities for Treatment and Rehabilitation of Narcotic Drug Users and Addicts. Am. J. Pub. Health, 57:1025-1033, 1967.

9. GEIS, G. The East Los Angeles Halfway House for Narcotic Addicts. Sacramento: The Institute for the Study of Crime and Delinquency, 1966.

10. CARRICK, R. W. Southmore House: Use of a Halfway House and Integrated Community Approaches in the Posthospital/Correctional Institution Rehabilitation of Narcotic Addicts, in Sells, H. F., ed. Rehabilitating the Narcotic Addict. U. S. Government Printing Office, Washington, D. C., 1966.

11. DOLE, V. P. and M. E. NYSWANDER. A Medical Treatment for Diacetylmorphine (Heroin) Addiction. J.A.M.A., 193:646-650, 1965.

120

12. DOLE, V. P., M. E. NYSWANDER and M. J. KREEK. Narcotic Blockade. Arch. Int. Med., 118:304-309, 1966.

13. DOLE, V. P. and M. E. NYSWANDER. "Methadone Maintenance and its Implication for Theories of Narcotic Addiction," in Wikler, A. ed. The Addictive States. Williams and Wilkins Co., Baltimore, 1968.

14. NYSWANDER, M. E. and V. P. DOLE. The Present Status of Methodone Blockade Treatment. Am. J. Psych., 123:1441-1442, 1967.

15. WIELAND, W. F. Methodone Maintenance Treatment of Heroin Addiction: Beginning Treatment on an Outpatient Basis. Paper read at the annual meeting of the American Psychiatric Association, 1968.

16. FREEDMAN, A. M. Toward a Rational Approach to the Treatment of Narcotic Addiction: Basic Notions, in Wikler, A., ed.: The Addictive States. Williams and Wilkins Co., Baltimore, 1968.

17. TERRY, J. G. and F. L. BRAUMOELLER. Nalline: An Aid in Detecting Narcotic Users. Calif. Med., 85: 299-301, 1956.

18. MARTIN, W. R. and M. D. GORODETZKY and T. K. McCLANE. An Experimental Study in the Treatment of Narcotic Addicts with Cyclazocine, Clin. Phar. and Ther., 7:455-465, 1966.

19. JAFFE, J. H. and L. BRILL. Cyclazocine, a Long Acting Narcotic Antagonist: Its Voluntary Acceptance as a Treatment Modality by Narcotics Abusers. Int. J. Addictions, 1:99-123, 1966.

20. FREEDMAN, A. M. and M. FINK, R. SHAROFF and A. ZAKS. Clinical Studies of Cyclazocine in the Treatment of Narcotic Addiction. Am. J. Psych., 124:1499-1504, 1968.

21. PATRICK, S. W. Our Way of Life: A Short History of Narcotics Anonymous, Inc., in Harms, E. Drug Addiction in Youth. Pergamon Press, New York, 1965.

22. CASRIEL, DANIEL. So Fair A House: The Story of Synanon. Prentice-Hall, Inc., N. J., 1963.

23. CHERKAS, M. S. Synanon Foundation: A Radical Approach to the Problem of Addiction, Am. J. Psych., 121:1065-1068, 1965.

24. MARKOFF, E. L. Synanon as a Fresh Approach to the Rehabilitation of Drug Addicts. Paper presented at the annual meeting of the American Psychiatric Association, 1965.

25. YABLONSKY, L. The Tunnel Back: Synanon. Macmillan Co., New York, 1965.

26. YABLONSKY, L. and C. E. DEDERICH. Synanon: An Analysis of Some Dimensions of the Social Structure of an Anti-Addiction Society, in Wilner, D. M.,

121

and Kassebaum, G. G., eds. Narcotics. McGraw-Hill Book Company, New York, 1965.

27. SHELLY, J. A. Daytop Lodge—A Two Year Report, in Sells, H. F., ed. Rehabilitating the Narcotic Addict. U. S. Govt. Printing Off., Washington, D. C., 1966.

28. HAGEMAN, L. L. A Neighborhood-Based Addict Rehabilitation Program: Exodus House, in Sells, H. F., ed. Rehabilitating The Narcotic Addict. U. S. Govt. Printing Off., Washington, D. C., 1966.

29. WILKERSON, D. The Cross and the Switchblade. Bernard Geis Associates, New York, 1963.

30. O'DONNELL, J. A. Research Problems in Followup Studies of Addicts, in Sells, H. F., ed. Rehabilitating the Narcotic Addict. U. S. Govt. Printing Off., Washington, D. C., 1966.

31. RAMIREZ, E. The Mental Health Program of the Commonwealth of Puerto Rico, in Sells, H. F., ed.: Rehabilitating the Narcotic Addict. U. S. Govt. Print. Off., Washington, D. C., 1966.

32. DUVALL, H. J., B. Z. LOCKE and L. BRILL. Follow-up Study of Narcotic Drug Addicts Five Years After Hospitalization, Public Health Reports 78:185-193, 1963.

The Treatment of Drug Addiction: Some Comparative Observations

WILLIAM N. DAVIS*

Current attempts to treat or rehabilitate the drug addict are characterized by a myriad of different philosophies, methodologies, and desired outcomes. In theory, such a multi-dimensional approach has its advantages since there is no widely recognized answer to the problem of drug addiction. Thus, it may be beneficial to experiment with a variety of different treatment orientations—in the hope of finding the most appropriate combination of therapeutic methods. However, in practice, utilizing very dissimilar techniques to try and solve the same problem can create significant disadvantages. For example, inter-agency competition for funds or recognition may become overly intense causing efforts at program evaluation to be diluted or distorted, and elevating the importance of political expertise to the point where it becomes an end in itself. All of this can and does occur, usually in the service of maintaining the integrity of one's own approach among a multitude of others.

What exactly *are* the differences that so divide the overall attempt to rehabilitate drug addicts? The discussion to follow is intended to provide some insight into this question. It is based entirely on clinical observations of the various treatment approaches being utilized in the New York City metropolitan area. For present purposes addiction will refer to heroin addiction. Addiction itself will be taken to mean any amount or frequency of heroin use, such that the user comes into contact with a treatment agency. A treatment program or agency refers to any organization, public or private, whose purpose is to treat or rehabilitate drug addicts. The paper is organized around three separate issues, or areas of disagreement: the nature of the addict; the treatment process; the nature of rehabilitation. Each of the issues are discussed in relation to three different models for the treatment of drug addiction. The models themselves are artificial conceptualizations; but they seem to provide a convenient, meaningful, and relatively inclusive framework from which to examine current efforts to help the drug addict.

ADDICTS AND ADDICTION

Underlying every treatment or rehabilitation program is a conception, or a set of beliefs about addiction, and about the kind of person that becomes an addict. These are probably *the* fundamental considerations that guide the development of a treatment effort. They provide a framework for deciding how an addict should be dealt with, in general as well as in very specific, practical terms. In this regard there are important differences of opinion among existing treatment agencies. It seems possible to differentiate three basic conceptions of the addict, and of addiction from the plethora of current points of view.

One widely accepted notion is that the heroin addict is emotionally disturbed. This is the crux of what might be called the psychiatric or "symptom" model. Using drugs is considered a surface manifestation, or a symptom, of an underlying psychological disturbance. Frequently the addict is seen as a passive, dependent person who turns to drugs in an attempt to satisfy his dependent longings and, at the same time, to defend against their full impact through heroin induced detachment and isolation.

Akin to this general orientation is the belief that the heroin user's addiction serves only as a defense, or only as a means of gratification. When addiction is thought of solely as a psychological defense it usually is felt that heroin is used to block from awareness overwhelming frustration or despair. Interpreted primarily as a source of gratification heroin is seen as an artificial means for obtaining feelings of euphoria, or power, or of being nurtured—sensations that otherwise would be impossible to attain.

Whether addiction is seen only as a defense or only as a method of gratification the implications regarding the nature of the addict are the same as when addiction is interpreted as a fully-fledged psychiatric symptom. The addict has an underlying problem that he attempts to solve, deal with, or make more palatable through the use of heroin.

In contrast to this point of view is another widely held belief about the addict. Instead of being emotionally disturbed, he is regarded as essentially a victim of both his psychological and sociological environment. This conception of the addict holds that there is nothing special or unusual about the personality characteristics or the behavior of an addict *before* he begins to use heroin. Relative to others in his sub-culture the pre-addict is regarded as a psychologically or emotionally normal individual. Addiction is believed to occur as a result of typical psychological phenomena, in combination with unfortunate sociological circumstances. Thus, adolescent curiosity, or the desire of adolescents to be accepted by their peer group, or the tendency of adolescents to identify with admired or prestigious adults may, in a high drug use neighborhood, lead to experimentation with drugs. Experimentation may then lead to frequent use and eventually to addiction as a result of continual peer pressure, misinformation about the effects of heroin, or a well-intentioned desire to please or impress significant adults. Thus, the addict becomes a victim of heroin. He falls prey, often unwittingly, to a drug that first overshadows and finally submerges his basically normal pre-addictive personality.

There is a variant to the "victim" model of drug addiction which has some superficial similarity to the notion that addicts are emotionally disturbed. It is that heroin creates a metabolic deficiency, of unknown etiology, in an addict's body that forces him to seek out more and more of the drug in order to satisfy a physiologically induced craving. As in the symptom model the addict is believed to have a disorder, and his addiction is seen as a surface manifestation of this disorder. Here, however, the addict is regarded as physically or medically ill rather than emotionally ill. Furthermore, the addict is considered a psychologically normal person whose physical composition, rather than his emotional makeup, is primarily responsible for his susceptibility to heroin. Addiction itself is the outcome of what are thought to be essentially accidental circumstances. Perhaps because of peer pressure, but in any case because of some fairly typical psychological phenomena, the pre-addict is exposed to heroin. Experimentation gives way to more frequent use and then to physical dependence as heroin has its effects on the metabolic system. An addict is victimized by heroin in the sense that its physiological consequences trap him into constant drug use regardless of his pre-addictive attitudes and needs.

A third widely recognized conception of the addict starts from a basic premise entirely unlike anything in the two models already discussed. Within this point of view the addict is considered a "hustler" or a "fiend", someone who is morally reprehensible because he has taken the easy way out by turning to heroin. The important implication here is that the addict could have chosen voluntarily and consciously *not* to become addicted. In other words, the pre-addict is presumed to be in full control of his behavior as he started to take heroin and then became addicted to it. This is in sharp contrast to both the symptom model and the victim model where the process of addiction is seen as out of the individual's voluntary control. In the symptom model internal conflicts of which the pre-addict is largely unaware propel him towards addiction; in the victim model external agents (e.g. peer pressure) or a disordered metabolism force the addict in the direction of constant heroin use.

Where the addict is seen as a hustler it is often thought that he first chose to use drugs because he wanted to avoid responsibility, wanted to live a daring adventurous life outside the law, wanted to gain a measure of prestige or status in his neighborhood, or some combination of all these. As with those who believe the addict is a victim of circumstances, the "hustler" model encompasses the notion that the pre-addict is a psychiatrically normal or average person. However, unlike both other models, the hustler point of view includes the belief that the addict is a morally deficient person because he decided to use drugs that have detrimental social consequences, and because he maintained his addiction through lawlessness and unscrupulous manipulations of his family, his friends, and complete strangers.

THE TREATMENT PROCESS

The question of how to treat an addict is closely, and perhaps necessarily, linked to one's ideas regarding the nature of addiction. Not surprisingly, therefore, there are sharp differences of opinion as to how the heroin user should be helped. The symptom model of addiction contains within it the belief that relatively traditional psychiatric techniques are the treatment modalities of choice. In other words, insight oriented psychotherapy is thought to be the preferred procedure because it focuses on helping patients to understand the underlying causes for their maladaptive thoughts, feelings, or behaviors. The importance of uncovering underlying causes follows directly from this model's conception of addiction as an overt, symptomatic expression of some relatively unconscious psychological difficulty. Generally speaking the treatment process is seen as one which goes from attitudinal and emotional change—as a result of increased insight—to behavioral change as newly-acquired insights are translated into action.

In practical terms, treatment agents who work within this model are likely to be more psychologically supportive of addicts, and less psychologically demanding of them than others working from different points of view. Also, addiction itself is not likely to be the primary focus of treatment, whereas theoretically relevant interpersonal relationships and significant emotional experiences are heavily emphasized. Treatment agents who consider the addict emotionally disturbed have had difficulty successfully engaging addicts in individual psychotherapy, and thus have turned to various group techniques such as group therapy and psychodrama as primary treatment modalities.

The victim model of addiction views the treatment process as one in which the addict is helped to eliminate or otherwise deal with the unfortunate circumstances that produced his drug dependence in the first place. Thus, environmental manipulation is often considered very important. Practically, this might mean removing the user from his former environment, or helping him to find a job, or encouraging him to develop new friendships. Here, little if any emphasis is placed upon psychotherapy in its traditional sense. Treatments agents are actively rather than passively supportive, and they concentrate on behavioral change without much direct regard for attitudes. The assumption is that sufficient opportunity will produce behavioral change and this in turn will have a constructive effect on whatever maladaptive feelings or attitudes an addict may have acquired as a result of his addiction.

When the addict is considered a victim in the sense that he is suffering from a metabolic deficiency the general principles of the treatment process are similar to the above. That is, the object of treatment is to remove the conditions which caused the addiction to develop. Again, there is very little interest in traditional psychotherapy; support is constant and very active; behavior change, rather than feeling or attitudinal change, is heavily emphasized.

However, in a medically oriented approach, the content of the treatment process is somewhat different from other approaches utilizing the victim model. A methadone maintenance program is a good example. Here, addicts are stabilized on high dosages of methadone, in order to blockade the narcotic effect of heroin. Theoretically, methadone corrects an addict's heroin-induced metabolic deficiency, thus enabling him to function adaptively once again. Supportive measures are utilized in addition to methadone maintenance to encourage an addict to make full use of his present and future capabilities—the same capabilities that were temporarily interfered with while heroin exercised its destructive impact.

The "hustler" model of addiction conceives of the treatment process in a fashion that is strikingly different from the other two models. Since the addict is looked upon as someone who has purposefully and immorally "copped out", the job of treatment is first to make him painfully aware of what he has done and second to push him gradually but firmly in the direction of assuming his proper obligations and responsibilities. The growth of awareness here has some relationship to gaining psychological insight—one of the foci of treatment within the symptom model. However, the assumption is not so much that the addict is dealing with unconscious conflicts which need to be slowly pointed out to him, but that an addict *must* be forced to recognize and admit how much of his life has been spent in manipulating others and avoiding responsibility. Implicitly, it is felt that the addict really knows what he has been doing, and that whatever lack of awareness he initially may show is likely to be another manipulation designed to avoid taking responsibility for his own actions.

Confrontation groups, where addicts are very directly, and sometimes brutally, reminded of the consequences of their drug-related activities are a frequently used treatment modality within this model. At times, such groups seem designed to force a "confession" of sorts. The addict is led to admit what a mess he has made out of his own life and the lives of others. Only at this point, after all the manipulations and deceptions have been exposed is an addict revealed for what he has become —a dope fiend; and only after this has occurred can the addict make real progress towards his own rehabilitation.

Rehabilitation proper usually takes place via a series of graded, well-structured steps where the addict is expected to assume specific responsibilities. Failing to meet these obligations is immediately interpreted as an attempt to fall back into the dope fiend's way of life—avoiding all responsibilities and living only in order to satisfy as quickly as possible one's own needs and desires. As addicts progress through this kind of treatment approach they are asked to assume more and more responsibility, much as a child is required to take on ever-increasing responsibility as he grows into a man.

Much more than the symptom or victim model, the hustler model makes severe psychological and behavioral demands on the addict. To mental health professionals steeped in traditional psychiatric methodology, the entire approach often seems callous, even destructive, or sadistic. In fact, this seems to be one of the reasons why relatively few professionals deeply involve themselves in treatment programs that utilize this model. In this regard, those who favor the hustler approach argue that the addict does receive support while undergoing treatment. They point out that peer support—from other addicts in the program—is constantly available, and that the treatment agents can and do offer protection if someone seems overwhelmed by the intensity of a particular confrontation. Furthermore, they argue that there is virtually no incidence of major psychological breakdowns among those addicts who remain in a program.

REHABILITATION

Every treatment program, unless totally disorganized, tends to emphasize a particular conception of the addict; growing out of this is some fairly specific notion of how best to treat the addict. Similarly, there follows from the nature of the treatment process that is emphasized, some fairly well articulated idea of what it means to rehabilitate an addict. This is the concept of "cure", or the goal toward which the treatment process is aimed. Since the three models of addiction that are being discussed include different conceptions of the addict, and of the treatment process, they should also differ with regard to the nature of rehabilitation.

Proponents of the symptom model believe that psychotherapy will lead to the resolution of those emotional conflicts that initially stimulated the addict's need to use heroin. Given that such conflicts are successfully dealt with, the addict's need to use heroin should simply disappear just as any psychiatric symptom is believed to fade away once the underlying psychological forces that forced its appearance

TABLE 1. DIFFERENCES OF OPINION AMONG THREE MODELS FOR THE TREATMENT OF DRUG ADDICTION

Model	Conception of the addict	Conception of the treatment process	Conception of treatment outcome
Symptom	emotionally disturbed	emotional conflicts resolved through relatively traditional psychotherapy	emotional rehabilitation
Victim	victim of circumstance and/or metabolically deficient	addictive circumstances removed through support and environmental manipulation (and where used through medical assistance—e.g. methadone)	relatively normal self reasserts itself
Hustler	morally deficient	dope fiend behavior confronted, admitted to, and replaced by responsible behavior	moral rehabilitation

are dissipated. The result, and this is the essence of rehabilitation for the symptom model, is an emotionally secure person who is able to function adaptively in whatever direction his conflict-free interests and attitudes seem to take him.

The victim model assumes that if an addict is removed from the sociological and psychological stresses that created his addiction, his relatively normal pre-addictive self will reassert itself. Then, with sufficient support and encouragement, he will be able to return to a useful position in society. Thus, for this model, rehabilitation means providing a millieu that allows an addict to make constructive use of his inherent capabilities.

Where the victim model includes the belief that addiction is caused by a metabolic deficiency the concept of rehabilitation is essentially the same. That is, it is thought that medical treatment enables the addict's relatively normal personality to naturally re-emerge. At present, in a methadone maintenance program, it is felt that the use of methadone to block the effects of heroin should be continued indefinitely. In other words, the metabolically generated craving for heroin should be kept under permanent control. As long as this is the case a former addict will be able to function adaptively and constructively in society.

The symptom model emphasizes emotional rehabilitation, and the victim model focuses on medical rehabilitation or rehabilitation through environmental manipulation. In contrast, the hustler model conceptualizes cure primarily in terms of moral rehabilitation. By participating in a treatment program geared to function within this model it is assumed that an addict will come to define himself as a sober, responsible individual who takes his obligations seriously, and who makes every attempt to follow through on them. Thus, here, rehabilitation means prodding an addict towards adopting a sober, industrious, socially acceptable way of life.

Table 1 recapitulates in outline form the major differences of opinion that have been discussed.

SOME IMPLICATIONS

Thus far this paper has focused on the disagreements that exist among various approaches to the treatment of drug addiction. Three basic points of view, or models, have been conceptualized. As mentioned, the models are artificial. It is true that many of the treatment programs in the New York City area tend to emphasize only one of the three presented; but this should not be taken to mean that proponents of, and components of several models do not co-exist within the same treatment program. On the contrary, this certainly does occur. The primary intention here is simply to offer a framework from which to identify divergent treatment programs, and to more clearly understand the issues that separate them.

However, there may be more to gain from the three models. Most important, there seem to be implications here for the future treatment of addicts. There is little doubt but that programs utilizing each of the models have had their share of successes and failures. That is, some addicts have benefited from treatment programs stressing the symptom approach, others from programs using the victim model, and still others from programs using the hustler model. On the other hand, programs embodying each of the models have also failed to help many addicts. It seems clear, therefore, that each approach can help some addicts but that none of them can benefit all addicts. Given that the three models actually lead to different treatment methods, this suggests that addicts are different kinds of people who bring varying needs, concerns, and reasons for using heroin with them when they enter treatment. An addict who is lucky enough to stumble upon a program whose methods are designed to deal with people like him may get some help; another addict who finds his way to a program not designed to work with him, and others like him, will very probably get no help at all. The point is that any treatment program that embodies a certain philosophy and certain procedures can actually treat only certain kinds of people—those who need the type of help that is most closely related to the type of help the program is implicitly or explicitly designed to provide.

Consequently, it seems extremely important to determine what kinds of people are best suited for treatment programs utilizing the symptom model, the victim, and the hustler model. Given the nature of the three models the following speculations seem worth considering. Treatment programs that emphasize the symptom model should be particularly effective for addicts who are relatively intelligent, and both willing and able to verbalize their inner experiences. Further, addicts who view their drug taking as an internal problem—as a driven, ego-dystonic activity, should benefit from the symptom approach. On the other hand, an addict who is not particularly uncomfortable about his drug use, or who comes to treatment because of external pressures probably would gain nothing from a program designed along the lines of the symptom model. Such a person might benefit the most from a program employing hustler concepts. The hustler model should also be particularly helpful for addicts who would benefit from feeling part of a community; who could use firm limit-setting, and a great deal of external structure to guide their behavior; who would respond favorably to both peer pressure and peer support. Finally the victim approach should be especially fruitful with addicts who are passive, highly suggestive, and who find it difficult to initiate activities on their own.

Regardless of the accuracy of these speculations, this is an area of investigation which must be pursued. By carefully and systematically evaluating the conditions under which each of the three models is most effective it should be possible to move beyond the intra- and inter-program bickering that is currently the rule rather than the exception. Eventually it should be feasible to develop a diagnostic center where every addict interested in, or compelled to undergo treatment would be carefully screened and referred to the treatment source that is most appropriate in his particular case.

Psychotherapy of Drug Dependence:
Some Theoretical Considerations*

M. M. GLATT

This paper is based in the main on over 15 years' experience working with alcoholics and drug abusers as a psychiatrist employing an eclectic, dynamically orientated approach. It would therefore seem necessary briefly to describe the types of patient, experience with whom the views expressed in this paper are based.

TYPES OF PATIENTS

As is well known by now, over the past decade or so a considerable shift has taken place on the English drug scene,[1] both as regards the type of patient seen, the predominant drug employed, and the method by which the drug is taken. In the 1950's the drug addicts seen in the London area were in the main middle-aged men and women, falling by and large into the groups of professional and "therapeutic" addicts, namely, belonging to the professions with easy access to the drugs, for example, doctors, nurses, chemists, etc.—or, on the other hand, patients who were introduced to drugs by their doctors for some "legitimate" medical indications, such as morphine for colics, barbiturates for tension and insomnia,[2] amphetamines for slimming purposes. Not infrequently one came across the "pseudo-therapeutic" drug abuser, e.g. middle-aged fairly obese women who had been advised by acquaintances to start amphetamines or phenmetrazine for slimming, and who soon experienced a feeling of heightened energy and uplift, and went on taking such drugs without a doctor's prescription or beyond the dose and length of time prescribed. These people took barbiturates and amphetamines by the oral route, though doctors who had become addicted to morphine, pethidine, etc., often injected the drug subcutaneously. Very occasionally one came across people, such as musicians, who were taking cannabis illicitly, or heroin and cocaine on prescription or illicitly.

Starting in the early 1960's the type of addict described above has been replaced more and more by another type of person, namely, youngsters in their teens to early twenties, who had started to take drugs for reasons quite different from those prevailing in the older type of addict—that is, much less often "pseudo-therapeutically" (such as lack of confidence) but much more often for reasons such as being bored and affluent at the same time. Having too much money in their pockets, too much time on their hands, and not knowing how to use their leisure time constructively, they had become independent of, and rebellious against, the advice and the values of their parents; or, seeing no meaning in life, had become curious

* Paper read at the International Conference on Drug Addiction in Quebec, 26 September 1968, and published in French in *Toxicomanies* (Quebec), 1969, II, and reprinted here with the kind permission of its Editors.

about the drug-taking habits of their peers—which often had been sensationally and glamorously depicted by the mass media. The drugs employed by these new-comers on the British drug scene included cannabis (first marihuana; in more recent years hashish), amphetamines, and heroin and cocaine. Cannabis was mainly smoked; amphetamines, often in the form of the famous drinamyl (a combination of an amphetamine and a barbiturate) taken by mouth; whereas heroin and cocaine takers often progressed from "sniffing" via "skin-popping" (intramuscular) to "mainlining" (intravenous) use. Cannabis and most of the amphetamines were obtained on the illicit market, whereas heroin and cocaine stemmed from a small number of overprescribing doctors—the surplus of heroin and cocaine prescribed by them to a relatively small (but gradually increasing) number of addicts being sold by the latter to young curious newcomers, so that in time a small heroin and cocaine epidemic came under way.[1] LSD and, over the past 18 months or so, methylamphetamine usually "mainlined" (i.v.), complete the list of drugs popular with the new young "non-therapeutic" drug abuser on the British scene. Unlike his American equivalent, the average young British drug user is not keen on "sleepers" (barbiturates). The slang terms used by addicts themselves, and quoted above, illustrate the emergence over the past years also in England of (or various types of) drug subculture.

ADDICTS—A HETEROGENEOUS CROWD

Thus, clearly even looking at only one country over a period of a few years, addicts form a very heterogenous group of people, differing greatly from each other in a great many aspects, such as age, underlying motivations for drug-taking[3] (for instance searchers for thrills and "kicks", or for oblivion or escape, rebels and "non-conformists" who at the same time want to belong to and conform with an anti-social subculture; therapeutic addicts, and so on), personality make-up, type of drug preferred (although the majority of modern young English drug abusers take a number of drugs simultaneously. There is no such person as "the" drug addict, and clearly there can be no one approach that is invariably the best for each and every addict. The method best suited, e.g., for the middle-aged, highly intelligent, professional or therapeutic addict—often highly skilled, married with a background of a good home and an integrated family—may require a completely different approach from the non-therapeutic young heroin addict who takes his drugs mainly for "kicks", who has left home and broken with his family, who has never learned a trade, and whose main allegiance is to an anti-social subculture. As one young drug addict recently put it in a group-therapy session, "You have to try to get at the roots of the individual addict's behaviour—you can't impose a blanket solution on everybody."

Not only may the best therapeutic approach be quite different in the various types of addicts, but also the therapeutic *goal* may be different. In the man with a basically fairly stable underlying personality (and such people *are* occasionally found among addicts—e.g. the therapeutic addicts, and the person who may have started his drug-taking career under the influence of his own subgroup in which drug-taking may have been the "in" thing at the time, for example when he was a student)[4,5] the therapeutic goal could obviously be much more ambitious than in the inadequate, immature, less intelligent youngster, or in the highly neurotic or psychopathic drug user. With many drug users one has to keep in mind that drug dependence—like alcoholism—is not only a relapsing disorder (so that relapses should not fill the therapist with utter frustration and guilt feelings, but should act as a spur to further endeavour), but also that one often has to be satisfied with a limited and often more modest result having sometimes to be grateful for small mercies. (It may be more doubtful to postulate as has been done to aim, a *priori*, at a goal of less than total freedom from taking drugs, and at a maintenance regime before initially attempting the goal of total abstinence from drugs.) In the British drug scene the question of maintenance without necessarily having to increase the dosage may mainly arise in the minority of therapeutic and (the probably very rare)[6] "stabilized" middle-aged addicts who have been able to keep at work steadily without increasing the dose, and possibly also in a few musicians who apparently had been able to take their drugs for years without increasing the dosage.

PSYCHOTHERAPY—ONE ASPECT OF A TOTAL THERAPEUTIC PROGRAMME

Like alcoholism, drug dependence has a multifactorial aetiology—factors pertaining to the mental and possibly physical make-up (the "host"), the environment (including ready availability of the drug) and pharmacological factors (nature of the drug) and so on, being more or less prominently involved in the given individual.[7,8] This illustrates again the need for a multidimensional, comprehensive therapeutic approach to be based on an assessment of the factors most important in the given patient. Because of the possible variety of factors involved, what is usually needed is an integrated, interdisciplinary therapeutic approach by a team of workers. Psychotherapy is thus only one of various methods employed, which has to take its place alongside physical, pharmacological, social, spiritual, and other approaches and treatments. It is however probably fair to say that whilst, e.g., drug treatments may be absolutely vital, especially in the initial stage, they are by and large no more than adjuncts to the more basic psychological and social techniques, although very often all these different methods will have to be applied simultaneously or consecutively. For example, tranquillizers in moderate doses may enable a tense, anxious, agitated individual to participate actively in the psychotherapeutic process, as may anti-depressants in the depressed individual, although it may often be difficult to decide at what stage anxiety may act as a spur and a stimulus, encouraging the individual to work towards a personality change, or at what intensity it becomes so intolerable and unbearable that it hinders the patient from making an active effort.[9] Drugs may also help in the establishment and maintenance of a relationship between the therapist and the patient by encouraging the addict to persist with the treatment process. To some extent, e.g., the new outpatient Treatment Centres in the United Kingdom have been established with the aim of encouraging the heroin/cocaine addict to obtain his supplies from psychiatrists rather than from the Black Market; and in order to motivate the addict to come along to these Centres and to undergo psychotherapeutic treatment, therapists in these Centres have found themselves, often with a somewhat bad conscience, continuing to prescribe such dangerous drugs as cocaine and methylamphetamine—though in ever decreasing dosage—the idea being gradually to reduce them whilst building a therapeutic relationship, and within this relationship to motivate the addict towards the acceptance of coming off drugs altogether. However, the methods adopted in these Treatment Centres is different from those employed in the past by a few General Practitioners in the London area who, rather than from the beginning trying to motivate the addict towards coming off drugs, attempted to form a relationship with him by prescribing drugs and waiting until the patient himself said he was ready to come off the drugs—and this in practice hardly ever seemed to happen.[1]

CHANGE IN ADDICT'S GOAL ORIENTATION—A SIGN OF PROGRESS

It is often interesting to listen to the young addicts' statements as to what they regard as the best method of treating addicts. In the initial stages of treatment these addicts often emphasize the necessity for Society to change its attitudes (cf. p. 59), become less "materialistic", more tolerant towards the individual and the young and to legalize allegedly "harmless" drugs such as cannabis and LSD, or the need to provide better social supportive services. They stress the need to discover or to prescribe equally potent but less addictive drugs. At various recent group therapy meetings, held in a prison, the answers given by the 6–10 addicts present—who were all of at least high average intelligence—all emphasized the above points—none of them even mentioning the need on their own part to learn to adjust themselves to reality by making an effort to understand their own motivations and to act less emotionally, less impulsively, and more rationally. The only treatment suggestion mentioned by one of this group of addicts was hypnosis—illustrating the widespread belief in a magical approach, with the patient playing a mainly passive role and circumventing the need of making an active therapeutic contribution himself. Without belittling the importance of the subject of Society defects mentioned by these addicts, it seems clear that the addict cannot really hope to make much progress until he realizes with the help of a psychotherapeutic approach, the overriding importance of making his own personal active contribution to the therapeutic process; and to work towards becoming to some extent at least "the Captain of his own fate"; the need not just to stand by and hope that environmental manipulation and support by society and welfare agencies, or to expect that a cure by the doctor's magical powers, will smooth the path for him. He will have to recognize the need to work towards emotional maturation and personality growth, so that he will be better able to stand inner and outer stresses whatever the attitude and state of his environment. This again illustrates the central function of psychotherapy within the comprehensive therapeutic approach; drug therapies provide the addict with a crutch, social therapies—e.g., helping the family to understand the addict's difficulties or their own contribution to the addict's dilemma—assist the addict towards making and maintaining his come-back, but obviously in the final instance it is up to the addict himself to make better use of his abilities and assets than before, and by approaching life in a more mature and realistic manner based on a better understanding of his personal defects (responsible for his need to prop himself up by drugs) and assets.* On the other hand, in this connection, the therapist has to be aware of certain pitfalls, e.g., the intelligent addict, knowing full well the difficulties involved in uncovering the reasons for his drug taking, and hiding behind such difficulties as an alibi against doing anything about his problem. As one addict put it complacently at a recent group therapy meeting held at an out-patient Treatment Centre, "I can surely not be expected to give up drugs until I have been told all the reasons why I am taking them," a view which got another addict to counter with the remark, "Too much importance has been put here as to why we become addicts. In a catastrophical situation you do something about the present situation first before delving to the roots."

THERAPEUTIC COMMUNITY (AND GROUP THERAPY) APPROACH TO DRUG DEPENDENCE

As individual and group psychotherapy with drug addicts will be discussed by other speakers at this Symposium, not much need be said about it at the present juncture. Group therapy in addicts may carry the risk that addicts might learn even more about addictive drugs than they already know. However, in our experience most addicts seem to like living in a therapeutic community where there are also other addicts present, and claim that they derive benefit from it.[10] Clearly, further research is needed to show whether, for example, it may be too risky to mix youngsters who have in the past taken drugs by mouth only (for example, amphetamines), or smoked cannabis, with others who have "fixed" narcotic drugs. Furthermore, a community formed by drug addicts only, runs the risk of perpetuating the subculture also inside hospital. At St. Bernard's Hospital we initially had to accommodate young drug abusers in the alcoholic ward for administrative reasons, as at the time nobody had been prepared for the new wave of addicts.[11] Certain difficulties did arise from that arrangement—the middle-aged alcoholics feeling that the young addicts were not really motivated and were not pulling their weight and were too undisciplined, too noisy, and so on, and the young drug addicts regarding the older alcoholics as "squares", etc. Despite this, in time most of the young drug abusers, however, stated that the more mature and more experienced alcoholics were of considerable help to them, as they shared with them the dependence on a drug, and preferred this arrangement of a "heterogeneous" group to a homogeneous one consisting of drug addicts only and to a heterogeneous one including other "mental" patients. Whether hetero- or homogeneous groups are preferable will again have to be the subject of much further research. From our own experience so far we feel that despite certain differences, a community formed by addicts may benefit from having assistance from older alcoholics who are willing to help and work with them. Incidentally, whilst we never had any difficulties in having middle-aged barbiturate and amphetamine abusers assimilated by a group predominantly consisting of alcoholics[12], young drug abusers do not fit in readily; thus, whilst a therapeutic community (where every experience of the patient could be used therapeutically) could be a mixed one containing both alcoholics and a

---

* It is often of value, and necessary, to emphasize the addict's abilities, and not merely to dwell on his defects, in view of his feelings of guilt, inadequacy, failure, and the hopelessness of his situation.

sprinkling of drug addicts, it would seem preferable to hold group therapy meetings separately. The great difference between various types of addicts as far as group formation and cohesion is concerned is again illustrated by this difference of being assimilated by the predominantly alcoholic groups between the middle-aged barbiturate and amphetamine abusers on one hand, and the young addicts on the other. This difference illustrates once more the need to adapt one's therapeutic approaches to the needs of the individual or at least to the type of drug addict concerned.

In general, like alcoholics, so also do drug addicts seem to be theoretically suitable for the group approach.[13] Like alcoholics, e.g., they have a common overriding problem and share many experiences; thus there is a natural common bond between them and they identify readily with each other—factors which, of course, outside hospital contribute to the ease of forming a special subculture. We have found the group approach with drug addicts helpful in a variety of settings, such as a special hospital unit, in prison, in a semi-private nursing home run by a religious organization, and in a new out-patient treatment centre. "Treatment in a therapeutic group can renew the capacity for social relationships and improve it" (Foulkes[14]), a factor which obviously is of great importance in drug addicts, (who so far have been able to communicate and to establish relationships only whilst and by, using drugs) provided the group-therapy takes place in a drug-free environment. This is difficult, or almost impossible to achieve in an open ward (such as the Alcoholism & Addiction Unit at St. Bernard's) where drugs may easily be smuggled in and where even the best motivated addict can readily fall by the wayside, e.g., by a conditioned reflex type of response when watching another addict "fixing" himself with drugs which he has smuggled in. From the aspect of providing a drug-free atmosphere, of course, prison (cf. p. 58) provides an advantage; (although drug dependence in itself should obviously be approached as an illness and not as a crime, and putting drug addicts in prison *per se* clearly is not treatment, for some reason or other drug abusers will often find themselves in prison), and in our experience group-therapy is quite feasible with addicts in a prison. Here, naturally enough, addicts often produce complaints about prison conditions, and the therapist's task would be made much easier by providing institutions with conditions and rules midway between those of hospital and prison, making the atmosphere within the prison as permissive as possible—by filling the prisoner's day with meaningful occupations, and by trying to establish a therapeutic community within the prison group-therapy, in our experience, so far seems also a promising tool under the system of the new English Out-patient Treatment Centres. Addicts come along in the main because of their need to obtain drugs which they are usually prescribed for in decreasing dosages, so that they are still taking drugs whilst attending therapy sessions, and a great deal of resistance is expressed, e.g., by "nodding" (after having taken drugs shortly before) as well as by missing sessions, coming late, and complaining about the therapist's lack of understanding in not giving the addict the amount of drugs which he wants, which (in his opinion) is the amount he needs. The same addict has occasionally been seen successively in the permissive hospital set-up, the out-patient centre and in prison, and often such an individual seemed to be to an outside observer at his best and to co-operate best in the drug-free prison atmosphere, and on the whole a somewhat less permissive set-up than the one so well suited in the case of alcoholics may be advantageous for the drug addict (e.g., a closed hospital ward with the atmosphere within the ward being a permissive and therapeutic one)—though the basic approach should also be in the case of the drug addict non-moralising, non-judgmental and non-punitive.

As in the case of the alcoholic at the present state of knowledge, the question in the treatment of drug dependence should not be physical *or* psychological methods, and as far as psychotherapy is concerned, not analytical *or* repressive-inspirational treatment, but there should be individual diagnosis, followed by choice of those forms of therapy best suited to the individual patient. Often the addict needs physical and psychological therapy, and a certain amount of insight as well as support. Like alcoholics, so also many drug abusers have a low frustration tolerance and lack of staying power; often they are not concerned with long-term goals, but want relief and satisfaction here and now. Because of this and because of the frequently low strength and immaturity of their ego, they are often averse to tolerate the more anxiety producing, orthodox psychoanalytic process; the drug provides relief here and now, and the addict therefore when faced with internal or external stresses may easily take recourse to the drug rather than struggling along with the analyst who may hold out hope for him not until the distant future, analysis moreover provoking further stress situations for the patient. As with alcoholics, the group approach may be less anxiety provoking, and therefore more bearable to the addict; and the supportive aspect of a predominantly dynamic or analytically orientated groups may enable the addict to tolerate also, and to participate with, the analytical aspect of such groups, and face the "uncovering" process better than he might be able to do in the individual confrontation with the therapist. In general, uncovering methods with alcoholics, and even more so with addicts to other drugs, have to be satisfied with a less ambitious aim than trying to discover the deepest levels of motivation. It may often suffice for him to acquire a certain amount of insight into the reasons for their drug use and their behaviour, and to learn the need for finding less destructive and more constructive means of coping with their difficulties and obtaining satisfaction. Among the goals a greater understanding by the patient of the nature of his personality problems and his illness, increase in socialization, insight into his favourite defence mechanisms, better adaptation to reality may often be possible, whereas the more ambitious goal such as emotional reorientation on deeper insight into his conflicts, and considerable modification of personality functioning may be possible only in a minority.

For patients who have difficulties in verbal communications, other methods may sometimes be helpful to enable them to express their feelings, attitudes, etc., such as painting—a method often very acceptable to addicts, with their frequent artistic leanings. Behaviour therapy, aiming at removal of the symptom without taking much notice of the underlying factors, has of course also been tried in the therapy with addicts (e.g., aversion treatment with apomorphine). In alcoholism, the often dynamically orientated professional group-therapy has been supplemented by the more repressive-inspirational therapy of the lay groups of Alcoholics Anonymous and certain such lay groups have also been formed by drug addicts. By and large the professional therapist has sympathy and understanding for the pre-addictive, symptomatic aspects of the addict's behaviour, whereas the addict himself, having had similar experiences, has empathy in the main for the secondary "addictive" features of the drug user's behaviour. Collaboration by the professional therapist with the recovered addict in the treatment of other addicts should therefore often prove helpful, though in our experience with the types of addict seen in England, non-professionals, on their own, may run into difficulties and require regular assistance from the professionally trained therapist much more often than Alcoholics Anonymous. This may be related to the fact that by and large the hypothetical "average" drug addict is likely to be an emotionally more disturbed individual than the "average" alcoholic. Among drug addicts, as well as among alcoholics, one may find all types of personalities, who very roughly can be divided into predominantly psychoneurotic, predominantly psychopathic, individuals, and a body of people who may not be greatly different psychologically as regards their pre-addictive make-up from the so-called "normal". However, it must not be forgotten that as alcohol is widely accepted by Society, even the average personality may run a risk of abuse, whereas the addict in order to start his abuse has to break rules of Society and the Law. Thus, by and large, the proportion of originally relatively stable individuals is likely to be much less among addicts than among alcoholics. Degree of co-operation, proportion of less disturbed and therefore recoverable patients, is thus likely to be higher among alcoholics than among addicts.

The older alcoholic after giving up his alcohol has often a former way of living to fall back on. On the other hand, among drug addicts, too, one finds people, such as professional addicts (with easy access to drugs) and therapeutic addicts (introduced to the drug quite legitimately by their General Practitioner) who may have started drug abuse without basically asocial or antisocial personality characteristics, and the same thing may hold good for the student who may have started to smoke cannabis in order to conform with the attitudes and habits of a special subculture (cf. p. 53).

PSYCHOTHERAPY UNDER "COMPULSION"

It is usually held that psychotherapy is possible only in the motivated patient and that compulsion is useless. It certainly would seem that not much progress can be made with the addict whilst he can easily get hold of drugs, so that some means of getting the addict away from his source of supply would logically have to be the first step. Thus compulsory treatment in a drug-free atmosphere may often enable the addict to participate with treatment in a not drug-befuddled frame of mind, and certainly some of our experiences seem to show that in some addicts beginning treatment even without motivation under a certain degree of compulsion is by no means hopeless. Our experiences in prison (cf. p. 56) and in Treatment Centres respectively confirm the impression that it might be helpful to give addicts the chance to co-operate in psychotherapy by placing them in an atmosphere where it is difficult or impossible to obtain drugs. Imprisonment by itself would tend to increase the addict's feeling of "defiant rage",[15] and of impotent embittered resentment, but with psychotherapy he may nevertheless become motivated into wanting help, and under an enlightened, not too restrictive regime he may learn the value of self-discipline, with gradual restoration of self-respect and self-confidence, based on a more realistic appreciation of his abilities, rather than on fantasy-based grandiose and often nebulous notions derived from over-compensation of inadequacy feelings.

PSYCHOLOGICAL AND SOCIAL DEPENDENCE

Psythotherapy is an intrinsic part of all stages in the treatment programme for the addict. From establishing rapport with the addict when first seen during the painful withdrawal phase (which gives the therapist the opportunity to provide support which should facilitate the building up of a relationship), throughout the hospitalization phase, and later on in after-care (for example, whilst staying in a Half-Way House, aimed among other objects at preventing the addict's immediate "fatal" return to his old haunts and his former drug using frends). An understanding, accepting, helping relationship may be more important than the particular method of treatment preferred by the therapist. The abstinence syndrome arising from physical dependence and necessitating drug therapy is the period most feared by the addict, but for the long-continued maintenance of drug abuse and for causing relapses it is the psychological dependence on the drug effect (apart from psycho-social dependence on the subculture) which seems most important, and to overcome psychological dependence psychotherapy is naturally the most potent weapon.

The drug addict is unable to find for himself a satisfying place in Society, partly because of his own feeling of inferiority and inadequacy which, rightly or wrongly, he projects to the state of Society (cf. p. 57), to its alleged failings, such as selfishness, its emphasis on materialistic values, on cold scientific and technological progress, on Society's attempts to make the individual conform with the "Establishment". Unable to find his niche, he escapes to drugs and into an asocial subculture which alienates him further from ordinary Society, but provides him with a feeling of belonging, and the satisfaction that here his views, ideas, and ideals are shared by others and that he is regarded as an equal who contributes actively to this group. In theory, finding his place in ordinary Society could be achieved or aimed at in two different ways; either by changing Society—aimed at creating an improved, better world with new ideals and goals with which the youngster could identify and where he could become involved and committed, thus helping him to get away from his close emotional involvement with subculture and drugs—or, on the other hand, by helping the addict to grow up emotionally and to adapt himself better to Society despite its imperfections.

The psychiatrist, whilst naturally also very interested in the first aspect, will in the main have to try to help the addict himself—although of course also being interested in attempting to help Society to attain a better understanding of addicts and addiction, leading to less ostracism and with it a lesser need for the addict to withdraw into an asocial subculture; and by involving the family in treatment—a task which may include a destruction of the family myth that the addict is the only family member who is sick.

DIFFICULTIES IN PSYCHOTHERAPY WITH ADDICTS

In the main patients co-operate with treatment only when they suffer from their affliction. However, many young addicts seem to enjoy their state rather than to suffer from it—as long as they can get hold of their drugs. This problem, for example, becomes almost insuperable in the case of cannabis: one may sympathize with the cannabis-takers' feeling that the punishment (e.g., prison) doesn't fit their alleged "crime" (i.e., possession) even though one objects to the legalization of the drug[16] but as the cannabis-taker doesn't feel ill and doesn't want treatment, what is the alternative? Likewise, with LSD, in spite of "bad trips", few LSD users want help to stay off the drug.

The addict tends to avoid the doctor unless he provides him with drugs—clearly because he gets something from the drugs which do something for him. Alcoholism and drug dependence are often described as forms of compulsive neuroses, but Matussek[17] has pointed out that in a compulsive neurosis the impulse is experienced as more foreign to the personality than in drug dependence; the compulsive neurotic's act cannot be enjoyed in the same way as the drug addict enjoys the drugs, even if the enjoyment is marred by guilt feelings and unwanted side- and after effects. Thus the drug addicts fights for his drug—defending its values against the therapist who attempts to withdraw the drugs, and he plays down the extent and the harmful effect of his drug-taking.

Not only does the addict avoid the doctor, the latter in turn avoids the addict who is an unsatisfactory patient, who is late for appointments—if he keeps them at all; who turns up at awkward times without appointments, making impossible demands; who makes promises and does not keep them; who relapses. Another factor, stressed by Schulte,[18] is the doctor's reluctance to feel himself forced into the role of supervisor, or even prosecutor—e.g., the doctor asked to work in the new English Treatment Centres may object to having to "dish out" drugs merely because of the "social" argument that if the addict is not given his drugs legally he will swell the ranks of those looking for illicit drugs, thereby increasing the risk of the emergence of a large-scale Black Market.

Other difficulties arise from certain personality characteristics of addicts, such as their narcissism, and their inability to tolerate anxiety and frustration (cf. p. 57). Analytical writers have stressed the early infantile roots[15] of drug dependence, of the drug taker's fixation in or regression to the oral phase of obtaining satisfaction, a too little rather than too much frustration in early life,[18] leading to oral insatiability, a hunger for excitement, a narcissistic regression from responsible partnership, a tendency to be mothered,[19] and so on.

On the other hand, a study group of the World Health Organization (1957)[20] expressed the view that the group of addicts with the characteristics described above is the "most difficult" one among addicts and requires intensive psychotherapeutic treatment, whereas many other types of addicts are reckoned to be easily amenable to treatment, i.e., those exposed to accidental stress in countries with easy availability of the drugs; those addicts whose dependence is mainly due to social, environmental or cultural factors; and members of asocial or antisocial groups and gangs where drug taking is a prerequisite of full participation, and where removal from this subculture often enables successful treatment and, furthermore, addictions resulting from temporary psychological or physical illness.

WHICH ADDICTS ARE ACCEPTABLE FOR PSYCHOTHERAPY?

Many addicts seen in England are from the intelligence and age aspects suitable in theory, despite the general lack of motivation (which first would have to be instilled in them as far as possible). In a Lexington study[21] carried out in 1955,

46 per cent of a sample of 100 narcotic addicts were considered acceptable for psychotherapy by three psychotherapists on the basis of their ability to verbalize feelings, spontaneously produce problems for discussion, and give evidence of original thinking; the addicts regarded as suitable were also more apt to ask for aid with their problems, and showed more evidence of previous ability to modify their patterns of living. Certain psychological measures, e.g., verbal intelligence tests and tests of degree of manifest anxiety were significant predictors of acceptability. Patients judged to be acceptable for therapy by psychiatrists could fairly accurately be selected from a larger group of patients by social service interviews and psychological tests.

WHEN IS ANALYTICAL PSYCHOTHERAPY INDICATED IN ADDICTS?

According to Bräutigam[19]* it is indicated in young addicts whose internal motivation is stronger than exogenous temptation, who experience their interpersonal relationship as disturbed and who themselves experience conflicts and inhibitions.

SUMMARY

The prognosis in many addicts cannot be regarded as good, and there are many difficulties which confront the therapist—so much so that in Schulte's view[18] it is no surprise that Freud has almost totally avoided the subject of psychotherapy in drug addicts. However, a certain amount can often be achieved by a patient, understanding, tolerant but yet firm, therapist using a comprehensive programme, at the core of which would be a psychotherapeutic approach. Just taking the addict off his drug and leaving him in a vacuum is obviously not enough. He uses drugs because his present personality functioning requires this. If he wants to learn to live happily and usefully without drugs there is need for a change of attitudes and of outlook, for new goals and satisfactions, so that he no longer requires drugs. He has to be made to feel that there is something in the world to give up drugs for. Important as other therapeutic methods are in the necessary comprehensive overall approach, psychotherapeutic methods will often play the most important role.

REFERENCES

1. M. M. GLATT, D. J. PITTMAN, D. G. GILLESPIE and D. R. HILLS. *The drug scene in Great Britain.* Edward Arnold, London (1967).
2. M. M. GLATT. *Bull. Narcot. (U.N.)* **14,** 20 (1962).
3. M. M. GLATT. In: *Drug dependence in Adolescence,* C. M. Wilson (Ed.), Pergamon Press, Oxford (1968).
4. M. M. GLATT. *Pax Romana J.* (6), 18 (1967).
5. M. M. GLATT. *New Student (Lond.)* 15 (Feb. 1968).

* The difference between "analysis" and two other psychotherapeutic techniques, persuasion and suggestion, is in Hart's words that analysis "is aimed at the causes responsible for the condition, and seeks to remove the condition by removing or rearranging those causes, whereas suggestion and persuasion are aimed solely at the symptom, and seek to remove the symptoms without reference to the causes which have produced them."[22]

6. *Drug addiction.* (Rep. of the Interdepartmental Committee), H.M.S.O., London (1961).
7. M. M. GLATT. *12th Int. Inst. Prev. Treatment Alcoholism, Prague, 1966,* Int. Council Alcohol & Alcoholism, Zurich (1967).
8. M. M. GLATT. *W.H.O. Chronicle* **21,** 293 (1967).
9. M. M. GLATT. *Br. J. Addict.* **55,** 111 (1959).
10. M. M. GLATT. *Nursing Times* **63,** 519 (1967).
11. M. M. GLATT. *Lancet* **ii,** 171 (1965).
12. M. M. GLATT. *Br. J. Addict.* **59,** 000 (1963).
13. M. M. GLATT. *Br. J. Addict.* **54,** 133 (1958).
14. S. H. FOULKES. *Introduction to Group-Analytic Psychotherapy,* Heineman, London (1948).
15. S. RUDO. *Comprehens. Psychiat.* **4,** 160 (1963).
16. M. M. GLATT. *Is It Alright to smoke Pot,* C.E.Y.C., London (1968).
17. F. HATUSSEK. *Nervenarzt* **29,** 452 (1958).
18. W. SCHULTE. *Dt. med. Wschr.* **89,** 223 (1963).
19. W. BRÄUTIGAN. *Nervenarzt.* **29,** 445 (1958).
20. STUDY GROUP, W.H.O. *Bull. Narcot. (U.N.)* **9,** 36 (1957).
21. A. McLEAN *et al. Archs Neurol. Psychiat.* **74,** 356 (1955).
22. B. HART. *Psychopathology,* p. 125, 2nd edn., Cambridge Univ. Press (1950).

Drugs, Hippies, and Doctors

Harry A. Wilmer, MD, PhD

The doctor-patient relationship is rapidly becoming pharmaceuticalized. Every physician has his own particular pharmacologic armamentarium. Armamentarium indeed! A formidable array of chemical weapons and chemical solace. The more drugs that have become available, the more physicians have felt relieved of the burden of taking a careful history, of listening to patients. Time is running short in the consultation room.

Physicians are increasingly dependent upon the prescription of drugs. It is a rare experience for a patient to leave a doctor's office without a prescription in his hand. Now, there are more specific drugs, more potent drugs in widespread use than there are patients, diseases, disorders, or symptoms. Every physician knows that his own attitudes and beliefs about drugs alter their effectiveness. Prescribing drugs has always been good medicine for doctors, often assuring them a good night's sleep. Tranquilized patients are "more amenable" to psychotherapy even though some appear as zombies, stiff parkinsonian automatons, or characterless dehumanized objects. But still, it is not all bad. There are fewer psychiatric patients climbing the walls, fewer assaultive patients. A more humane atmosphere exists, and it is one that is vastly preferable to the nightmare scene of mass electroshock, cuffs, belts, straightjackets, locked bare cells, camisoles, pentylenetetrazol (Metrazol), lobotomy.

Drugs are an essential element of the effectual practice of medicine, but the point I wish to emphasize is that, considering the extraordinary dependency of physicians on drugs, it is not at all surprising to find patients and nonpatients alike looking to drugs as a means of curing themselves or as a way of making their lives more livable.

It is a truism to say that we live in a drug culture. We also live in violent times, often mad times, times of drastic social change, times ripe for countless "miracle drugs." But the miracles rarely pay off, and the human striving for the real miracle drug continues.

The Drug Culture and the Hippie

In this atmosphere a conspicuous group of young people are experimenting with the self-administration of drugs in an attempt to solve personal and social problems. Such a subculture exist in the Haight-Ashbury district of San Francisco, where "any drug offered is taken, no questions asked." It is with this drug-culture microcosm, made up of young people dependent on amphetamines, hallucinogens, and marijuana, that I concern myself.

In July 1967, to study this phenomenon, a treatment center was established at Langley Porter Neuropsychiatric Institute, at the University of California School of Medicine nine blocks away from Haight-Ashbury. It is called the Youth Drug Study Unit and is, as far as I know, the first such unit in a community mental health center in the United States. It accepts for treatment young people taking psychoactive drugs other than hard narcotics.

Between July 1, 1967, and March 12, 1968, 58 patients were admitted to the Youth Drug Study Unit, 36 males and 22 females with a mean age of 18.5 years. Twelve patients were from San Francisco, 7 from Oakland, 2 from Berkeley, and 14 from the Bay Area and Peninsula from Santa Rosa to Monterey; 6 were from Southern states, 8 from far Western states, 3 from the Midwest, 3 from the Atlantic Coast states, 2 from Los Angeles, and 1 from Canada.

Drugs used were lysergic acid diethylamide (LSD) plus marijuana in 21 instances; amphetamines plus LSD plus marijuana in 11 instances;

"all or everything" in 9 instances; marijuana alone in 4 instances; amphetamines and marijuana in 3 instances; LSD alone in 1 instance. Drug history of the others was not reliable.

Of the 58 patients, 12 were treated with tranquilizers, 4 were offered tranquilizers and refused. For the remaining 42, no medication was prescribed.

Referrals were made by the Haight-Ashbury Clinic in 16 instances; by former patients or friends in 12 instances; from Bay Area psychiatric hospital units in 6 instances; by private physicians in 4 instances; by LSD Rescue and Huckleberry (for runaways) in the Haight-Ashbury area in 3 instances. The remaining patients were referred by clinics, parole agents, parents, and physicians at Langley Porter.

The patients remained on the ward from one night to six months, with a mean between one and two months. Five patients remained more than two months, and six remained one week or less.

As to family background, 32 came from original, intact families, 6 from divorced parents, 4 from separated families, 1 was adopted, 1 was illegitimate, 1 had lost a father, one had lost a mother, and the remainder were from separated and remarried parents. Four were grammar school graduates, 9 high school dropouts, 18 high school graduates, 9 college dropouts, 5 college graduates, and the remainder unknown.

Three of the patients were married (one common law), 5 were divorced; in 2 instances marital status was unknown, and 49 were single.

Accepting, Evaluating, and Discharging Patients

The unit operates 24 hours a day, seven days a week. Patients who are referred to us meet with an evaluation team which accepts and discharges patients. It is composed of a resident psychiatrist, a nurse or social worker, and two patients. During the patients's stay on the ward he meets with this team at the end of his first month, or sooner if necessary. When the time for discharge comes, he meets with a similar four-person team which makes its recommendation to the total community. Thus, patients have a say in who comes to the unit, a stake in each other's motivation, and a sense of responsibility. Even our psychotic patients behave rationally on such committees.

We require that the patient give up drugs to be accepted. He is admitted if he acknowledges that he has a drug problem, and if he genuinely wants help. From the very beginning, there is no question but that we aim at getting the patients to give up their drugs. However, in our completely open ward so close to the drug scene, we expected some patients to revert to drugs under stress and provocation. The only way to keep patients completely off drugs would be to lock up the patient and maintain maximum security.

Moreover, we want to study patients who have free access to the streets. With our "free-floating" youngsters, we nonetheless maintain clear limits on behavior within which they can be free, and can trust us. We do not allow drugs on the ward, and anyone pushing drugs is discharged. If someone comes onto the ward or into groups "stoned" on marijuana or LSD, it would be foolish to boot him out. After all, this is his "hang-up" as we see it; this is his symptom. We must examine it as assiduously as we would any symptom. Naturally, this gets some staff members "up tight," as they say. But it gives us a unique opportunity to study the interaction of the square and the hippie culture.

It is obvious to anyone who has tried to modify an institution that the institution reacts to change with enormous resistance. Delinquent patients, barefoot patients, long-haired, bizarrely dressed patients, patients doing Yoga exercises on blankets by the elevators, patients lying down on the lobby floor, and patients playing their guitars in the halls evoke strong institutional counterforces. Still, as the patients say, the "vibrations" from the ward are good. So they keep coming and keep referring their friends.

There is a steady flow of patients coming from the streets referred by physicians, hospitals, clinics, parole agents, schools, and the Haight-Ashbury Medical Clinic. They stay. At first our problem was the transient nomadic tendencies of these young people. They came for a day or two and "split." Now they stay and are reluctant to leave. Therefore, the total operation is now continually dealing with the problems of dependency and separation anxiety.

Why Drugs?

Why do our patients take drugs? Some do it just

for kicks and for belonging in a clique or group; we rarely see this type. Others take drugs to cope with depression, violent impulses, and fear of insanity. Our patients have seriously altered states of consciousness; we find in them indications of arrested psychosocial development. There are often signs of organic brain change. It appears to us that some residual permanent defect will be the lot of many of our patients.

In the families of almost all of our patients, there is serious discord. The parents reject their children or give them "contingent love." The children perceive this as sham; in adolescence they reject their parents' moral and ethical values, shaming them by their dress and strange behavior. Since they are denied real love, it is no wonder that they trade the sham of love for the illusion of love and nurture it with drugs.

A Multimedia Community

Beginning as a traditional therapeutic community modeled after the first therapeutic community for acutely psychotic patients,' we are developing entirely new treatment and social learning methods. Enormous energy was spent to create an innovative program that is in tune with the youngsters' lives on the streets and with what is happening in their heads. Treatment is within the framework of a living-learning exprience, more like a school than a hospital.

Breaking with traditional psychiatric methods, we emphasize developing the creative potential of patients. We believe that a new kind of awareness, a new kind of consciousness' expansion can substitute for the drug experience. An objective of our therapy is to invoke as many dimensions of sensory experience and imagination as possible. The usual "insight" psychotherapy is deemphasized. We rely on television, film making, photography, motion pictures, telephone talk-shows, stereo-audiotapes, as well as music, art, and creative writing as therapy. Once a week we have a creativity seminar to which we invite writers, philosophers, and artists of all kinds as guests.

We hypothesize that through multiple sensory experience, the individual is provided the opportunity for positive synthesis of imagination and feeling. It is what I call *synesthetic psychotherapy*.

Synesthesia, the unification of sensory and imaginative life, is a term McLuhan uses in describing the television experience.[2]

Innovative Television Techniques

Our program revolves around group psychotherapy. The small and large groups, the seminars, psychodrama, families in group therapy and interviews are videotaped.[3,7] Patients and staff take turns operating our television equipment. Ten- to fifteen-minute segments are immediately played back to all participants for a discussion that focuses on patient and staff behavior. This kind of collaborative review, however painful, has a humanizing effect on everyone.

We symbolically offer "options" with television. Originally we videotaped groups using one camera. Viwers often reacted to this resentfully, as if the monitor dictated to them what they must watch. So we began using two cameras and two videotape recorders. On replay the participants watch two monitors; they have a choice of watching themselves or others.

We feel that our most significant innovation is that of the patient talking to the camera alone. Each new patient talks to the television camera in a room all by himself for 20 minutes. By eliminating the interviewer the patient emerges in "pure culture." This tape is replayed to him alone, after which he decides for himself whether he wants to show this or have it erased. The patients do more than talk to the camera, they use the experience as a kind of free wheeling individual psychodrama; they talk, act, use props, play, sing, walk away, pantomime. These tapes are extraordinarily revealing and often beautifully expressive.

This aroused our curiosity about the possible distorting effect of the second person in a videotape session. Therefore we experimented as follows: A volunteer patient was interviewed by five different people for ten minutes each. He talked to a professor of criminal law, a jungian psychoanalyst, a policeman in plain clothes, a newspaper reporter, and a policeman in uniform. The patient did not know the identity of his interviewers except for the uniformed policeman. Each interviewer was given written instructions to "ask the patient in your own way about his problem, drugs, his hospital experience, and his future." The patient responded differently to each interviewer. This session was taped by four cameras recording from different positions. These tapes were played back simultaneously on four monitors stacked in a block. Now we found that not only did the patient's behavior change with each interviewer, but each of the four monitors recorded this same piece of behavior in a different way. This raises questions as to the possible manipulative use of videotape as clinical evidence.

Television, because of its two-dimensionality, is a medium that is overwhelmingly preferable to audiotape. One feels the inadequacy of a one-sense dimension when one plays the videotape without sound. In Santayana's words, "The same battle in the clouds will be known to the deaf only as lightning and to the blind only as thunder." And even with television it is obvious that we are often blind to what we do not want to see and deaf to what we do not want to hear.

Problems of the Staff

Our main problem in managing this unit centers around the staff, and more particularly with doctors than nurses or technicians. In the self-revealing techniques we employ, the doctor has more to lose than the patient. This is particularly anxiety-provoking to the psychiatric resident who finds himself suddenly functioning in a pressure-cooker microcosm of social change. Once trained to act with authority, to write and give orders, to work at the peak of a power hierarchy, now he finds his role identity and value systems are shaken.

Another stressful factor for the psychiatric resident is that the therapeutic program is geared to group psychotherapy. While the resident is free to meet with patients individually at any time, particularly in crises, he does not have the usual one-to-one continuous psychotherapeutic relationship. His psychotherapeutic technique is brought into the open in groups where it may be challenged. Thus the resident becomes a "deprived person" and may, in his identification with the patient, himself "act out."

There is enormous resistance to self-observation by psychiatrists and psychiatric residents." The patient may be seen as having delinquent tendencies— but the staff?

149

There is the rub. The attitudes of the staff are often covertly moralizing, condemning, evasive, deceptive, or punitive. Our young patients perceive this no matter what words are spoken. Given the opportunity to express their honest feelings, they do so. All to the good. But it is a difficult thing for the physician to face up to this kind of frank exchange. Some of the attitudes of the staff which we find self-defeating with this patient population are those of laissez-faire, indifference, ambivalence about saying "no," and covert fostering of delinquency.

The crucial issue of staff attitudes in tolerating and treating delinquent youths is the latent delinquency of the staff itself. Unless the physician can acknowledge in himself seeds of delinquency, the game is lost.

Female nurses and technicians struggle with their problems. Given a new kind of responsibility and freedom, their skills become evident and their inadequacies obvious. Some of these women have great difficulty resolving authority and identity conflicts, and these conflicts are especially provoked by adolescent patients. The new freedom, for which their training has poorly prepared them, is a burden to some women who are passive-dependent or obsessive-domineering. Senior staff members often become scapegoats.

Results

It is too early to give more than a general impression of results. In our follow-up of the 58 patients we have studied, results are generally favorable. Patients leave feeling more confident, thinking more critically about drugs. Some of those who "dropped out" have dropped back in. In the Youth Drug Unit they have found a home where they do not feel alienated, and this is a unique experience for most of them.

Summary

Our multimedia therapy for young people involved with psychoactive drugs focuses on the examination of social behavior. Our electronic feedback systems facilitate open communication. Group therapy and group creative activities offer "options out." The constant critical evaluation of staff as well as patient behavior is at the heart of the program.

The use of innovative techniques gives the ward its spirit and morale. The sharing of "toys," ideas, and feelings helps to establish trusting relationships. We feel that in attracting and keeping these youngsters who have little or no trust in the establishment, we are taking a significant step.

Acceptance of the basic tenet that there are delinquent tendencies in all of us, patients and staff, is crucial if the program is to succeed.

References

1. Wilmer, H.A.: A Psychiatric Service as a Therapeutic Community, *US Armed Forces Med J* 7:640-658 (May) 1956.
2. Wilmer, H.A.: Ten-Month Study in the Care of 939 Patients, *US Armed Forces Med J* 7:1465-1469 (Oct) 1956.
3. Wilmer, H.A.: *Social Psychiatry in Action*, Springfield, Ill: Charles C Thomas, 1958.
4. McLuhan, M.: *Understanding Media: The Extension of Man*, New York: McGraw Hill Book Co., Inc., 1965, chapter 31.
5. Wilmer, H.A.: Television: Technical and Artistic Aspects of Videotape in Psychiatric Teaching, *J Nerv Ment Dis* 144:207-223 (March) 1967.
6. Wilmer, H.A.: Practical and Theoretical Aspects of Videotape Supervision in Psychiatry, *J Nerv Ment Dis* 145:123-130 (Aug) 1967.
7. Wilmer, H.A.: Television as Participant Observer, *Amer J Psychiat* 124:1157-1163 (March) 1968.
8. Wilmer, H.A.: Innovative Use of Videotape on a Psychiatric Ward, *Hosp Community Psychiat* 19:129-133 (May) 1968.
9. Glover, E.: Psychology of the Psychotherapist, *Brit J Med Psychol* 9:1-16 (Jan, pt 1) 1929.

Merging the Treatment of Drug Addicts into an Existing Program for Alcoholics[1]

Donald J. Ottenberg, M.D. and Alvin Rosen, D.O.

SUMMARY. *An inpatient hospital, treating exclusively alcoholics by confrontation group techniques in a therapeutic community atmosphere, experimentally began to admit other drug addicts. Initial divisiveness among the patients gave way to successful joint therapeutic benefits when appropriate modifications in rules of the groups and the whole community were introduced. The results with alcoholic patients remain the same as before the merge and the results with all but older hardcore drug addicts appear promising.*

D URING the past year and a half we have gradually introduced patients addicted to drugs other than alcohol into an existing inpatient treatment center for alcoholics.[2] The present communication reports some of our observations in the course of this experiment.

Three major influences stimulated us to try this combined approach: (1) Our experience with alcoholics at the Eagleville Hospital and Rehabilitation Center in the past 4 years convinced us that alcoholics are very much like other troubled persons and are amenable to the same kinds of therapeutic approaches, once the cycle of addictive drinking is interrupted. We assumed, and wished to confirm, that this would be as true of other types of addicts. (2) Among the alcoholic patients we found a significant proportion who either currently or in the past were abusers of other drugs. Dual addiction and the substitution of one substance for another

---

[1] Presented at the International Institute on the Prevention and Treatment of Drug Dependence, 8–11 June 1970, Lausanne, Switzerland.

[2] For convenience of expression we will refer to them respectively as "addicts" or "drug addicts" and "alcoholics."

were by no means rare. (3) As one of the few sizeable and professionally staffed private nonprofit hospitals devoted exclusively to the rehabilitation of alcoholics, we were under increasing pressure from the surrounding community to "do something" about the burgeoning drug problem, especially in youth. We believed that a carefully pursued attempt to treat alcoholics and other addicts together would be of general interest and might provide a useful example of how an existing alcoholism facility could respond to a new and growing community need.

INITIATION OF THE JOINT PROGRAM

We assumed that despite obvious differences such as age and life style, persons with problems related to other drugs are similar to alcoholics in make-up and responses. We therefore undertook to treat both types of patients in the same way. We decided to maintain a ratio of one addict to three alcoholics in the patient population, believing this would provide a buffering effect on the behavior of the addicts. Patients were assigned to therapy groups without regard to substance used, except that we attempted to maintain the same ratio as in our over-all patient population. This policy fitted into the philosophical framework of the Eagleville therapeutic community, which encourages staff and patients alike to appreciate all members of the community for human qualities that are considered more basic than maladaptive behavior tagged as "addict" or "alcoholic." The existing program at Eagleville was centered around group therapy of an "encounter" type, carried out in the atmosphere of an interdisciplinary therapeutic community. In addition to daily group sessions of 2 to 4 hours' duration, we utilized time-extended group therapy in the form of "minithons," which usually last 12 to 18 hr, and marathons of 40 to 60 hr with a 4-hr break for sleep at the end of about 20 hr.

Underlying the intensive therapeutic confrontation were the principles of honesty, openness, and responsible concern of one person for another. Eagleville's cardinal rules were that there could be no use or threat of violence and no unauthorized use of drugs or alcohol.

In the 32 months prior to the admittance of addicts, 1342 men alcoholics had been treated in our 110-bed institution. Between 1 July 1969 and 31 March 1970 we admitted 201 addicts, of whom 29 (14%) were women, and 484 alcoholics, of whom 34 (7%) were women. We have a small separate 13-bed ward for women, and so can admit only few women at this time. The average age of the addicts was 23 years, and of the alcoholics, 42. Among the addicts 83% were between 16 and 29 years old, while among the alcoholics 83% were between 30 and 59.

Group Differences

Certain differences in the attitude and behavior of the addicts and alcoholics were obvious immediately. We had been accustomed to the alcoholics who usually arrived "beaten down" by their families, employers, and society in general. Except when there was a particularly aggressive alcoholic in a therapy group, the therapist had to play the role of provocateur and confronter in order to get the passive, withdrawn patients to participate.

In contrast, the majority of addicts were active, aggressive and even hostile. They were part of an unspoken conspiracy which tried to defeat the system in general and Eagleville in particular. Few arrived with strong motivation to "kick the habit," and few felt that there was anything wrong in their use of drugs, despite serious personal and social difficulties which may have resulted from the use. This differed from the alcoholics, many of whom felt guilty and contrite, wanting above all to solve their drinking problems, albeit usually without giving up the drinking.

Another notable difference between addicts and alcoholics had to do with the way in which addicts acted out their impulses. While most of the alcoholics were passive and resigned, a large proportion of the addicts were aggressive and impetuous. They showed the impulsiveness and brash irrationality that characterize immaturity and that one expects to find in the young. As an example, addicts characteristically would violate the rule against use of unauthorized drugs, and then scheme to deny having done so and defend themselves against accusation and penalty in order to remain in the program. Alcoholics who drank would usually leave voluntarily, or remain, but put up no defense. Part of this difference might be accounted for by the fact that many more addicts were in the program as a result of considerable pressure from outside forces such as courts and probation and parole officers. Another part of the difference is the difficulty in detecting the illicit use of drugs. Much more than the alcoholics, the addicts belonged to a well-defined subculture with its own language, mythology, codes and hierarchy.

Individual Effects. Initially the two segments of the population viewed one another with suspicion, disdain and, occasionally, open hostility. Addicts tended to look on alcoholics as deteriorated "squares" who "couldn't make it" in life, while the alcoholics saw the addicts as "wild kids," with a tendency toward violence and criminal behavior. At times these distorted perceptions were reinforced by a few staff members who also had stereotyped views of the addicts. A few alcoholics were sufficiently frightened to sign themselves out of the hospital; an equally small number of addicts left after a short stay. They rationalized their departure by an inability to get along with one another. Other alcoholics admitted being fearful. Their response was to withdraw from active participation and concentrate on protecting themselves rather than dealing with their problems.

Group Effect. The early effect of the addicts on the therapy groups was divisive. It was as if there were two opposing teams. Few patients were able to accept the idea that the substance used was not the most important issue. Unless the therapist was able to channel the ferment into productive therapeutic interaction, the addict minority tended to "take over" the group and push the alcoholics into the background. The group found itself almost totally occupied with matters concerning the addicts, especially their "acting out" behavior.

The addicts in some groups kept the center of attention for many weeks, while older alcoholics slowly built up anger at the turmoil created by the new members. Eventually, the alcoholics expressed their feelings and in doing so became more actively involved in the group process. The group therapy began to function across barriers of age, differences in substance used, life style, and language. Much of this renewed activity came from the members themselves rather than being initiated by the therapist, who was now more occupied in guiding dynamic activity than creating it.

As the group process intensified and addicts and alcoholics found new areas of identification, the interaction revealed that many of the alcoholics also had a "pill problem" and that a significant number of the addicts were also either alcoholics or problem drinkers.

As group members began to understand one another the emphasis shifted from the substance used to the person who was using. Participants were viewed as people with problems rather than as alcoholics or drug addicts. Through psychodrama and role playing with alcoholics, addicts had new insight into the feelings of their parents. Alcoholics often could begin to deal with problems concerning their own children of similar age. Ultimately, the patients developed a sense of allegiance to the group, along with concern and responsibility for one another. A new family or subculture transcended the subculture of the addict or the alcoholic. The therapy groups interacted more productively with one another in the various program activities within the larger Eagleville community.

Community Effect. The admittance of addicts changed everyday life at Eagleville by providing a succession of broken rules and acts of misbehavior with which the community had to deal. This presented a formidable challenge. Consistent with the Eagleville philosophy, we adopted an approach of moral persuasion and shared responsibility. We chose not to rely primarily on policing from without in our attempt to create a drug-free environment. This would have required authoritarian and suppressive measures that go counter to the spirit of mutual trust on which the Eagleville program depends.

After much deliberation the existing automatic-discharge rule for drinking or taking drugs was replaced by a rule that put the authority for handling violations within the therapy group of the violator. The group and therapist together decided whether the individual was to be discharged or allowed to remain. Specific commitments might be required of an individual as his part of the decision. An important feature of the revised mechanism was that every decision concerning a rule infraction had to be reported promptly to the entire Eagleville community. Many of the meetings were stormy sessions, but over a period of a few months Eagleville began to adjust to the presence of the addicts and the problems they introduced. Gradually the antagonism between addicts and alcoholics began to abate.

Measures Instituted

With the introduction of the addict population other changes were made. We began to hold community meetings every morning, attended by all residents and staff, where each therapy group reported on progress and problems. The community as a whole reacted freely to the reports but agreed to abide by any decision made by the individual therapy group. Rule violations were reported much more frequently among the addicts than among the alcoholics. Sometimes as many as four or five addicts would use drugs illicitly together, bringing down on them the anger of the entire community. These emotionally charged incidents served to involve everyone in community issues, which was helpful in combating the inertia observed in many alcoholics. The regular therapy groups which followed the daily community meetings were often much more productive as a result of what had transpired earlier.

Not long after we opened our program to addicts, we found ourselves admitting a significant number of older "hard-core" addicts who had spent considerable time in prison. This group tended to view the hospital as another prison and set about organizing the other addicts into a prison-type subculture. The younger addicts followed their lead, partly out of fear and a kind of hero worship. This was a particularly difficult period. The community meetings were helpful in dealing with the crisis by bringing into the open the subgrouping that was occurring along with subtle threats of retaliation against community members who uncovered illicit use of drugs by other residents. The street ethic and the Eagleville ethic met head on. Solid support from the alcoholics and the staff enabled some of the younger addicts who had been frightened to speak up and break the grip of the few hard-core addicts on the community. A few of the disruptive older addicts were discharged.

We found it necessary to institute weekly random urine analysis for detection of illicit use of drugs. We did so because in the face of adamant denial by the patient it is difficult to be certain whether drugs have been used, and also as a requirement of receiving Federal funds from the National Institute of Mental Health to support part of our program. In addition to the routine checks the urine test was carried out on request of any staff member when he thought it was indicated.

Challenging the addict population with a urine test began to separate the patients and worked counter to our philosophy. Negative feelings and suspicions about the addicts on the part of staff and alcoholic patients were repeatedly reinforced. Furthermore, the test disturbed the relationship of some group therapists with the addicts in their groups by providing a frequent reminder, a piece of paper with a positive test report on it, that the addict was not "doing well," or was deceiving the group. No such obstacle was placed between the therapist and the alcoholics.

Addicts as a rule received disciplinary discharges more frequently than alcoholics and after shorter periods of time in the program. An alcoholic member of the group may have shown as little therapeutic progress as an addict member, but the therapist, the group, and the entire community, knowing the results of the urine tests, were likely to subject the addict to earlier discharge.

The urine tests did not disturb other therapists who philosophically viewed it as a deterrent for the addicts. It was considered another control to help remind the addict not to use drugs, much as the disulfiram (Antabuse) tablet reminds the motivated alcoholic.

The urine test also proved to be somewhat of an equalizer in the group setting. Whereas the alcoholic was quite obvious if he drank, his fellow group member, the addict, was not easily detected when he used drugs. Urine tests balanced out this discrepancy.

Policies governing the use of methadone for detoxication at the time of admission were another factor that affected the merging of the two types of patients. Some of the staff felt that the addicts should be withdrawn "cold turkey," even though it always had been our policy to administer tranquilizers for a few days to alcoholics in withdrawal. This inconsistency probably was related to the patients' attitude on admission, referred to earlier. We tend to be more sympathetic toward the "beaten down" alcoholic asking for help than to the addict, who is frequently coerced into the hospital by the courts. Another influence on staff attitudes toward the use of methadone was that in the early days of our experience we were frequently "conned" into using more methadone than was necessary. Furthermore, we admitted a number of patients addicted to methadone itself and encountered considerable difficulty in withdrawing them. These factors had a negative effect on some staff members, who felt that addicts had to demonstrate their motivation for help, a prerequisite not usually applied at Eagleville to alcoholics.

Preliminary Comparisons

Comparing 488 alcoholic patients admitted to Eagleville prior to the initiation of the addict program with 484 alcoholics admitted after we mixed the two groups, we find that 59% of alcoholics completed the inpatient phase of treatment after the merger, and 56% did so before. Before the merger 39% were given irregular discharges ("eloped," or "left against medical advice," or "disciplinary") and 33% after. The "disciplinary" discharges of alcoholics decreased by 2.6%. These results indicate no adverse effect of the merger on the alcoholics, at least by these measures. The average length of stay in the inpatient program (51 days) also was essentially unchanged.

When we compare 201 addicts and 484 alcoholics in the combined program, there are some marked differences. The average length of stay of the addicts was 30 days, of the alcoholics, 48. Only 2.9% of the alcoholics received disciplinary discharges after an average stay of 50 days for this discharge category, whereas 22% of the addicts received disciplinary discharges after an average stay of 24 days. The major factors in this difference were the acting-out behavior of the addicts and the routine urine tests for detection of illicit use of drugs. Length of stay in the other discharge categories was similar in the two types of patients. For example, addicts who completed the inpatient phase averaged 60 days and alcoholics 62.

Comparing results during the last 6-month period, 1 December 1969 to 31 May 1970, with the immediately prior 6-month period, we find a decrease in positive reports of urine tests from 35% to 19.5%, indicating stabilization of the program as we gain experience.

Discussion

Merging the treatment of alcoholics and addicts at Eagleville has been a rewarding experience. We believe the advantages outweigh the disadvantages, although we do not at this time have sufficient follow-up data that could validate the efficacy of the program. Six recovered addicts who came through the program are now working on our staff; five of them have been free of drugs for more than a year. Others are doing well in the outside community. Having begun to admit addicts about a year and a half ago, we consider that we are still learning how to accomplish what we set out to do. The program is not mature enough to be judged strictly on the basis of treatment results.

On the positive side we can say that the presence of addicts along with alcoholics has resulted in a more stimulating atmosphere. Any outsider who visited Eagleville before and after the merger is aware of the difference. People are more active, more engaged in what is happening, be it recreational and social activities or occupational and industrial therapy. Alcoholics Anonymous meetings and Narcotics Anonymous meetings held twice weekly in the evening at the hospital are usually well attended.

Having a good many younger people present undoubtedly contributes to the more vigorous pace. We have found the two-generation population a great advantage in our therapeutic work. Eagleville is now much more like a family, having old, middle-aged and young members. This creates tensions around different values and life styles, all of which abounds in therapeutic opportunity. Furthermore, the whole community has the ambience of a good large family where people care for and help one another despite conflicts and differing needs.

The prejudgments that alcoholics and addicts make about each other, which keep them widely separated in the outside world, are a frequent source of interpersonal conflict at Eagleville, but we use these naturally occurring incidents as a point of entry into the therapeutic process of the groups. We always have found alcoholics using their self-conceived difference from other people as a defense against recognition of their drinking problem and attempts to help them overcome it. Addicts, with their intense allegiance to a culture of their own, exhibit the same defense. Forcing both groups to interact as persons unlabeled "addict" or "alcoholic" has been therapeutic.

One of our reasons for accepting addicts was to be responsive to a surrounding community which is faced with a growing addiction problem and meager resources to combat it. We are winning confidence, gratitude and growing participation from that larger community. We consider this an important dividend. Now we are able to extend our work into the larger community where efforts to bring generations together in tolerant understanding, if not in values and attitudes, may be the most important approach one can make toward prevention.

If we look at the less optimistic side of our experience, we must speak first of the recurrent turmoil and crisis that followed the addicts into our usually tranquil hospital. Not always were we sure our program could withstand the shock waves of feeling and counterfeeling. Patients, staff and administration all were upset at times, and it was not always easy to keep "professional" perspective. Now we feel confident that we have passed through the most critical period and will survive. Most of the staff have overcome their initial feelings of threat and frustration and are now enthusiastic. A few have left. Possibly a few others do not consider the entire experience worth the anguish.

The fact that addicts need tighter external controls than alcoholics creates a difficult problem. Special measures, such as a urine surveillance program, tend to be divisive and work against the principle of accepting one another as persons, without regard to the substance used. Positive reports from urine tests, being such tangible evidence of behavior that is self-defeating and threatening to the community, inevitably results in different handling of behavioral problems.

From what we have learned up to now we would encourage others to try combined programs if they have the impulse and the opportunity. Our strongest caution would be to prepare the staff, patients, administration, and surrounding community carefully before the program is put into operation. Then the process of integration ought to be undertaken slowly. One must allow time to respond to the problems that inevitably will arise—and time for staff and patients to become comfortable with the new situation.

Few precedents will be available to help resolve a variety of difficulties. This means a need for a staff and a hospital community capable of rising to the occasion with innovative approaches. At the same time it is necessary to be watchful that new methods of meeting problems do not tend to separate addict from alcoholic and polarize the community.

Older "hard-core" addicts with prison experience pose a special threat. The hospital community needs a considerable degree of openness and trust to prevent the development of an infrastructure of power and authority like that seen in prisons.

Mixing older and younger patients we see as an advantage, provided one draws the line at age 16 or 17. Transgenerational communication is important not only within the therapeutic encounters but in helping families of patients and in offering an approach to the prevention of addictive problems in the community at large.

We offer these opinions and recommendations out of our everyday observations and experiences, not on the basis of hard data. The tentative conclusions must be substantiated in a more objective fashion. For the moment we believe that treating addicts and alcoholics together in an inpatient program along the lines of a therapeutic community is both feasible and desirable and ought to be tried more widely.

CROSSVALIDATION OF THE HILL-MONROE ACCEPTABILITY FOR PSYCHOTHERAPY SCALE FOR ADDICT MALES

JURIS I. BERZINS   WESLEY F. ROSS AND JACK J. MONROE

PROBLEM AND METHOD

Over ten years ago, Monroe and Hill[4] published a 46-item scale designed to predict the acceptability of addict patients for psychotherapy. In the original study, acceptability for psychotherapy (AP) was defined chiefly by the clinical judgments of three psychiatrists who, in the course of three one-hour interviews with 100 addict patients, made global ratings regarding the patients' acceptability[3]. An initial pool of true-false questionnaire items which empirically discriminated acceptable from less acceptable patients was eventually reduced to the 46-item AP scale.

The present study reexamined the validity of the AP scale in a therapy-analogue experiment in which male psychiatric aides conducted 20-minute interviews with male addict patients, shortly after the latter had undergone withdrawal ($N = 40$ dyads). The aides' task was to elicit as much "in depth" information from patients as possible, following an outline of 12 suggested topic areas. The interviews were tape-recorded and were later independently rated by two judges (graduate students) for (a) the number of areas explored by interviewers, and (b) the "adequacy" of patients' self-disclosures within areas covered. Interrater reliability coefficients were .86 and .80 respectively.

162

Although this experiment was designed to examine the effects of several compatibility and situational variables upon patients' self-disclosures [2], the selection of patients for the study in no way involved the AP scale. After the experiment was completed, however, it was possible to obtain complete psychometric data from the admissions testing battery on 37 of the 40 patients in the study. The admissions battery consists of the 14 standard scales of the MMPI, the Lexington Personality Inventory (LPI) [5], the Verbal Facility Scale (VO) which is an unpublished test of verbal intelligence, and the Rotter I-E Locus of Control Scale (IE) [6]. Included in the LPI are the AP Scale, a scale to measure acquiescent response (AQ), a scale of criminal psychopathy (SM), an impulse control scale (IM), an addict response scale (AA) which differentiates addict patients from Hathaway's MMPI standardization sample of males, a self-concept measure of intellectual orientation or status (IO), a favorability of self-concept scale (FA-1), and 9 other criterion derived and/or construct validated scales.

RESULTS AND DISCUSSION

Among the 32 variables included in the admissions battery, the AP scale proved to be the best single predictor of patients' self-disclosures in the interview ($r = +.52$, $df = 35$, $p < .01$). Table 1 shows the relation of AP scale scores to (a) other

TABLE 1. CORRELATES OF THE AP SCALE FOR ADDICT MALES

Item or scale	Pearson r
(a) PREINTERVIEW (ADMISSIONS) TESTING VARIABLES	
Education	$+.49$****
Rotter Locus of Control scale (IE)	$+.35$**
Acquiescent responding (LPI AQ)	$-.34$**
Infrequency scale (LPI IF)	$-.33$**
Verbal facility (VO)	$+.41$***
Criminal psychopathy (LPI SM)	$-.48$****
Impulse control (LPI IM)	$+.33$**
Favorability of self-concept (LPI FA-1)	$+.28$*
Addict-like responding (LPI AA)	$-.36$**
Intellectual status (LPI IO)	$+.44$****
Masculinity-femininity (MMPI MF)	$+.34$**
Hypomania (MMPI Ma)	$-.38$***
(b) JUDGES' RATINGS OF PERFORMANCE IN INTERVIEW	
Adequacy of patients' self-disclosure	$+.52$****
Number of topics covered by interviewers	$-.07$
(c) JUDGES' RATINGS OF PATIENTS' CHARACTERISTICS	
Self-confidence	$+.45$****
Sophistication	$+.52$****
Professionalness	$+.53$****
(d) INTERVIEWER'S POSTINTERVIEW REACTIONS TO PATIENTS	
Ease of communication	$+.35$**
Liking	$+.30$*
Degree of compatibility	$+.28$*
Saw patient as "active"	$+.34$**
Saw patient as "warm"	$+.41$***
Saw patient as "open"	$+.30$*

$*p < .10$, two-tailed; $**p < .05$; $***p < .02$; $****p < .01$.

variables measured at admission (following withdrawal), (b) performance in the interview, (c) judges' ratings of patient characteristics (from the tape recordings), and (d) aides' (interviewers') post-interview reactions to patients. It is evident that patients scoring high on the AP scale were perceived by their interviewers as warm, easy to talk to, active, likeable, open, and "compatible". Judges also saw the high-

AP patient as more self-confident, sophisticated, and "professional."[1] Inspection of the scales included in the admissions battery indicates that, relative to low-AP scorers, high-AP scorers are better educated, believe in internal control of reinforcement[6], are more verbally facile (VO), show greater impulse control (IM), present themselves more favorably (FA-1), are more intellectually-oriented (IO), and show less typically "masculine" interests (MMPI *MF*). The high-AP scorers were also lower in acquiescent (AQ) and "deviant" response styles (MMPI *F*). Their responses had little in common with the responses of addicts-in-general (AA), criminally-psychopathic addicts (SM) and high scorers on the MMPI *Ma* scale. The impression one gets from this constellation of characteristics, both intellectual and emotional, is that the AP scale measures some aspects of general "social competence".

This impression is corroborated by an inspection of the loadings of the AP scale on the first six varimax factors extracted in a principal axis factor analysis of the admissions battery scores of 836 male addicts at the Clinical Research Center (unpublished data). The AP scale basically defined one of the six factors, along with infrequency (IF, negative loading), MMPI *F* scale (negative loading), and verbal facility (VO, positive loading). FA-1 and IO, which correlated with AP in this study (Table 1) also loaded positively on this factor, and the label of "social competence" does not appear inappropriate for this dimension.

It may be concluded that the AP scale shows satisfactory behavioral validity in even this brief experimental interview, and that the behavioral component which differentiates high from low scorers on this scale ostensibly involves a dimension of social competence. It should be noted, however, that these conclusions apply only to drug-dependent patients and only to these patients' *initial* response to treatment-like situations. The ego-strength (Es) scale[1], developed as a prognostic index for neurotic outpatients, correlated only .17 (NS) with the AP scale in this study; its relation to the adequacy of self-disclosure measure was actually negative ($r = -.31$, $p < .10$). Within these limitations, however, the AP scale may prove useful as a variance-reducing ingredient in the design of future studies of the addict patient.

SUMMARY

The validity of a 46-item true-false acceptability for psychotherapy (AP) scale for male narcotics addicts was reexamined in a therapy analogue experiment. Forty psychiatric aides conducted 20-minute interviews to obtain "in depth" information from 40 patients. Post-hoc analyses of various admissions testing data showed that the AP scale was the best single predictor of patients' self-disclosure in the interview. The behaviors associated with varying AP scores appeared to involve a "social competence" dimension.

REFERENCES

1. BARRON, F. An ego strength scale which predicts response to psychotherapy. *J. consult. Psychol.* 1953, *17*, 327-333.
2. BERZINS, J. I., ROSS, W. F. and COHEN, D. I. The relation of the A-B distinction and trust-distrust sets to addict patients' self-disclosures in brief interviews. Unpublished manuscript, NIMH Clinical Research Center, Lexington, Kentucky, 1969.
3. McLEAN, A., MONROE, J. J., Yolles, S., HILL, H. and STORROW, H. A. Acceptability for psychotherapy on institutionalized narcotics addicts. *Arch. Neurol. Psychiat.*, 1955, *74*, 356-362.
4. MONROE, J. J. and HILL, H. E. The Hill-Monroe inventory for predicting acceptability for psychotherapy in the institutionalized narcotic addict. *J. clin. Psychol.*, 1958, *14*, 30-36.
5. MONROE, J. J. and MILLER, J. S. Experimental test manual. Unpublished material, NIMH Clinical Research Center, Lexington, Ky., 1968.
6. ROTTER, J. B. Generalized expectancies for internal versus external control of reinforcement. *Psychol. Monogr.*, 1966, *80* (1), (Whole No. 609).

---

[1]This rating may sound strange when applied to patients. It was originally selected to apply to aides, but judges rated patients for this attribute as well.

AN ANALYSIS OF A PEER NETWORK USING PSYCHEDELIC DRUGS*

BY EDWARD F. FOULKS, M.D., AND RUSSELL EISENMAN, Ph.D.

For the past two years the authors have met weekly with habitual users of psychedelic drugs.** Meetings were held at a user's apartment or "pad," and the authors observed his peer network interaction. Group size varied from 5 to 15 members, and our observation typically lasted about two hours per weekly meeting.

In a recent article[1] we outlined some preliminary observations concerning the interactions in the peer networks of habitual users of psychedelic drugs. We observed that many groups were initially formed by individuals with a common background of severe psychic stress, many having been treated for psychiatric disturbances. Such groups usually remained cohesive for a period of 10 weeks to 52 weeks. During this period, drugs were used frequently as part of the group's socializing, and group discussion often centered around the restructuring of a system of moral values. Following this period of cohesiveness, we observed significant movement in most members toward greater adaptation to society. It was this rejoining of society-at-large which reduced membership in the peer network, and eventually broke up the group. Since individual group members seemed to possess greater social adaptive capacity after their experience in the network of drug users than before, we proposed that a therapeutic process had taken place. We termed this process the "phoenix phenomenon,"*** and characterized it as including an initial state of psychic stress, followed by a state of psychic searching, and completed by a state of psychic and social reintegration. We speculated that the "phoenix phenomenon" may represent a capacity of mankind in general for adaptive change. Recently Wallace has clarified the universal aspects of this process in his cultural and historical analysis of the psychic notion of the "trip."[2] He points out that in many

From the Department of Psychiatry, Hahnemann Medical College, Philadelphia,
* Grant #MH14943-03 from the NIMH, Ross V. Speck, M.D., Principle Investigator.
**By the term "psychedelic drugs" we are referring to a group of drugs used commonly in series or combination which include marijuana, hashish, L.S.D., D.M.T., occasionally heroin, amphetamines, and barbiturates.

***The phoenix is a legendary bird of Egyptian mythology which was consumed in fire by its own act, only to rise again from its ashes in youthful freshness. It is usually represented as a bird-of-fire, and used as symbol of immortality and resurrection.

cultures throughout the world humans have likened the process of spiritual growth to the experience of making a trip. The metaphor is so commonly used, that he suspects it represents a basic human process of psychic adaptation which is perhaps best communicated to others by likening it to a trip.

Recently we have had the opportunity of observing a peer network while they were under the influence of psychedelic drugs. Such meetings are necessarily of long duration, ranging from 7 to 16 hours. The lengthened period of observation has enabled us to investigate each member in a more detailed manner. In addition, we have observed a group communication process which suggests a mechanism for the therapeutic experience described in the "phoenix phenomenon."

THE PEER NETWORK

Before this peer network began to smoke marijuana, the five members were given a battery of psychological tests in the following order: Bender-Gestalt test,[3] Multiple Affect Adjective Check List,[4] Blacky Pictures,[5] Gordon Personal Profile,[6] and the Draw-A-Person test[7] (the subject was first requested to draw a full length picture of a person from head to toe, and next to draw a person of the opposite sex from the one just drawn). A subject-by-subject interpretation encompassing all the members of the peer group revealed the following.

Sam, our host, is the oldest of six children and a college graduate. His Bender is adequately done, and indicates the absence of brain damage. The Multiple Affect Adjective Check List can be taken under either a *state* set, in which the subject describes how he feels presently, or under *trait* instructions, in which the subject describes how he generally feels. The adjectives checked give an indication of anxiety, depression, and hostility. The peer group was instructed to describe how they felt now, which refers to their present emotional state. Sam is clearly within the normal limits on all three subtests, indicating that at the time of our meeting he was not particularly anxious, depressed, or hostile. Much more revealing was his Blacky Pictures performance. This psychoanalytically derived test is a projective assessment of certain psychodynamic drives, obtained by having the subject tell stories to cartoons of a dog, Blacky, and his friends. Sam performed in an extremely compulsive fashion in that he "obeyed" the instruc-

166

tions which included what's happening, what led up to it, and how it all comes out (present, past and future, respectively) by writing "what's happening" at the start of his story, "what happened" in the middle, and "what will happen" near the end. He did this for all of the first nine cards, and followed the same format, without actually writing in the instructions, on the last two cards. The stories are short, often hostile, and contain oral cravings as well as a smattering of humor.

The Gordon Personal Profile contains scores for ascendency, responsibility, emotional stability, sociability, and a total score which indicates whether the subject tended to describe himself favorably or unfavorably. Sam scored average in emotional stability and in the 60th percentile (he scores equal to or better than 60% of the population) on ascendency, indicating leadership tendencies. He is markedly low in responsibility (23rd percentile) and sociability (19th percentile) and overall tends to admit to negative features about himself. He drew a side view of a male with arms in motion for his first drawing, and an upside-down, rather strange-looking female. If we hypothesize that the figure drawn first indicates sexual identification, Sam is identified with the male sex. However, the strange picture of the female may indicate hostility to or problems with females.

Ed was the only member of the group dressed in a notably "hippie" fashion, with granny glasses, atypical vest and tie, and an overall impression of being dressed nonconformist. He is the oldest of four children and has completed two years of college. His Bender was well done; but on design 1, instead of copying all the dots, he copied six and then wrote "etc." This probably summarizes a major feature of this group: They are able to conform to many conventional expectations, but choose not to. He was normal in anxiety, depression, and hostility. His Blacky stories were well-written and contained many direct sexual references—e.g., one dog says, "If you are going to fuck me be gentle." They tended to be clever stories and read like those of a rather creative, literary-oriented person. Ed is extremely high in ascendency, indicating that he is probably the real leader of the group. In fact, recent arrangements for our continued meeting were made by Ed rather than by Sam, who had been the initial contact and host. Ed is rather low in sociability, and markedly low in responsibility and emotional stability. He draws a caped male first and a ghost-like figure of a female, suggesting negative feelings toward females.

Freddy is an only child who has completed ½ year of college. His Bender is well done, and he is not unusual in the indicators of anxiety, depression, or hostility. His Blacky pictures reveal a great concern with "hodology," a topic which will be discussed later in this paper. Freddy is slightly below average in sociability, but extremely low in ascendency, responsibility, and emotional stability. In fact, he describes himself as about as emotionally unstable as it is possible to describe oneself on the Gordon. His male figure drawing has the head and feet of a duck, while the female was also duck-headed and had no hands. Of the three members of the peer network discussed thus far, Freddy appears to be the most disturbed and withdrawn. He said little during the testing session or before, but came alive some during the smoking of marijuana and laughed frequently at the non-verbal communication (see below).

Hank reported spending the last several years in therapy with various therapists. He is the third of eleven children, and completed only the ninth grade, although he communicates at a much higher level. His Bender seemed to reflect less than maximal effort, but it was adequately done with no indications of brain damage. He seemed more hostile on the adjective check list than had other subjects, but not markedly anxious or depressed. Hank's Blacky stories are often clever and make references to L.S.D., as well as sex. Although normal in ascendency, he is low in sociability, and extremely low in responsibility and emotional stability. His responsibility score places him in the lowest possible percentile. His drawings of both the male and the female are of juvenile figures, instead of comparable 18-year-olds, possibly indicating immaturity.

The fifth member of the peer network was Sidney, who was on dexedrine that day. He spent many hours on the Blacky test and never finished. Consequently, we do not have Gordon Personal Profile or Draw-A-Person data on this subject. His Bender is adequately performed, and he is normal in anxiety, depression, and hostility. This 21-year-old, married subject, with a child, showed the effects of dexedrine on his Blacky test, where he wrote what probably appeared to him to be profound comments but which, to an outside observer, seem superficial. He repeated words for emphasis and engaged in contrasts, such as pondering over the meaning of black and white. Apparently the effect of dexedrine was to allow him to lose himself in concentration and to feel good about his efforts without, however, resulting in high level performance. He spoke to one of us during the testing and thereafter, and communicated adequately.

The overall portrait of the group is that of a rather asocial bunch, both in terms of small tendency to mingle with others, and in terms of conformity to society's conventions. There seem to be creativity and humor despite the frequently admitted feelings of emotional instability. Their primary difference with society seems to be one of motivation: It is not that they cannot conform, but that they choose not to.

PEER NETWORK INTERACTION
UNDER THE INFLUENCE OF PSYCHEDELIC DRUGS

The five group members and the authors sat on the floor or a low day couch in a tight circle, each member almost touching the members next to him. High grade, finely-strained marijuana was rolled into paper by Ed. The cigarettes were lighted and smoked one at a time, being passed from one member to the next around the circle. As the group became more and more intoxicated with marijuana, we observed that their communication with one another changed quality. Before intoxication their conversation followed the laws of secondary process* and could be followed by us without difficulty. As the drug took effect, however, it became increasingly difficult for us to follow the group's conversation, which was apparently quite intelligible to them. A single word or shrug of the shoulders would produce a highly affective response from other group members, a response which was impossible for us to appreciate. They stated that they could not convey the significance of their communication to us because we had never "tripped" with them. We entertained the notion that what we were observing was a group of individuals who, through

*"... We have found that the processes in the unconscious or in the id obey different laws from those of the preconscious ego. We name these laws in their totality the primary process, in contrast to the secondary process which governs the course of events in the preconscious, in the ego." (p. 164)

"... Our theory makes use of [condensation and displacement] in defining the character of the primary process we have attributed to the id." (p. 168) Freud's *An Outline of Psychoanalysis* (1940) Hogarth Press. London. 1964.

using psychedelic drugs together 30 to 50 times, had developed an ability to communicate primary process material to one another. This notion was confirmed several weeks later when Sam acknowledged that each member gains from the group an increased sense of communicating to other group members his authentic feelings, whether they be socially appropriate or inappropriate. He stated that this communication develops from "tripping" together frequently, and gives each person the feeling that he is more deeply understood by the others. His sense of being appreciated and his appreciation of the other members correspondingly increases.

This communication system is termed by the group, their "hodology," a concept borrowed from Kurt Lewin.[8] Hodology as defined by Lewin is a geometric model for which the vectors are defined in dynamic psychological terms. Direction from one hodological region to another is defined. not by the shortest distance, but by the dynamic properties of the two regions. The "shortest distance" is the one traversed with the least effort.

In psychotherapy and in close social relationships such as love affairs the communication of primary process is both the medium for and the expression of gaining the intimacy required to bring the relationship to a humanly satisfying state. So too with relationships of less intensity, it would appear that the satisfaction gained from the relationship is proportional to the degree of mutual communication of primary process either through gesture or word. Primary process material is always affect laden, and it seems reasonable to assume that its effect is related to the mutual transmission of authentic affect. From such relationships we acquire a sense that others are not rejecting of our authentic selves. Without the experience of such relationships one is left in the position of forever questioning the appropriateness of his feelings and desires; and usually because of social values and taboos, one finds them quite unacceptable. Without having the experience of trying out his feelings and finding them understandable and often appreciated by others, one is left considering himself an enigma, a person without authentic identity.

Expression of one's authentic self to others for their consideration and acceptance is a process found informally in love affairs and intimate social relationships. where no one would deny its therapeutic effects. Many individuals for various reasons are unable to enjoy this process to the degree required for self identity and satisfaction. Social institutions have therefore been created to foster this process. They are numerous and varied in form; however, a listing might include religious testimony and confession, Alcoholics Anonymous, Day Top Village, Psychoanalysis, and, it appears, the peer networks of habitual users of psychedelic drugs.

While each member of the peer network is able to consciously attest to the therapeutic values of his experience in the group, we are continuing our observations longitudinally in an attempt to document more objectively the changes in personality which may or may not ultimately occur.

In past studies[1] we have pointed out that the majority of habitual users of psychedelic drugs observed by our research group gave histories of overt psychiatric difficulties. However, we cautioned that our sampling may have been biased, since the initial contact with a given group member came through a psychiatric outpatient clinic. The peer network analyzed in this paper was the first one contacted through sources other than a psychiatric agency. The degree of psychopathology found in this group is consistent with our belief that some users of psychedelic drugs are attempting to deal with psychic stress via their drug use, with the peer group support playing an important, therapeutic-like part.

REFERENCES

1. Foulks, E., and Eisenman, R.: A spontaneous therapeutic process in habitual users of psychedelic drugs. Manuscript submitted for publication, in possession of Department of Psychiatry, Woman's Medical College of Philadelphia, 1968.
2. Wallace, A. F. C.: The trip. Presented to Symposium on Psychedelic Drugs. Hahnemann Medical College, Philadelphia, Pa., November 23, 1968.
3. Bender, L.: A visual-motor Gestalt test and its clinical use. American Orthopsychiatric Association, Research Monographs, #3, 1938.
4. Zuckerman, M., and Lubin, B.: Multiple affect adjective check list. Today Form, Educational and Industrial Testing Service, San Diego, 1965.
5. Blum, G.: The Blacky pictures: A technique for the exploration of personality dynamics. Psychodynamic Instruments, Ann Arbor, Mich. 1950.
6. Gordon, L.: Gordon personal profile. World Book Co., Yonkers, N. Y. 1951.
7. Machover, K.: Personality projection in the drawing of the human figure. Thomas. Springfield, Illinois. 1949.
8. English, H., and English, A.: A Comprehensive Dictionary of Psychological and Psychoanalytical Terms. P. 141. Longmans, Green. New York. 1958.

Hypnosis and the Adolescent Drug Abuser[1]

FRANZ BAUMANN, M.D.

This paper reports the results obtained with an accidentally discovered technique of hypnotherapy over a five year period with adolescent drug abusers in private practice. Results appeared to depend markedly upon the motivation of the subjects. Those who really wanted to make a change because of possible harm to their physical health were more likely to succeed than others who felt that their drug was essentially harmless. This is the probable explanation for the fact that marijuana smokers were not significantly helped, whereas users of LSD, amphetamines and barbiturates made considerable improvement. The methodology and outcome are described and discussed.

The use of drugs to alter feelings is not new. Opiates have been used in the Orient for 5,000 years. The American Indian has long been using psychotrophic drugs as part of his religious ceremonies. Even in modern religions alcohol plays a definite role in the form of wine. Within the past decade, however, the excessive use of illegal drugs has spread to the teenage group to such an extent that subcultures have developed which are centered around certain drugs. The incidence of the use of marijuana for instance has been reported to be as high as 30 or 40% in junior high school and 80% or more at the college level. Brunstetter (1969) quotes a recent issue of a California high school newspaper in which the students themselves had conducted a survey to determine the extent and nature of marijuana use. Forty-five percent reported that they have tried marijuana and 31% indicated that they continued to use the drug. In the graduating class, 57% stated they had experimented with marijuana, and 47% stated they continued to do so. To the question "Which constitutes the greatest threat to your health following excessive use?", 44% answered alcohol, 37% nicotine, and only 13% marijuana and 6% caffeine. Inasmuch as the sale, possession or use of this particular drug is punishable by law to an extent that exceeds the punishment for serious crimes, it becomes apparent that the passage of laws may not be an effective means of controlling the abuse of this particular drug. If these laws were indeed enforced they could provide a criminal record for a great number of college students, whose careers would then be interrupted. This could entail a great threat to an entire generation. Some of these generalizations might also apply to the other so-called "mind altering drugs."

In this preliminary report no attempt will be made to describe therapeutic experiences with the members of communes of our drug using subculture. The patients to be described came from my private practice and were mostly of white, middle class origin. One-fourth or less were referred because of the use of drugs *per se*.

[1] Presented at the Twelfth Annual Scientific Meeting of the American Society of Clinical Hypnosis, San Francisco, California.

Almost all of them were living at home. They were using drugs more frequently than so-called curious experimenters. An arbitrary number of ten "trips" or episodes of drug use was required to be included in this series. The five youngest patients were in the sixth grade, and the greatest number in the 10th and 11th grade. The number of boys and girls was roughly equal. None was seen in the office during a period of acute intoxication, although a few were "talked down" by telephone when they were "high." I believe that all of these young people had the sincere belief that there was a drug or pill for everything. I suspect that television and other advertising media may have helped to produce this kind of thinking.

I have used visual imagery as an induction technique for many years. In 1964 I asked a 15-year-old girl to think about the happiest time she had ever had and then to re-orient to that time with her eyes closed. I told her that perhaps she could relive this time. She went into a rather deep hypnotic state during which she recognized and solved several of her problems. After the hypnotic state was terminated, I invited her to tell me what this happy time had been. She told me it had been a "pot party" during which she had become very "high." In reliving this party in her imagination she re-experienced the good feelings she had had during the original social event. These good feelings included a euphoric component, a sense of social ease, a feeling that she could communicate with everyone else there, and the feeling that she could make "small talk" without being the least bit uncomfortable. At the same time she felt that life was beautiful, that all people were friends and that only the present was important. Everyone at the party was beautiful; their minds, their thoughts, their words and their concerns were also very beautiful. She felt happy and forgot about her poor relationships at home and her inadequate schoolwork. Her reaction could perhaps be described by saying that she was "floating on air" and "feeling no pain."

Since she had been able to relive this past episode so vividly, I asked her to repeat the whole process, but to intensify the enjoyment, to multiply the pleasure she had experienced, in other words, to make it far better than the original event had been. She obligingly went back into a deep hypnotic trance, which she was obviously enjoying. When she roused up a few minutes later she informed me that this was more beautiful than anything she had experienced in the past. The same process of intensification was repeated four or five times. At the end of this she informed me that now she knew that she no longer needed to smoke marijuana. She had come to the realization that she had the capacity *within herself* to produce the good feelings and hallucinations which she was seeking. It was quite simple to teach her self-hypnosis, attaching the usual precautionary suggestion that she could utilize this technique only when it was safe. Since this girl had been referred to me for reasons other than the use of marijuana, it goes without saying that her problems of adjustment were dealt with by using hypnoanalysis, individual psychotherapy without hypnosis and family therapy. Eighteen months after the first visit described above she was functioning well at home and in school, and was not using any drugs. I felt that "hallucinating hallucinogens" might be worth trying on as large a scale as private practice permitted.

The accidental recognition that a drug experience or "trip" could be utilized as an induction technique was then tried out on 80 patients who were frequent users of marijuana, 42 patients who were frequent users of LSD (acid heads), 17 patients who had used intravenous methedrine (speed freaks), 28 intermittent users of oral amphetamines or "uppers," 10 patients with a history of recurrent barbiturate ingestion or "downers," and 2 who had used heroin at intervals but had not become addicted. In general, the technique consisted of the following steps:

1. History and physical examination with a sincere attempt at establishing rapport.
2. Induction of hypnosis usually by revivification of a previous "good trip" or happy drug experience.
3. Having the patient develop this hallucinated drug experience into one which, in his or her opinion, was more rewarding, more intense, more profitable than the original.

The advantages were obvious: a self-induced hallucinated experience was not against the law, it was free and totally under the subject's control (only *he* could turn it off and on), and thus I felt would help the adolescent's need for independence, without depriving him of the kick, adventure or escape previously supplied by injection or ingestion of illegal, expensive drugs with unpredictable present or future effects. Short term psychotherapy was offered to all patients and accepted by most. In a number of instances this included referral to a competent psychiatrist.

RESULTS

Of the 80 patients who were frequent smokers of marijuana approximately one-half felt that they no longer needed this drug. About ten percent did not know whether they would use the drug in the future or not. One year after treatment 40 of the 80 patients were still using marijuana, although some claimed to be using it less frequently. I felt that this approach to the marijuana problem had indeed produced 40 cures, and that there would be 40 less young people entering adulthood with a criminal record, if detected. This left me with a rather good feeling until I decided to sample 80 other adolescents in my practice whom I had not treated for this problem. No attempt was made to match treated and untreated groups. Approximately one-half of the untreated group also had abandoned the use of marijuana. The reasons given by the members of this group ranged from "boredom" and "it's not worth it" or "it didn't really do anything for me" to "I'm not going to get caught with any of that stuff on me." The reasons given for continuing the use of marijuana in both the treated and untreated group were basically the same. I concluded from these answers that these young people consider marijuana a purely social drug which, they feel, is the equivalent of the adults' cocktail hour. Most of them emphasized that the dangers of marijuana are less serious than those of alcohol, the use of which is legalized (California Medical Association, 1969).

They also stated time and again that "the establishment" was taking this drug much too seriously. Many of them felt that they could no longer trust their elders because they had lied to them about the dangers of marijuana.

To me it is obvious that my brand of hypnotherapy has not been successful with marijuana smokers. It appears that they were not motivated to begin with and could not be influenced in any way to abandon a drug which they feel is only *legally* dangerous, and which they believe to be relatively harmless to body and mind (Public Health Service, 1969).

Motivation for making a change seemed to be the key to the success in all the remaining groups. Of 42 teenagers who were "dropping acid" (LSD), it was difficult to help the 12 who had been on bad trips with this technique without adapting it to their needs. Those whose trips had been "good" enjoyed their visits with me; there was, however, some resistance prior to the widely publicized likelihood of chromosomal damage. They did want to have normal children some day, and, oddly, were far more concerned about physical damage to themselves or their offspring than any kind of harm to their mental or emotional health. Many of the so-called acid heads resembled the original flower children who had come to San Francisco in search of beauty. Introspection and better self-understanding is part of their "thing." Once they discovered in hypnosis they could accomplish what they wanted far more effectively without ever having to wait for a drug to wear off, they were more than willing to give up LSD. Of the 30 who had experienced only good trips, 26 have definitely stopped ingestion of drugs. The four who have not stopped have cut down on the use of drugs, but are using mixtures of dubious content, ingesting medication without prescription. Some of these young people have only been treated recently, and I expect some reversals.

My group also included 17 patients who were "shooting speed" (amphetamines). They had the same ability as the other patients to relive the drug taking experience in their imagination. The psychological and physiological changes I was able to observe in the office situation during the hallucinated injection were so severe that on several occasions I found it necessary to suggest that "the drug is very weak today." The slogan "speed kills," which the patients themselves quoted very frequently, implies the possibility of damage to their bodies and therefore a certain amount of motivation for making a change existed. In more recent months this motivation has become far greater because of the taking over of the amphetamine market by organized crime.

There has been a great deal of violence and a number of killings in San Francisco during the past year. All 17 patients have abandoned the intravenous use of amphetamines; four of them, however, are still taking amphetamines by mouth but, hopefully, not frequently.

The group of oral amphetamine users consisted of 28 young students who took overdoses, but were interval users. Of these, 20 were improved in that they reduced the dosage and prolonged the intervals. Six stopped altogether and two remained unchanged.

Ten patients used overdoses of barbiturates at frequent intervals. Of these, nine can be considered to be much improved, although six of the nine are occasional users of marijuana now. The drugs used had been secobarbital, pentobarbital, or a mixture of secobarbital and amobarbital. Strangely, all the capsules I was shown were originals with the markings of reputable drug houses. This small group did not lend itself to hypnotic revivification, since the original experiences had left no memory. I felt that their drug intake was primarily intended to produce a shock to the parents, or represented a cry for help much as a scratch on the wrist had been used for this purpose by others. There was, of course, also an element of need for escape from reality, which was more pronounced in this group than in any of the others. Hypnotherapy was used in this group primarily to help these youngsters use other ways of "shocking" the parents without harming themselves, and to acquire insight via hypnoanalysis. Conjoint family therapy could then be used to open communication.

There is also another group, that of multiple drug users, who knowingly used more than one drug simultaneously. They often do not know the name of the drugs ingested. I appear to have failed to recognize the majority of these young people and am aware of only two such patients in my practice. Neither one of these returned; follow up is therefore not available.

Lastly, there were two patients, one a doctor's son, who had been intermittent users of heroin without becoming addicted. It was most intriguing to see one of these patients relive in his imagination (in hypnosis) the experience of an intravenous heroin injection. The patient developed reversed peristaltic waves in his epigastric area, which resembled those seen in infants with pyloric stenosis. In fact, vomiting seemed imminent. The patient described this as a very pleasant experience and referred to it as a "gastric orgasm." Treatment in these two young people was directed toward the solution of their many personal problems. One of them had been taking drugs for eight years. He was what he describes as an "alcoholic" at the age of twelve and ended up in a well known treatment facility on the East coast, where he learned more about narcotics and other drugs. Not long ago he took an overdose of two kinds of sleeping pills, along with a bottle of vodka. He ended up in an intensive care unit and survived. The other boy no longer lives in this area and was not available for follow-up. I cannot say that my management of these two occasional heroin users has been of value.

COMMENT

Hypnotherapy of the type described appears to be a valuable adjunct in the management of many young drug abusers provided they are or can be motivated. In this preliminary report it was most helpful for the users of LSD, amphetamines, and barbiturates. It was not of value in the largest group, that of marijuana smokers, probably because of lack of motivation. I am now planning to study the application of this technique to groups of young drug users. This may provide information about more patients in a shorter time. It is hoped that other therapists will become interested in using hypnosis as a tool in the management of drug abusers of all ages. Successful treatment of this growing population group would be likely to reduce the need for criminal acts arising from the increasing cost of illegal drugs.

REFERENCES

BRUNSTETTER, R. W. Comments on the physician's role in drug abuse work. *California Medicine*, 1969, 110, 383–388.

CALIFORNIA MEDICAL ASSOCIATION. What is the most commonly used depressant? In *Damaging Effects of Drug Abuse*. Published as a public service by the California Medical Association and the California Interagency Council on Drug Abuse, 693 Sutter Street, San Francisco. July, 1969.

PUBLIC HEALTH SERVICE. *Marihuana*. Publication No. 1829. U. S. Dept. of Health, Education and Welfare; Public Information Branch, National Institute of Mental Health, Chevy Chase, Maryland, March, 1969.

Hypnosis in Living Systems Theory:

A Living Systems Autopsy in a Polysurgical, Polymedical, Polypsychiatric Patient Addicted to Talwin[1]

FRED T. KOLOUCH, M.D., PH.D.

A 50 year old, married female patient who responded well to combined medical-psychiatric treatment, including hypnotherapy, is presented. The total medical situation, illnesses, diagnoses, and treatments are viewed in the model of living systems theory. The position of hypnosis in living systems theory is discussed.

Hypnosis is a controversial medical tool of limited medical acceptance. Several national hypnosis organizations exist. Their membership covers professionals of many disciplines. The programs of the meetings of this and the other similar groups interested in the medical and other applications of hypnosis suggest it is an exceedingly valuable therapeutic modality.

In spite of an active national medical interest in hypnosis, very little time is devoted to it at meetings of the American Medical Association, the American College of Physicians, the American College of Surgeons, or the American Psychiatric Association, indicating in general, hypnotists talk to hypnotists instead of to their colleagues who do not use this method of treatment.

It has been difficult for me to evaluate hypnosis in relationship to other forms of mental therapy, e.g., the ordinary doctor-patient relationship with cognitive communication, psychoanalytic psychotherapy, behavioral conditioning, organic therapies,

suggesto-therapy, autogenic training, and many other varieties of medical relationship and communication.

As I have listened to hypnotist-physicians describe their experience with hypnosis in the treatment of a variety of illnesses, I have been impressed with the potential of being misled relative to the importance of the role of hypnosis in the overall recovery of the patients discussed. I have been biased in my own use of hypnosis and, doubtlessly as a result, have overvalued its effects. Some of my biases are published. (Kolouch, 1962, 1964, 1965; Titchener and Levine, 1960).

A conceptual model, living systems theory, exists which has allowed me to take a more realistic, less biased view of my own use of hypnosis as an adjunct in psychotherapy.

A very complex patient who has responded well to combined medical-psychiatric treatment including hypnotherapy, will be presented to illustrate the role of hypnosis in her apparent improvement. Her case history will be followed by the total medical situation, illnesses, diagnoses and treatments viewed in the model of ·living systems theory. A living systems

[1] Presented at the Twelfth Annual Scientific Meeting of the American Society of Clinical Hypnosis, San Francisco, 1969.

autopsy will be done to show the factors leading to her improvement and the place of hypnosis in her total treatment. The position of hypnosis in living systems theory will be discussed.

CASE REPORT

The patient is a 50-year old, married female, of the Mormon faith, who was referred to me by a psychiatrist for hypnotherapy in the hope it would relieve intractable upper abdominal and lower chest pain, and frequent migraine headaches of 20 years duration. As one reviewed her life story, the frightening complexity of her illness was soon obvious.

The illness started in 1949 with upper abdominal pain attributed to gallbladder disease. A cholecystectomy was done. Her pain persisted and a series of upper abdominal surgical procedures failed to relieve her. She was treated medically and psychiatrically with many evaluations and unsuccessful treatments. She became iatrogenically addicted to both opiates and sedatives. In spite of all surgical, medical and psychiatric attempts to alleviate her symptoms, she continued to have pain. She became depressed, suicidal and on one occasion was hospitalized in the Utah State Hospital following a suicidal attempt.

Her past history could not be documented accurately. Summaries of her hospital records of all hospitalizations after 1940 were obtained for review.

Some of her physicians were contacted and cooperated with our requests for information. It was estimated she had utilized more than 100 physicians, 4 clinics, and 8 hospitals in her search for comfort.

She had been in a nearly continuous medical relationship since birth, being treated for physical and psychological symptoms, and syndromes involving all body systems. She was classified as a polysurgical, polymedical, and polypsychiatric patient.

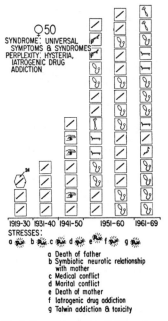

Fig. 1. Summary of Hospital Experience.

Her total hospital experience is summarized in Figure 1. Each square is a hospital admission. The symbolic key in Figure 2 explains the medical specialty responsible for her care: A knife in the square represents a surgical admission; the couch, psychiatry; the stethoscope, medicine, etc. "Pow" is the symbol for a serious psychological stress. Her principal stresses are listed at the bottom of Figure 1.

The geographical distribution of her surgical procedures both in relationship to her body and her country are shown in Figure 3.

Her present illness, the focus of this discussion, is summarized in Figure 4. It started with a medical admission in the University of Utah Medical Center in October, 1967. She had a thorough medical workup including the usual laboratory and X-ray studies. No organic basis for her

178

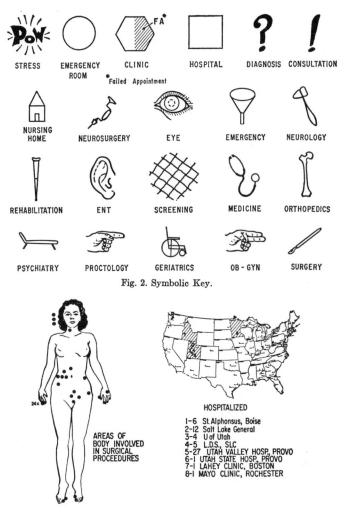

Fig. 2. Symbolic Key.

STRESS   EMERGENCY ROOM   CLINIC   HOSPITAL   DIAGNOSIS   CONSULTATION

*Failed Appointment

NURSING HOME   NEUROSURGERY   EYE   EMERGENCY   NEUROLOGY

REHABILITATION   ENT   SCREENING   MEDICINE   ORTHOPEDICS

PSYCHIATRY   PROCTOLOGY   GERIATRICS   OB - GYN   SURGERY

AREAS OF BODY INVOLVED IN SURGICAL PROCEEDURES

HOSPITALIZED

1-6   St. Alphonsus, Boise
2-12   Salt Lake General
3-4   U of Utah
4-5   L.D.S., SLC
5-27   UTAH VALLEY HOSP, PROVO
6-1   UTAH STATE HOSP, PROVO
7-1   LAHEY CLINIC, BOSTON
8-1   MAYO CLINIC, ROCHESTER

Fig. 3. Geographic Distribution of Surgical Procedures.

symptoms was found. A psychoneurotic personality disorder with a hysterical reaction, complicated by iatrogenic drug addiction was listed as her discharge diagnosis. Psychiatric consultation had been obtained. Psychiatric evaluation and treatment were offered. This finally led to two psychiatric admissions in April, 1968. She had another medical admission in May, 1968 in the Utah Valley Hospital and a neurological admission in the LDS Hospital in July, 1968. Her last hospitalization was in Feb-

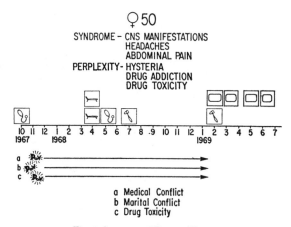

— CNS MANIFESTATIONS
          HEADACHES
          ABDOMINAL PAIN
PERPLEXITY- HYSTERIA
          DRUG ADDICTION
          DRUG TOXICITY

a Medical Conflict
b Marital Conflict
c Drug Toxicity

Fig. 4. Summary of Present Illness.

ruary, 1969 in the University of Utah Medical Center on Neurology with transfer to the Psychiatric Service.

Her presenting complaints during all of these admissions were about the same. They were excruciating upper abdominal and lower chest pain, recurring headaches, blackout spells, periods of confusion, weakness, diplopia, dizziness, numbness of the extremities, and transient motor paralyses of the right side of her body. These symptoms had been treated by her family doctor with a variety of medications to relieve her symptoms. Just previous to her last admission, she had received Talwin, Nembutal and Leritine. Arlidin and Librium had been used for a few months.

During her April, 1968 hospitalizations, the patient and I became acquainted and discussed the potential of hypnotherapy. She was an intelligent, angry woman who had become disenchanted with the medical profession. She had seen one medical hypnotist and her experience had been fruitless. On one occasion she had been offered prefrontal ultrasonotomy or cordotomy. She had refused both treatments after investigating the merits of the procedures.

I was candid with her. I told her I would be willing to work with her, but we would have to judge the results from the experience itself. I was willing to try to help her, if she would be willing to cooperate with me. She agreed to try hypnosis again. During the hospitalization, she proved to be a fair subject, and I felt hypnotherapy should be continued.

After leaving the hospital in April, 1968, I saw her in my office at weekly intervals for four visits. She soon became a good subject. Through hypnoanalysis and symptom substitution, she was able to achieve a great degree of comfort while in hypnosis. She would feel good for a short period of time, but her pain symptoms would recur soon after leaving the office.

Both the patient and I became disappointed with the transitory results of her hypnotherapy. She continued to be symptomatic, and was advised to continue on the medications administered by her family doctor. Her CNS symptoms were becoming worse, and she was advised to see an otologist for her dizziness and a neurologist for an evaluation of her rather ill defined CNS symptoms.

180

In May, 1968 she was hospitalized in her local hospital for a severe headache. She was finally admitted in the LDS Hospital by a neurologist for a complete neurological workup in July, 1968. On the basis of his evaluation, including head X-rays and an EEG, she was told she had cerebral arteriosclerosis as the basis of her symptoms. She received Arlidin to improve her cerebral circulation and Librium for her anxiety.

She returned to the care of her family doctor, from July to February, 1969. She continued very symptomatic, utilizing large doses of Talwin, Nembutal, Librium and Arlidin. Her symptoms increased. In October, 1968 she saw an internist who felt she needed more exercise but agreed she had cerebral arteriosclerosis. At this point her family doctor disagreed with both the neurologist and internist and told her the problem was purely emotional, and that if Talwin did not help, she could add Leritine to her medications, which she did. Her illness became worse. She became anorexic, constipated, and lost weight. She was also confused, dizzy, diplopic, had transient blackouts, had a unilateral motor weakness of her right arm and leg, was too weak and uncertain to walk, and fell occasionally. She continued to have intermittent abdominal pain and headache. She suffered anomie, a sense of hopelessness, and was depressed.

In February, 1969 she again consulted me. She appeared very ill. She was in a poor state of nutrition, unable to function, with all of her symptoms present. A review of her recent medical treatment revealed that the patient was very angry about the mixed message she had from her doctors concerning her diagnosis and treatment. She did not know whether she had an emotional illness or cerebral arteriosclerosis. This created a serious medical conflict. She really wanted to know whether her problem was organic or functional. She demanded a realistic prognosis.

At this point, I was forced by her critical condition to take another view of the patient. She appeared to be an ideal case for investigation of Balint's tenet (1957), the complex patient requires a holistic approach for successful therapy. In our first relationship, I functioned as a consultant using hypnosis to relieve a symptom, pain. This had failed. In our second encounter, I committed myself to a complete therapeutic relationship with the patient. I became her primary physician. She agreed to this readily, since she was very hostile toward her previous physicians.

She agreed to hospitalization on the Neurological Service. We started a search for all of her past records. It was impossible to extract the past medical information from the medical system in view of the archaic methods of data processing, storage, and retrieval utilized in doctors' offices, clinics, and hospitals. Our medical system was in part responsible for the difficulties her many doctors had viewing her holistic medical picture. This has certainly contributed to her continuing illness.

She was hospitalized as a neurologic problem. Another neurological workup preceded transfer to Psychiatry for evaluation and treatment.

The patient and I discussed her past medical conflicts, which had created a confused concept of her illnesses, great insecurity, and unresolved anger. Discussing her present medical situation, we agreed that she should receive a clear medical message, with both her physicians and the patient commonly and mutually understanding an acceptable concept of her illness and the treatment plan.

Following her neurological and psychiatric evaluations, the neurologist and I together discussed our impressions with her to give her a unified medical message.

Our conclusion was she had a psychoneurotic personality disorder (hysteria), complicated by iatrogenic drug addiction. We felt there was no evidence of arteriosclerosis. We suggested her treatment consist of detoxification by drug withdrawal, plus psychotherapy. We felt all of her symptoms were conversion phenomena. The patient seemed to agree with our diagnosis and the proposed therapy.

She was hospitalized for two weeks. All medications were gradually withdrawn. After discharge, she was treated as an outpatient, initially every two weeks, but recently on a monthly basis. Psychotherapy, including hypnoanalysis utilizing ideomotor questioning was carried out. She was taught self-hypnosis as a relaxing technique and a substitute for medication. An effort was made to improve her marital situation. Brief family therapy was done. Her religious beliefs and the social aspects of her relationship to her friends and church were explored. Her social and economic state were discussed. Some decisions were made relative to her living style both in relationship to work and play. Considerable time was spent allowing her to ventilate her anger toward physicians who had treated her in the past. In time, she seemed to resolve her marital, medical, social, and religious conflicts.

The patient rapidly improved. She learned to utilize self-hypnosis well. She was usually able to control her conversion phenomena when stressed. After she was being seen on a once a month schedule, she understood she could call me, or the psychiatric resident on call, at any moment she became distressed, if her symptoms recurred.

On two occasions she became anxious, her pain returned, and she took Talwin. Both times she became very ill and developed all of her previous CNS symptoms.

Up to this point we had been treating her hysteria, and felt that psychotherapy and hypnosis were controlling conversion phenomena related not only to her pain but also to her bizarre CNS symptoms. She confronted me in an angry, hostile manner, carrying the drug insert describing Talwin toxicity. She had underlined all of her symptoms. A review of her records revealed that on several occasions she told us Talwin was causing her CNS symptoms, but she did not get through our bias regarding the primary hysterical character of her illness. No one listened to her views of her illness. She had proven by a clinical experiment that Talwin toxicity was also a part of her syndrome. She changed our medical diagnostic agreement to include Talwin toxicity. After ventilating her anger, she felt much better and now knew she could not use Talwin.

She was doing very well until she developed a severe migraine headache. This responded to hypnotherapy and the ventilation of anger toward her husband.

Later in June, 1969 she developed severe abdominal pain which she said was similar to the pain that led to her cholecystectomy. This responded to hypnotherapy. In hypnoanalysis she revealed she was very concerned about the fact that I would not be available for two months and drugs were no longer available for her discomfort. She accepted the psychiatric resident as a person she could see (a substitute for me) if distressed, and had no more pain.

Following these experiences, she finally leveled with me about the seriousness of her drug addiction. It was her real problem. She said she was as addicted to Talwin as she had been to the opiates. The toxic effects angered her since she had suspected Talwin as the basis of her symptoms but no one, including me, would listen to her. We made a new agreement on her diagnosis. Hysteria, Talwin addiction, and Talwin toxicity most accurately described her syndrome. By stopping the Talwin injections (up to 30 cc daily) her health had been restored. I had been treating her under the illusion that psychotherapy and hypnosis had removed her CNS symptoms.

Currently, the patient is totally asymptomatic, functioning normally as a housewife and enjoying her family and social relationships. She has regained her weight, is attractive, and has a great desire to live out the rest of her life in a useful, self-fulfilling fashion.

She uses self-hypnosis daily for relaxation and self-analysis. When she feels anxious, she goes into hypnosis and reviews her current activities and relationships to understand her stress.

In my therapeutic relationship with this patient, I never pressed her for information regarding drugs. Neither her records nor her history related to me indicated the magnitude of her drug dependence. She recently wrote a letter to me concerning the extent of her addiction; the following excerpt is revealing:

I have been on hard narcotics for years and years—Demerol, Leritine, Dilaudid, Pantopan, Morphine, Talwin—you name, I have had it. I have also been on barbituates—Seconal, Carbital, Tuinal, Nembutal, etc. I have gone through all the torture and torment, the hell and horror of withdrawal—the cramps, sweats, shaking, nausea, convulsions, and anxieties. I have done every rotten thing in the book to get drugs. It is true, I didn't get them at gunpoint, as I was fortunate, if you can call it that, to always have a doctor or druggist who would give them to me. If one doctor turned me down, I could always go to another drugstore and call another one. This wasn't very often necessary as there was always one doctor who would give me all I wanted.

The role of the nonjudgmental therapeutic relationship between the patient and myself as a factor in her recovery is evident in the next excerpt:

Words by Virgil best describe the addict's plight: "Easy is the descent to Hell; night and day the gates stand open, but to reclimb the slope and escape to the outer air, this indeed is a task." To endure anxiety and tension and resist temptation while the magic needle or the soothing pill is near is a real fight, but worth every agonizing moment,

if there is someone near who understands and really cares. You gave me the feeling that someone cared and you gave me a chance to show I cared for someone else. It has paid off a thousand fold. How can I help someone else to find this happiness and security?

The therapeutic success in this patient has many facets. I had really been treating an iatrogenically addicted, sociopathic personality. She was a medical addict who fooled and manipulated her doctors, using them as pushers. It is difficult to be certain whether her pains are really conversion phenomena or malingering means to obtain drugs. At this point in her clinical course, it is unimportant.

LIVING SYSTEMS THEORY

Living systems theory offers a model for a broad systems view of this patient in her complex illness, its myriad of treatments and the present therapeutic success. It allows a view of both the patient and her physicians as well as the disease and its treatment. It offers a way out of a medical maze that she has wandered around in due to our current medical delivery system. Until her present treatment, there was no effective medical coordination of her case. In living systems theory one can put the therapeutic value of hypnosis in its proper perspective.

Space does not permit a detailed discussion of living systems theory. The reader is referred to basic articles on the subject (Bertalanffy; Buckley, 1968; Miller, 1965a, b, c; Shannon and McCarthy, 1956). A brief review of the essentials of living systems theory will establish the means to take a broad look at our patient and her treatment.

Living systems theory is the application of the principals of general systems, communication, and information theory to biological systems.

A living system consists of an organism whose function depends upon the integrated

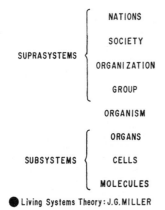

Fig. 5. Living Systems Hierarchy of Organization.

action of its unitary subsystems. It is separated by a boundary through which it relates, and is a component of its immediate suprasystem or environment. A person is an organism whose subsystems consist of organs, cells, and molecules. The organism is a functional component of suprasystems identified as groups, organization, society, nations, and the universe. Information, matter, and energy are the ingredients serving the organization and function of the structure and processes of an orga-

nism's living system. The hierarchial systems organization of an organism is illustrated in Figure 5.

LIVING SYSTEMS AUTOPSY

In order to assess properly the impact of all of the demonstrable events relevant to this patient's medical failure and success, a living systems autopsy has been devised, which will allow a simultaneous investigation of a substantial segment of her medical experience in relationship to her illnesses, the therapies, and the therapists. It will show clearly the core need for a holistic approach to this patient. Included in her therapies are my own past failure and present success.

Her lifetime medical experience will be reviewed on the basis of a living systems model. It will be reviewed relative to her present illness and her past history. Finally, a discussion of her medical relationships will demonstrate the crucial changes in her diagnosis and treatment which led to her improvement.

Her present illness viewed in the living systems model, the living systems autopsy (Figure 6), presents pathology in all hierarchies of her living system. The singular interest in the pain aspects at the

LIVING SYSTEMS AUTOPSY (Present Illness ♀ age 50 yrs.)

DIAGNOSIS:
Iatrogenic Drug Addiction, Hysteria, Polymedicine, Polysurgery, Polypsychiatry

Systems Hierarchy	Involvement	Pathology
UNIVERSE	+	RELIGIOUS CONFLICT
NATIONS	+	DRUG ADDICT
SOCIETY	+	MEDICAL CONFLICT
ORGANIZATION	+	COMMUNITY CONFLICT
GROUP	+	DEATH OF MOTHER MARITAL CONFLICT
ORGANISM	+	ANOMIE – PAIN – ANGER – DEPRESSION HOPELESSNESS – SUICIDAL
ORGANS	+	PAIN – ABDOMEN and HEAD – CNS POLYSYMPTOMS
CELLS	+	DRUG DEPENDENCE
MOLECULES	+	DRUG TOXICITY – PSYCHOLOGIC REACTION

Fig. 6. Patient's Present Illness viewed in a Living Systems Autopsy.

organ level of her living systems presentation leaves large areas of untreated pathology both in her suprasystems and subsystems. Her drug addiction and personality problems permeated all levels and defeated the goals of physicians with unitary interest in relief of her pain. As they prescribed drugs, they unwittingly created her addiction, toxic reactions, and prolonged her illness. I was a member of the group until we developed a relationship in which she could comfortably discuss her basic drug addiction with me.

The failure of her continuous treatment by the entire medical system over the years can be seen by a living systems investigation of her past history. In view of the enormity of the data and our incomplete recording of her past medical treatment, this synthesis must be an abstraction. It is quite informative in spite of serious and obvious limitations and defects.

In Figure 7, one can at a glance visualize pathology involving all vertical hierarchial levels of her living system and also pathology has been present horizontally in all of her organ systems, their cells and molecules.

Table 1 shows the details of much of her organ systems involvement recorded in her old medical records after 1940. Before 1940, we depended on the patient's memory for medical information.

It is obvious that a living systems autopsy is the only way one can clearly visualize the basis of constant medical, surgical, and psychiatric failure in this patient. The lack of appreciation of her sociopathic tendencies concerning her drug needs, her conflicts in all hierarchial levels, the poor communication between her many doctors and druggists who provided her drugs, the medical conflicts between the various specialists who guarded their biases and did not coordinate their findings in behalf of her treatment, her freedom to exploit the medical system to support her drug habit, all contributed to medical failure. Her basic neurosis started the chain of events but it became lost in the medical maze, and actually in the end was an untreated label. The impact of her medical and drug expense on her marriage and family was never appreciated. The drug addiction and the marital conflict plus her feeling of rejection by many doctors were her most serious stresses. Her pain treated by medicine, surgery, and psychiatry, insured her drug supply. It is impossible to determine whether the pain was a hysteri-

LIVING SYSTEMS AUTOPSY (Past History ♀ age 50 yrs.)
DIAGNOSIS:
Iatrogenic Drug Addiction, Hysteria, Polymedicine, Polysurgery, Polypsychiatry

Systems Hierarchy	Involvement	Pathology
UNIVERSE	+	RELIGIOUS FANTASIES
NATIONS	+	DRUG ADDICTION 20 yrs.
SOCIETY	+	SOCIAL and MEDICAL CONFLICTS
ORGANIZATION	+	FAMILY RELIGIOUS CONFLICTS
GROUP	+	NEUROTIC FAMILY RELATIONSHIPS –MARITAL CONFLICT–MEDICAL ECONOMIC RUIN
ORGANISM	+	ANOMIE –PAIN–ANGER–DEPRESSION HOPELESSNESS– SUICIDAL
ORGANS	⊞	
CELLS	⊞ }	POLYMEDICINE–POLYSURGERY–POLYPSYCHIATRY
MOLECULES	⊞	

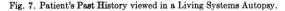

⊞ CNS ⊞ CR ⊞ GI ⊞ GU ⊞ ENDO ⊞ MS

Fig. 7. Patient's Past History viewed in a Living Systems Autopsy.

185

TABLE 1

ELABORATION OF DETAILS OF INVOLVEMENT OF HORIZONTAL ORGAN SYSTEMS DEPICTED IN FIG. 7

CNS—Central Nervous System
  1912—Meningitis
  1950—Migraine headaches
  1952—Psychasthenia with hypochondriasis
  1953—Transthoracic splanchnicectomy
  1954—Psychoneurosis
  1956—Conversion hysteria
  1957—Right thoracolumbar sympathectomy
  1957—Left thoracolumbar sympathectomy
  1958—Intractable pain syndrome
  1961—Psychogenic pain (was offered and refused both prefrontal ultrasonotomy and cordotomy)
  1962—Crainiotomy for subdural hydroma
  1965—Narcotic dependency
  1967—Chronic hysterical conversion reaction, Barbituate addiction
  1968—Depressive reaction
  1968—Psychophysiologic syndrome—severe—chronic (Was told by neurologist she had cerebral arteriosclerosis)
  1969—Hysterical neurosis with hysterical fainting and dizziness, Polysurgery
  1969—Drug addiction, Iatrogenic (Talwin), Talwin toxicity, Hysteria?—Sociopathy?—Polymedicine, Polysurgery, Polypsychiatry
Endo—Endocrine System
  1936—Thyroidectomy
MS—Musculo-skeletal System

  1919–1921—Recurring osteomyelitis of finger with 24 surgical procedures under local anesthesia
  1932—Ingrown toenails
  1945—Teeth extracted
  1946—Groin herniorrhaphy
  1953—Ingrown toenails
  1953—Arthritis of spine
  1956—Hand infection
  1960—Hip ulcer
  1962—Fracture vertebrae T-7
CR—Cardio-Respiratory System
  1932—Tonsillectomy
  ? —Pneumonia
GI—Gastro-intestinal System
  1930—Appendectomy
  1949—Cholecystectomy
  1950—Choledochotomy with celiac neurectomy
  1955—Choledoctotomy
  1955—Acute pancreatitis
  1956—Chronic pancreatitis
  1957—Visceral epilepsy
  1957—Biliary dyskinesia
  1961—Chronic pancreatitis
  1963—Acute large bowel obstruction
GU—Genito-urinary System
  1936—Oophorectomy
  1941—Bartholin abscess
  1944—Delivery of normal child
  1944—G.U. infection
  1947—Hysterectomy

cal conversion phenomenon or a manipulative, malingering means to support her drug dependency. She exhibits many features of both hysteria and sociopathy.

When Talwin replaced her other drugs, she developed a serious toxic reaction. Her living situation became unbearable and this led to her willingness to try psychotherapy. She has found a useful and harmless substitute for drugs in self-hypnosis. I feel a unified approach to her medical communication by the neurologist and myself, and a willingness to develop an agreement with the patient concerning her diagnosis and treatment based on our therapeutic relationship, has also contributed to her continuing improvement.

HYPNOSIS IN LIVING SYSTEMS THEORY

In view of this living systems autopsy, what was the role of hypnosis in her recovery?

Hypnosis was utilized as a form of psychotherapy. Essentially, in the living systems model it was involved at the organism level as a form of personal relationship and communication. To clarify the position of the modality hypnosis in the living systems model, the patient-doctor relationships at all levels are listed in Figure 8. Hypnosis can be viewed as a method for communication by suggestion at a personal organism level. As information influences the psychophysiological

LIVING SYSTEMS MODEL
Human Relationships in Medical Transactions

Systems Hierarchy	Relationships	Patient ♀ age 50 yrs.	Doctor
UNIVERSE	Mystical	⊞	IDIOSYNCRATIC VARIES WITH PERSONALITY, TRAINING, AND BIAS.
	Spiritual	⊞	
NATIONS	Ethical	⊞	
	Legal	⊞	
SOCIETY	Social	⊞	
	Economic	⊞	
ORGANIZATION	Geographical community	⊞	
	hospital	⊞	
GROUP	Role	PATIENT ⊞ DOCTOR	
	Family	⊞	
ORGANISM	Person Relationship	⊞	
	Communication	⊞	
ORGANS	Mechanical	⊞	NEUROLOGIST SURGEON
CELLS	Physiological	⊞	INTERNIST
MOLECULES	Psychological	⊞	PSYCHIATRIST

Fig. 8. Human Relationships in Medical Transactions.

LIVING SYSTEMS AUTOPSY (Medical Relationships in Present Illness)

DIAGNOSIS:
Iatrogenic Drug Addiction, Hysteria, Polymedicine, Polysurgery, Polypsychiatry

Systems Hierarchy	Relationships	Patient ♀ age 50 yrs.	A	B	C	D Doctors*
UNIVERSE	Mystical	⊞				⊞
	Spiritual	⊞				⊞
NATIONS	Ethical	⊞	⊞	⊞	⊞	⊞
	Legal	⊞	⊞	⊞	⊞	⊞
SOCIETY	Social	⊞				⊞
	Economic	⊞	⊞	⊞	⊞	⊞
ORGANIZATION	Geographical community	⊞	⊞			
	hospital	⊞		⊞	⊞	⊞
GROUP	Role	⊞	⊞	⊞	⊞	⊞
	Family	⊞				⊞
ORGANISM	Person Relationship	⊞	⊟	⊟	⊞	⊞
	Communication	⊞	⊟	⊟	⊞	⊞
ORGANS	Mechanical	⊟	⊟	⊞	⊟	⊟
CELLS	Physiological	⊞	⊟	⊟	⊟	⊞
MOLECULES	Psychological	⊞	⊞	⊞	⊞	⊞

*A-GENERAL PRACTITIONER B-NEUROLOGIST C-2nd NEUROLOGIST D-PSYCHIATRIST

Fig. 9. Medical Relationships in the Present Illness.

manifestations of organs, cells, and molecules, hypnosis is operative. Currently, we do not understand the role of information in psychophysiologic mechanisms. As communication enables an organism to resolve suprasystem conflicts, hypnosis is also operative.

Returning to the living systems autopsy in Figure 9, we will review her medical relationships during her present illness involving her family physician (A), the first neurologist (B), the second neurologist (C), and the psychiatrist (me) (D). The patient is involved at all levels of relationship occurring in her living system. On the basis of her story, her expressed hostility toward doctors A and B, she exhibited a patient-doctor role relationship, but it was negative at a personal level. Her communication was confused, Dr. A telling her she had cerebral arteriosclerosis and Dr. B telling her her problems were emotional. Dr. C, the second neurologist, also had an impersonal role relationship. His cognitive communication was positive, and she understood she had no mechanical obstruction to the circulation of her brain. In the psychiatric relationship with the patient there was involvement at all levels. Initially, I felt her problem was primarily psychological, but she finally convinced me by her experiment with Talwin, and her confession of profound drug addiction, that we also must consider our relationship at the physiological level.

In view of this it seems our interpersonal relationship, as she defines it as caring, plus good communication, both cognitive and in hypnosis, with a relationship at all levels of her living system, created the difference between therapeutic failure and success. I do believe her ability to relax and control her anxiety as a substitute for chemical relaxation has been extremely helpful in maintaining her ability to overcome her psychological drug dependence. It is here that hypnosis is operative.

Conclusions

The case illustrates the validity of the ancient medical model which has established that an accurate diagnosis must precede successful treatment. Balint's model, relating to the need of an holistic medical diagnostic and therapeutic approach which includes the psychological parameter along with the physical, is also supported. Many of Balint's points relating to problems in the relationship and communication of the patient with the medical community are visible. The resolution of medical conflicts and a medical agreement with the patient concerning her diagnosis and treatment led to recovery.

Hypnosis was initially unsuccessful when used primarily as a therapeutic agent in her case. It was only when a correct diagnosis and holistic systems treatment was used that hypnosis seemed of value. It has been a segment of a very broad psychotherapeutic and neurologic approach to her therapy.

The difficulties encountered in the care of this patient and the search for her medical data support the contention that our entire system of the delivery of medical practice needs revision. The medical system itself could not coordinate and control this patient's treatment. She was free to use her doctors as pushers and her druggists as suppliers, and this kept her from necessary psychiatric treatment. Probably all iatrogenically addicted patients need a living systems autopsy to identify the pathology that needs treatment. At the moment, it is an extremely difficult task to gather medical information for this purpose. When medical data is processed, stored and easily retrievable, the polymedical, polysurgical, polypsychiatric addicted patient will be easier to treat.

The role of hypnosis in medical treatment should be viewed on the basis of a broad living systems model. It has value at the organism level for control of the communication by suggestion. As a relaxation type of therapy, self-hypnosis has been very useful in this patient. It has replaced her drugs.

REFERENCES

BALINT, M. *The doctor, his patient, and the illness.* New York: International Universities Press, 1957.

BERTALANFFY, L. VON. The theory of open systems in physics and biology. *Science,* 3, 23–29.

BUCKLEY, W. *Modern systems research for the behavioral scientist.* Chicago, Ill.: Aldine Publishing Co., 1968.

KOLOUCH, F. T. Role of suggestion in surgical convalescence. *American Medical Association Archives of Surgery,* 1962, 85, 304–315.

KOLOUCH, F. T. Hypnosis and surgical convalescence: A study of subjective factors in postoperative recovery. *American Journal of Clinical Hypnosis,* 1964, 7, 120–129.

KOLOUCH, F. T. The role of the patient in surgical convalescence. *Journal of the Iowa Medical Society,* 1965, 363–368.

MILLER, J. G. Living systems: Basic concepts. *Behavioral Science,* 1965, 10, 193–237. (a)

MILLER, J. G. Livings systems: Structure and process. *Behavioral Science,* 1965, 10, 337–379. (b)

MILLER, J. G. Living systems: Cross-level hypotheses. *Behavioral Science,* 1965, 10, 380–411. (c)

SHANNON, C. E. AND McCARTHY, J. (Eds.) *Automata studies.* Princeton, N. J.: Princeton University Press, 1956.

TITCHENER, J. L. and LEVINE, M. *Surgery as a human experience: The psychodynamics of surgical practice.* New York: Oxford University Press, 1960.

189

Diagnosis and Treatment of Drug Dependence of the Barbiturate Type

BY ABRAHAM WIKLER, M.D.

A CCORDING TO THE DEFINITIONS proposed by the World Health Organization(18):

Drug dependence of the barbiturate type is described as a state arising from repeated administration of a barbiturate, or an agent with barbiturate-like effect, on a continuous basis, generally in amounts exceeding therapeutic dose levels. Its characteristics include: 1) a strong 'desire or need to continue taking the drug; the need can be satisfied by the drug taken initially or by another with barbiturate-like properties; 2) a tendency to increase the dose, partly owing to the development of tolerance; 3) a psychic dependence on the effects of the drug related to subjective and individual appreciation of those effects; and 4) a physical dependence on the effects of the drug requiring its presence for maintenance of homeostasis and resulting in a definite, characteristic, and self-limited abstinence syndrome when the drug is withdrawn.

Although patients who display any or all of the first three characteristics are also in need of medical and psychiatric attention, the development of the fourth characteristic, physical dependence, may be fraught with danger to life and therefore demands immediate and skillful treatment. This article will therefore begin with a discussion of the diagnosis and treatment of physical dependence on drugs of the barbiturate type.

Physical Dependence on Barbiturates

Understanding of the clinical course and predictable outcome of chronic barbiturate intoxication was greatly advanced by the experimental studies of Isbell and associates(14), Wikler and associates(17), Fraser and associates(8, 10), and Belleville and Fraser(2). Using former narcotic addicts without psychosis, epilepsy, or other central nervous system disease as subjects (all volunteered for the research), these investigators demonstrated that tolerance, though only partial, does develop to the effects of barbiturates on the central nervous system; and that abrupt withdrawal of secobarbital, amobarbital, or pentobarbital after prolonged (one or more months) continuous intoxication results in a characteristic abstinence syndrome. The severity of the latter is at least in part directly related to the daily dose level attained before drug withdrawal.

Table 1 summarizes the essential features of the "full-blown" barbiturate abstinence syndrome as it develops on abrupt withdrawal of the so-called short-acting barbiturates following chronic intoxication at daily dose levels of 0.8 to 2.2 gm. For convenience in discussion the clinical phenomena may be classified as "minor" (apprehension, muscular weakness, tremors, postural faintness, anorexia, and twitches) and "major" (seizures, psychosis).

As indicated in the table, the minor abstinence phenomena are observable within 24 hours after administration of the last dose of barbiturates and continue beyond the appearance of the major abstinence phenomena which, if they develop, emerge between the second and eighth days.

Among the minor abstinence phenomena,

TABLE 1

The Barbiturate Abstinence Syndrome

(After abrupt withdrawal of secobarbital or pentobarbital following chronic intoxication at dose levels of 0.8 to 2.2 gm. per day orally, for 6 weeks or more)

CLINICAL PHENOMENON	INCIDENCE	TIME OF ONSET	DURATION	REMARKS
Apprehension	100%	1st day	3-14 days	Vague uneasiness, or fear of impending catastrophe.
Muscular weakness	100%	1st day	3-14 days	Evident on mildest exertion.
Tremors	100%	1st day	3-14 days	Coarse, rhythmic, nonpatterned, evident during voluntary movement, subside at rest.
Postural faintness	100%	1st day	3-14 days	Evident on sitting or standing suddenly. Associated with marked fall in systolic and diastolic blood pressure, and pronounced tachycardia.
Anorexia	100%	1st day	3-14 days	Usually associated with repeated vomiting.
Twitches	100%	1st day	3- ? days	Myoclonic muscular contractions; or spasmodic jerking of one or more extremities. Sometimes bizarre patterned movements.
Seizures	80%	2nd-3rd day	8 days	Up to a total of 4 grand mal episodes, with loss of consciousness and postconvulsive stupor.
Psychoses	60%	3rd-8th day	3-14 days	Usually resemble "delirium tremens"; occasionally resemble schizophrenic or Korsakoff syndromes; or acute panic states may occur.

Note: These data are based on a series of 19 cases of experimental addiction to barbiturates. Four developed seizures without subsequent psychosis; one exhibited delirium without antecedent seizures. Three escaped both seizures and delirium.

192

postural faintness (orthostatic hypotension) is of particular value in differentiating the developing barbiturate abstinence syndrome from ordinary anxiety states, but often the differential diagnosis is difficult to make at this stage. The presence of coarse, rhythmic intention tremors in the upper extremities is also a useful but less specific sign of barbiturate abstinence. Other minor abstinence phenomena include insomnia, profuse sweating, and tendon hyperreflexia. Even if overt major abstinence phenomena do not develop, paroxysmal discharges may be found in the electroencephalogram after the second day of abstinence in a majority of the patients abruptly withdrawn from such dose levels(5, 17).

When major abstinence phenomena do appear, the seizures are invariably of the clonic-tonic grand mal type clinically indistinguishable from those of idiopathic grand mal epilepsy. It is curious that in the experimental studies on which this discussion is based, no subject had more than four seizures, and the interseizure electroencephalograms were characterized by recurrent 4 per second spike-wave discharges. Also of interest is that none of the subjects having seizures could recall any aura.

The psychoses that develop as major barbiturate abstinence phenomena are more variable. In severe cases the psychosis is indistinguishable from that of alcoholic delirium tremens (also a withdrawal phenomenon) with disorientation, agitation, delusions, and hallucinations (usually visual, sometimes also auditory). Rising core temperature is an ominous sign prognosticating a fatal outcome if not combated vigorously(9). Milder cases may be characterized by hallucinations with relatively clear sensorium, a Korsakoff-like syndrome, or by extreme anxiety.

The data in table 2, also obtained in experimental studies on former narcotic addicts who volunteered for research, show the relationships between daily dose level and duration of intoxication on the one hand,

193

and the incidence of major and minor abstinence phenomena following abrupt withdrawal of barbiturates on the other. It will be noted that of 20 subjects who were withdrawn from daily barbiturate dose levels of 0.4 gm. or less, none developed major, and only one developed significant minor, abstinence phenomena. On the other hand, of 23 subjects withdrawn from 0.6 to 0.8 gm. daily, three had convulsions, one displayed hallucinations, and 14 showed significant degrees of minor abstinence phenomena.

It may be inferred therefore that chronic intoxication with barbiturates at daily dose levels of 0.6 to 0.8 gm. for periods of 35 to 57 days is sufficient to produce a clinically significant degree of physical dependence. The data in table 2 also indicate that higher daily dose levels of barbiturates induce stronger physical dependence. Thus all of 18 subjects withdrawn from 0.8 to 2.2 gm. daily had minor abstinence phenomena, 14 had convulsions, and 12 had delirium (some subjects had both).

Although there is a direct relationship between daily intoxication dosage and severity of barbiturate abstinence phenomena, more information is needed about the relationships that may exist between duration of chronic barbiturate intoxication per se (daily dose level held constant) and the severity of abstinence phenomena.

Initial treatment of patients chronically intoxicated with barbiturates is directed toward withdrawal of the drug in such a manner as to prevent the appearance of the major abstinence phenomena altogether and to minimize the severity of minor abstinence phenomena. To this end the procedure developed by Isbell(13) has proven to be safe, simple, and reliable. Essentially it consists of stabilization of the patient on a so-called short-acting barbiturate (e.g., pentobarbital) at doses (0.2 - 0.4 gm., orally if possible, intramuscularly if necessary) at four- to six-hour intervals, regulated in such a manner that no abstinence phenomena and a minimal degree of barbi-

TABLE 2

Summary of Data on Relationship of Dosage of Secobarbital or Pentobarbital to Intensity of Physical Dependence

TOTAL NO.	PATIENTS — NO. RECEIVING		DAILY DOSE OF BARBITURATE, Gm.	DAYS OF INTOXICATION IN HOSPITAL	NO. OF PATIENTS HAVING SYMPTOMS		
	SECOBARBITAL	PENTOBARBITAL			CONVULSIONS	DELIRIUM	MINOR SYMPTOMS OF SIGNIFICANT DEGREE
18	16	2	0.9-2.2	32-144	14	12	18
5	5		0.8	42-57	1	0	5
18	18		0.6	35-57	2	0	9
18	10	8	0.4	90	0	0	1
2	1	1	0.2	365	0	0	0

(Reprinted from J.A.M.A., Vol. 166, 1958, pp. 126-129, by permission of the editor; see Ref. 10.)

195

turate-type signs of intoxication are observed.

After two to three days of such stabilization the barbiturate is withdrawn *slowly* at a rate not exceeding 0.1 gm. a day regardless of the daily stabilization dose level. If more than the mildest minor abstinence phenomena appear, the reduction schedule is suspended until these signs and symptoms subside, after which it is resumed at the same rate or a slower rate, e.g., 0.05 gm. daily, if orthostatic hypotension, marked tremulousness, and/or persistent insomnia develop.

In clinical practice, initiation of this stabilization and reduction procedure will depend of course on the status of the patient on admission. Should the patient be grossly intoxicated or comatose on arrival, no barbiturates are given until these effects have receded completely, but if there is a clear history of chronic barbiturate intoxication or if this is strongly suspected on other grounds, one should not wait until severe minor or any major withdrawal phenomena are observed before instituting the "stabilization" procedure.

In doubtful cases a test dose of 0.2 gm. of pentobarbital may be given after all signs of intoxication have disappeared, and if no signs of barbiturate effect (positive Romberg sign, gait ataxia, finger to nose incoordination, nystagmus, slurred speech, drowsiness) are observed one hour later, the same dose may be prescribed every six hours around the clock. During the next 24 hours the patient should be observed for signs of abstinence just *before* each dose and again for signs of barbiturate intoxication one hour *after* each dose.

If during this period clear abstinence phenomena and no signs of barbiturate intoxication are observed, the dose and/or the frequency of administration should be increased and then manipulated upwards or downwards until optimal stabilization is achieved. Often optimal stabilization takes more than 24 hours, but in no case should systematic reduction of daily dosage be initiated before the patient is stabilized.

On the other hand, if the patient reacts to the initial test dose of 0.2 gm. of pentobarbital with gross signs of barbiturate intoxication, the diagnosis of physical dependence on barbiturates should be questioned. To be safe it is usually advisable to continue the "assay" at reduced dosage—e.g., 0.1 gm. of pentobarbital every six hours with the same observations before and after each dose as already described. If during the next 24 hours no abstinence phenomena are observed and especially if the patient shows signs of increasing barbiturate intoxication, the diagnosis of physical dependence may be rejected and barbiturates may be discontinued altogether.

This testing and stabilization procedure may also be applied to patients who on admission display minor abstinence phenomena. In the case of patients who have already had one or more seizures, the initial dose of pentobarbital should be somewhat larger (0.3 to 0.4 gm.) and the stabilization procedure should be accelerated beginning with 0.2 gm. of pentobarbital every four hours, and dosage and frequency manipulated thereafter as indicated.

The presence of delirium on admission calls for a somewhat different approach. This condition is not easily reversible in the sense that the stabilization state can be readily achieved. Rather, the aim should be to sedate the patient heavily so that agitation, insomnia, and above all hyperpyrexia are suppressed. To accomplish this, pentobarbital may have to be given intramuscularly or intravenously in whatever amounts may be found necessary for three to five days, after which the degree of sedation may be lightened gradually and slow reduction carried out as in stabilized patients.

Because of its longer duration of action, sodium phenobarbital may be preferable to pentobarbital. Indeed, the Danish workers(16) have used the very long acting barbiturate, barbital (Veronal) with excellent results in the treatment of alcoholic delirium tremens since 1909; probably this venerable agent would be equally effective in the management of barbiturate withdrawal delirium. However, the very long duration of action of barbital may be a disadvantage to physicians who have had little experience with it.

In addition to specific therapy as described, it is of course necessary to ensure that patients displaying barbiturate abstinence phenomena, and especially delirium, are protected from injury. They should be provided with very low beds or mattresses on the floor and should receive adequate fluids and electrolytes, calories, vitamins, and, when indicated, antibiotics.

While theoretically such drugs as paraldehyde or chloral hydrate should readily substitute for pentobarbital in specific therapy, there appears to be no valid reason for employing certain other agents that have been advocated from time to time. Thus neither diphenylhydantoin (Dilantin) nor chlorpromazine (Thorazine) prevents barbiturate withdrawal seizures in the dog(4, 6), and systematic studies on the effectiveness of meprobamate (Miltown, Equanil) or chlordiazepoxide (Librium) in the management of the barbiturate abstinence syndrome have not yet been made.

Dependence on Nonbarbiturate Sedatives and Minor Tranquilizers

To date, systematic experimental studies on the physical dependence-producing properties of nonbarbiturate sedatives and minor tranquilizers in man have been reported only for meprobamate(11) and chlordiazepoxide(12). However, individual case reports, reviewed by Essig(3), indicate that barbiturate-type abstinence phenomena, both of the minor and major kind, can supervene when not only these agents but also glutethimide (Doriden), ethinamate (Valmid), ethchlorvynol (Placidyl), or methyprylon (Noludar) are withdrawn abruptly after periods of chronic intoxication at high daily dose levels of these drugs.

All of these agents are central nervous system depressants, and the abstinence phenomena that develop after their abrupt withdrawal under the conditions stated closely resemble the barbiturate abstinence syndrome. It may thus be inferred that to a considerable extent at least, there are common neurochemical mechanisms that underlie physical dependence on barbiturates, nonbarbiturate sedatives, and minor tranquilizers. If so, then barbiturates should substitute readily for nonbarbiturate sedatives and minor tranquilizers both in assaying the degree of tolerance and physical dependence that may have developed in patients chronically intoxicated on the latter two categories of drugs and in the clinical management of drug withdrawal.

This principle was applied by Bakewell and Wikler(1) in a study on the incidence of nonnarcotic addiction in a Southern university hospital psychiatric ward, using pentobarbital exclusively as the drug of substitution in the same manner as already described for the diagnosis and treatment of physical dependence on barbiturates. Inasmuch as the earlier studies of Fraser and associates(10) had indicated that the critical daily intoxication dose level for development of physical dependence on barbiturates is 0.6 to 0.8 gm., Bakewell and Wikler(1) adopted as a criterion for classifying patients as physically dependent on nonbarbiturate sedatives and/or minor tranquilizers the ability of the patient to tolerate (i.e., become stabilized on) 0.8 gm. of pentobarbital or more daily.

On the basis of this criterion, they found that nine of 132 consecutive patients (6.8 percent) admitted to the psychiatric ward over a 14-month period were physically dependent on nonnarcotic central nervous system depressants including glutethimide, meprobamate, chlordiazepoxide, diazepam, paraldehyde, and barbiturates, alone or in various combinations (table 3).

199

TABLE 3
Case Summaries

PATIENT NO.	SEX	AGE (YEARS)	DRUGS OF ABUSE		DAILY PENTOBARBITAL STABILIZATION-DOSE LEVEL (ORAL, MG.)
			AGENT	ESTIMATED AVERAGE DAILY INTAKE (MG.)	
1	M	36	Glutethimide	2,500	800
2	F	59	Glutethimide	5,000	1,200
3	F	44	Glutethimide	2,000	900
4	M	60	Glutethimide	4,000	1,200
5	F	49	Glutethimide Meprobamate	1,000 4,000	800
6	F	60	Glutethimide Chlordiazepoxide	? 100?	800
7	F	53	Amphetamine-amobarbital (elixir) Pentobarbital (elixir) Aprobarbital (elixir)	? ? ?	800
8	M	61	Secobarbital Pentobarbital Butabarbital Phenobarbital Propantheline and phenobarbital Diazepam	? ? ? ? ? ?	1,000
9	M	29	Paraldehyde	?	800

(Reprinted from J.A.M.A., Vol. 196, 1966, page 711, by permission of the editor; see Ref. 1.)

200

It is of interest that Ewing and Bakewell(7) concluded from a chart study that in 7.6 percent of 1,686 patients admitted to another Southern university hospital psychiatric ward over a three-year period, the diagnosis of drug dependence was made either on admission or during hospitalization. In their series, however, the drugs implicated included not only barbiturates, nonbarbiturate sedatives, and minor tranquilizers, but also bromides, amphetamines, alcohol, and narcotics.

Theoretically the testing, stabilization, and slow reduction procedures could be carried out with the nonbarbiturate sedative or minor tranquilizing drug on which the patient had become physically dependent rather than with pentobarbital. But since far less is known about the duration of action of the drugs in the former classes, the pentobarbital substitution method is preferable, at least at the present time.

However, differences in duration . of action between pentobarbital on the one hand and certain of the nonbarbiturate sedatives and minor tranquilizers on the other may require some modifications of the stabilization and slow reduction procedures described when pentobarbital is substituted for drugs in the other two categories. Thus, patients physically dependent on glutethimide or chlordiazepoxide may seem to be well stabilized on a given daily dose of pentobarbital, only to have convulsions a day or two later while still stabilized, or after a modest reduction of pentobarbital dosage has been made. In the cases of primary physical dependence on glutethimide or chlordiazepoxide, therefore, it might be well to delay initiation of pentobarbital reduction for a few days after initial stabilization.

Psychotherapy and Rehabilitation

As the series studied by Bakewell and Wikler(1) and Ewing and Bakewell(7) consisted of patients admitted to psychiatric wards, it is not surprising that all of those

201

judged to be dependent on drugs were also found to have antecedent emotional and/or characterological disorders, presumably rendering them addiction prone. However, it is remarkable that 93.2 percent of the patients in the first series and 92.4 percent in the second were *not* drug-dependent.

Whether or not the drug-dependent and the non-drug-dependent populations differed significantly in respect to particular kinds of emotional and/or characterological disorder cannot be decided on the basis of available data. However, it would seem reasonable to suppose that such disorders do play a role—if not a sufficient one—in the genesis of drug abuse. In any case, the existence of emotional and/or characterological disorder calls for treatment of these conditions by whatever means may be indicated.

Generally, psychotherapy of other than the supportive type will be more effective after drug withdrawal has been accomplished. Indeed, "painless" drug withdrawal may facilitate development of a favorable psychotherapeutic relationship between physician and patient. It has also been the author's impression that ignorance on the part of the patient, his relatives, and sometimes his physician of the dangers involved in escalation of dosage and/or frequency of administration of central nervous system depressant drugs has contributed to the development of physical dependence. Appropriate education is certainly indicated in such cases.

A difficult question to answer is the extent to which barbiturates, nonbarbiturate sedatives, and minor tranquilizers may be used in the treatment of addiction-prone patients, especially if they had become physically dependent on such drugs on one or more occasions in the past. Generally, these drugs should be avoided or, if used at all, they should be prescribed in therapeutic doses and for only short periods of time with rigid limitation of prescription refills.

In some cases daytime reduction of anxiety may be achieved with small doses of chlorpromazine, or with imipramine or amitriptyline if depression is a prominent symptom. According to Overall and associates(15), thioridazine possesses not only tranquilizing but also antidepressant properties, and therefore this phenothiazine derivative may be effective in some cases. Persistence of anxiety and/or depression, however, poses a challenge to the psychiatrist's skills which is not met by resorting to the unregulated use of drugs with physical dependence-producing properties, such as barbiturates, nonbarbiturate sedatives, and minor tranquilizers.

Summary

An abstinence syndrome characterized in its complete form by the appearance of tremulousness, anxiety, insomnia, diaphoresis, postural hypotension, tendon hyperreflexia, convulsions, delirium, and hyperpyrexia can ensue when barbiturates, nonbarbiturate sedatives, or minor tranquilizers are withdrawn abruptly following prolonged periods of intoxication at daily dose levels that exceed therapeutically recommended amounts. Regardless of the drug category involved, withdrawal of these agents may be accomplished safely by initial stabilization on pentobarbital alone in amounts and at intervals that suppress abstinence phenomena throughout. the day and night and produce mild signs of barbiturate intoxication. This should be followed by gradual reduction in pentobarbital dosage at a rate not exceeding 0.1 gm. daily.

If delirium has already developed when the patient is first seen, the immediate aim of treatment is not stabilization but heavy sedation with pentobarbital or phenobarbital, sufficient to suppress agitation, insomnia, and hyperpyrexia. Such heavy sedation is maintained for three to five days with appropriate supportive medical and nursing care, after which the degree of sedation is lightened gradually and slow reduction of the barbiturate is carried out as in the stabilized patient.

Psychotherapy and other treatment of psychiatric disorders associated with drug dependence of the barbiturate type is of course indicated, with due regard for the dangers involved in treating addiction-prone individuals with drugs that are capable of producing physical dependence.

REFERENCES

1. Bakewell, W. E., Jr., and Wikler, A.: Symposium: Nonnarcotic Addiction—Incidence in a University Hospital Psychiatric Ward. J.A.M.A. 196:710-713, 1966.
2. Belleville. R. E., and Fraser, H. F.: Tolerance to Some Effects of Barbiturates. J. Pharmacol. Exp. Ther. 120:469-474, 1957.
3. Essig, C. F.: Addiction to Nonbarbiturate Sedative and Tranquilizing Drugs, Clin. Pharmacol. Ther. 5:334-343, 1964.
4. Essig, C. F., and Carter, W. W.: Failure of Diphenylhydantoin to Prevent Barbiturate Withdrawal Convulsions in Dogs, Neurology 12:481-484, 1962.
5. Essig, C. F., and Fraser, H. F.: Electroencephalographic Changes in Man During Use and Withdrawal of Barbiturates in Moderate Dosage, Electroenceph. Clin. Neurophysiol. 10:649-656, 1958.
6. Essig, C. F., and Fraser, H. F.: Failure of Chlorpromazine to Prevent Barbiturate-Withdrawal Convulsions, Clin. Pharmacol. Ther. 7:466-469, 1966.
7. Ewing, J. A., and Bakewell, W. E., Jr.: Diagnosis and Management of Depressant Drug Dependence, Amer. J. Psychiat. 123: 909-917, 1967.
8. Fraser, H. F., Isbell, H., Eisenman, A. J., Wikler, A., and Pescor, F. T.: Chronic Barbiturate Intoxication: Further Studies, Arch. Intern. Med. 94:34-41, 1954.
9. Fraser, H. F., Shaver, M. R., Maxwell, E. S., and Isbell, H.: Death Due to Withdrawal of Barbiturates: Report of a Case, Ann. Intern. Med. 38:1319-1325, 1953.
10. Fraser, H. F., Wikler, A., Essig, C. F., and Isbell, H.: Degree of Physical Dependence Induced by Secobarbital or Pentobarbital, J.A.M.A. 166:126-129, 1958.
11. Haizlip, T. M., and Ewing, J. A.: Meprobamate Habituation: A Controlled Clinical Study, New Eng. J. Med. 258:1181-1186, 1958.

12. Hollister, L. E., Motzenbecker, F. P., and Degan, R. O.: Withdrawal Reactions from Chlordiazepoxide (Librium), Psychopharmacologia 2:63-68, 1961.

13. Isbell, H.: Manifestations and Treatment of Addiction to Narcotic Drugs and Barbiturates, Med. Clin. N. Amer. 34:425-438, 1950.

14. Isbell, H., Altschul, S., Kornetsky, C. H., Eisenman, A. J., Flanary, H. G., and Fraser, H. F.: Chronic Barbiturate Intoxication: An Experimental Study, Arch. Neurol. Psychiat. 64:1-28, 1950.

15. Overall, J. E., Hollister, L. E., Meyer, F., Kimbell, I., Jr., and Shelton, J.: Imipramine and Thioridazine in Depressed and Schizophrenic Patients—Are There Specific Antidepressant Drugs? J.A.M.A. 189:605-608, 1964.

16. Sørensen, B. F.: Delirium Tremens and Its Treatment, Danish Med. Bull. 6:261-263, 1959.

17. Wikler, A., Fraser, H. F., Isbell, H., and Pescor, F. T.: Electroencephalograms During Cycles of Addiction to Barbiturates in Man. Electroenceph. Clin. Neurophysiol. 7:1-13, 1955.

18. World Health Organization Expert Committee on Addiction-Producing Drugs: Thirteenth Report. WHO Technical Report Series no. 273, Geneva. 1964.

TREATMENT OF DRINAMYL ADDICTION

Two Case Studies

TOM KRAFT, M.B., D.P.M.

In opposition to the generally accepted view that true drug addiction is always chemically based, the present paper seeks to emphasize underlying personality disorder as a cause for some forms of addiction. The two young patients described in this paper were addicted to Drinamyl (Dexamyl in the United States), and both have recovered from their underlying disturbance and no longer need the support of addictive drugs.

The systematic desensitization of the patients' social anxieties formed an integral part of a much wider therapeutic program, which included training these patients to go to areas in London where drugs are freely available, and to be able to resist buying these drugs when they were offered by their friends. This led to the uncovering of phobic symptoms of which they had previously been unaware and made possible a treatment in much greater depth than could have been conceived at first examination. The final recovery of these two addicts is unusual in that both are working full time, no longer need addictive drugs, and have made satisfactory life adjustments. The argument is put forward that an important factor in their recovery is that the therapeutic value of the treatment session under deep hypnosis could adequately replace the desired effects of the drug. The patients themselves equated the effect of a treatment session with that of a dose of Drinamyl, but it was only when the patients felt that a treatment session had exceeded the value of the original Drinamyl that one could be sure that he would not return to the drug. All statements from the patients were supported by evidence from other members of the family, since addicts' statements tend to be somewhat unreliable and should always be corroborated by supportive evidence from less subjective sources.

It is widely believed by the general public that young addicts take their drugs for "kicks," but a case might be made that they are attempting to reach a level at which ordinary people function without needing the assistance of drugs.

When the addict has been deprived of his drug, he describes himself as being unable to make contact with other people and

The author wishes to thank Dr. John Denham for his permission to publish this paper.

as feeling so desperate that he is compelled to return to the drug. This feeling of isolation may well explain the high rate of relapse after treatments which remove the addictive drug, without treating the personality disorder.

The introduction of aversive techniques in the treatment of drug addiction (9–12), has directed attention on the addictive drug rather than to the underlying disorder responsible for the patient's addiction.

The treatment described in the present study was based on the assumption that when young addicts have overcome their social difficulties, they will no longer crave their drug of addiction. The social difficulties of the two patients described in this paper were treated by desensitization, but it was found, during this process, that the patients developed a marked dependence on the therapist, and this needed a separate course of treatment.

This report describes the treatment of two young male Drinamyl addicts, who appear to have made a complete recovery and no longer need their drug of addiction.

METHOD OF TREATMENT

The treatment is based on Wolpe's (13) method of systematic desensitization, and relaxation is induced by hypnosis. A standardized stimulus hierarchy, developed by the author, is used for all patients being treated for social anxieties, whether or not these are associated with alcoholism or drug addiction (6, 7).

Initially, the patient, when deeply hypnotized, is asked to imagine talking to one person on the ward, with whom he feels entirely at ease. The patient might be given the following instructions: "I want you to imagine talking to Ken. It does not matter what you imagine talking to him about, but I want you to indicate whether you feel entirely at ease in this situation." Although the patient may have stated that he has no anxiety talking to this particular patient, he may nevertheless admit to anxiety when he is hypnotized.

If the patient signals that he feels anxiety, or if his facial expression betrays evidence of tension (for example, furrowing of the brow, biting of lip), the stimulus is repeated until he seems completely free from anxiety. This may be achieved merely by withdrawing the stimulus, allowing the patient to relax, and repeating the stimulus once more. However, the patient finds it much easier if, on withdrawing the stimulus, he is given a "relief response," for example, listening to his favorite record, and

then the stimulus which had previously given rise to anxiety is reintroduced. In this way, the patient enjoys the treatment session, and progress is more rapid. The type of relief response employed varies from one patient to another, but the essential element is that it should have a high capacity for counteracting anxiety.

It is only when the therapist is convinced that the patient is completely anxiety-free that he proceeds to the next step in the hierarchy. Throughout the treatment, the patient does not need to rehearse the actual conversation, but is only required to *imagine* talking to people.

The second stimulus consists of talking to 2 patients on the ward, one male and one female. In order to ensure that the patient will finally make a satisfactory life adjustment, the treatment must be carried out in a mixed general ward. The therapist may now give the following instructions: "I want you to imagine talking to Ken and Lilian." When the patient is completely anxiety-free in this situation, other patients or members of staff are added, one at a time, until the patient can imagine being with 20 people he knows on the ward, 10 male and 10 female, talking to some of them, and not feeling anxious. At this stage of the treatment, it is helpful to the patient if the therapist commences each session with the easiest item, i.e., being with 1 person only, and then increasing the number of people present. In this way, the patient rapidly gains confidence, and the therapist can present the stimuli more rapidly on each occasion. It is important that the therapist refers to each person individually by forename, and that the sequence of people listed in the hierarchy remains constant, unless the patient makes a specific request for an alteration to be made, which is then always accepted by the therapist.

When the patient feels at ease with 20 people on the ward, the therapist now refers to the group as a "nucleus." Strangers are now added, 10 at a time, until he can imagine being with 20 people he knows well plus 80 strangers at the hospital social. Later, the number of friends accompanying him to the hopsital social is reduced, 1 at a time, until he can imagine going to the social on his own. He is then required to imagine approaching a girl and asking her to dance, which seems to be an extremely difficult task for these patients. Immediately after rehearsing these situations in treatment, the patient is expected to practice these in the life situation.

Once the patient has become socially competent within the hospital, treatment is now directed toward traveling to areas in town where drugs could be obtained. The patient is told that if he feels at ease in town, he may stay as long as he pleases, but if he feels anxious or develops a strong desire to buy drugs, he must return immediately to the hospital. He may now recognize that, without his drugs, phobic symptoms have been uncovered, of which he was previously unaware.

The patient is required to travel to Piccadilly, the center of drug addiction in London, both in the daytime and at night, all situations first being rehearsed under hypnosis. The patient must be able to resist the temptation to buy drugs, even when these are offered to him by his addict friends, an exceedingly difficult task. Also, he must be able to enjoy a party, without the assistance of drugs. During this part of the treatment, the therapist must ensure that, even when the patient is exposed to those situations which would normally have led to drug taking, he can now face these without drugs, and without developing either anxiety or nausea, because such symptoms will lead to avoidance of such situations later, and a less complete recovery. Gradually, he is allowed more freedom, and he is encouraged to remain outside the hospital for increasing periods of time.

When the patient has been freed of all his social anxieties and can move freely in the center of town without anxiety or a need for drugs, it is found that he has become extremely dependent on the therapist. The second phase of the treatment, designed to counteract this dependence, consists of a graded series of time intervals spent away from the therapist. In the treatment session, he is asked to imagine coping on his own for increasing intervals of time, and at first, he is given a highly structured program for this period, but later, the patient is expected to make his own arrangements. The time interval between successive treatment sessions is increased first from 24 to 48 hours, and then gradually up to 14 days.

In the first stage of the treatment, the patient has been given five 60-minute treatment sessions per week, but now the number of hypnosis sessions is reduced, and these are replaced by discussion sessions. Gradually, his need for hypnosis diminishes, with improvement in his life adjustment, and the patient now wishes to return to work. When he can cope on his own for 14 days, the individual treatment is complete, and he may then attend the Post Behavior Therapy Club, which meets weekly, and here the therapist is present throughout the evening (2). He is then allowed to attend the club for an indefinite period.

CASE HISTORIES

Case 1: A 20-year-old, single, male patient was admitted to hospital with a 5-year history of drug addiction (4, 5). His reason for requesting admission to hospital was that he could no longer tolerate the paranoid toxic effects associated with excessive Drinamyl ("purple hearts") intake. At first, he had no intention of seeking treatment for his drug addiction, but he later changed his mind when offered an intensive course of treatment.

The relationship with his father had always been poor: he had never been able to discuss the drug addiction problem with him, though he had no difficulty discussing it with his mother.

He was first introduced to drugs at the age of 15, when he bought five Drinamyl tablets from a friend. He took all the tablets at once and immediately felt "high." He found that he could talk to everyone, and he was happy that he could achieve this with the aid of drugs. He also found that he could dance all night, where normally he was too shy to dance.

He continued buying Drinamyl tablets each week, but on the second occasion, he decided to buy 10 tablets rather than the original 5. For the next 2 months, he continued buying 10 tablets each week, and then, for the next 6 months, he bought 15 tablets each week. By the age of 16, he started buying 20 tablets each week. He now found that he needed to take 15 tablets on a Saturday night and a further 5 tablets on a Sunday morning. It was not until he was 17 years old that he started taking Drinamyl on weekdays, and he would take 2 tablets each day, in addition to 20 at the weekend.

From the age of 17 to 20, his consumption of Drinamyl gradually increased, so that by the time he was admitted to hospital, he was taking 80 tablets during the course of a weekend and a further 20 tablets during the week. For 5 weeks prior to his admission to hospital, he had worked at a wholesale chemist, where he consumed Drinamyl while working, enjoying its easy availability.

In addition to his Drinamyl addiction, he has enjoyed smoking cannabis from the age of 17, but he has little interest in alcohol, as he tends to vomit when drinking to excess.

For the past 2 years, the patient has suffered from the toxic effects of Drinamyl each weekend. He believes then that people are plotting against him, and he remains in a constant state of apprehension that something undefined but sinister is about to happen to him. He has become very disturbed by "the horrors," and it was on account of these that he sought treatment.

He recognized that he was anxious in social situations and felt embarrassed in the company of both sexes (4). He was worried when people looked at him, and this gave rise to blushing and profuse sweating. These symptoms interfered with traveling by public transport, particularly on the London Underground, where sitting passengers face one another. Although he could not connect the drug taking with his social difficulties, he was prepared to consider a course of treatment designed to counteract his social anxieties. The first phase of the treatment required 15 treatment sessions, and a further 11 sessions were devoted to the second phase of treatment. His treatment was completed in 3 months.

After his first hypnosis session, he commented that he "felt marvelous" and as "a normal person should feel." He could talk readily to members of the staff, and he equated the session with five to six Drinamyl tablets, with the important difference that it did not interfere with his appetite. Before desensitization was commenced, he could only consider the advantages of taking Drinamyl, but after the first session, he could think only of all its disadvantages. He could see no reason for continuing drug taking. In the evening, he went to the hospital social and enjoyed dancing there.

In his second treatment session, he commented that the induction of hypnosis was very similar to the effect of Drinamyl. After the session, he felt "terrific," an effect which persisted for 48 hours, but as the effects began to wear off, he became disinclined to speak and could not pay attention to conversation. Though this would normally have precipitated drug taking, he could now avoid taking any tablets and wait for the next treatment session.

After the third session, he went out drinking with his friends but left before closing time, because he feared that if he remained in the public house, he would be sorely tempted to buy Drinamyl tablets. He decided it was "safer" to return home.

After the fifth session, he reported that he could now talk to 1 person at a time without any difficulty. After the next session, the situation having been rehearsed, he felt comfortable celebrating a patient's birthday when there were 12 people sitting around the table.

After the seventh session, he went to a public house in the West End of London with his girl friend, and he found that he could talk *without* the assistance of drugs, in a group of 15 people, when there were about 150 people present altogether. At closing time, his addict friends all went to buy drugs, but he could now resist the temptation to do so, and he returned home.

After the 12th session, he said that he had no further need to take drugs, and when talking to his addict friends, the thought of drugs would disappear entirely.

In the 15th session, although feeling socially competent, he was concerned that the treatment was nearing completion. He felt perfectly well in all normal social situations, and he tried to work out the source of his remaining anxiety. He recognized that he still needed the therapist, but he could not understand the nature of this attachment. He was reassured that patients normally develop a strong dependence on the therapist, and that this would be treated separately.

By the second session on dependence, he equated the treatment session with 40 Drinamyl tablets, and in the fifth session, he said that a treatment session was worth a great deal more than 100 Drinamyl tablets.

The interval between successive treatment sessions was gradually increased, at first from 24 to 48 hours, and eventually up to 14 days. When the patient found that a discussion session with the therapist could adequately replace a hypnosis session, his desire for hypnosis rapidly declined. He now felt that he had developed beyond the stage where he needed hypnosis, and this attitude was encouraged by the therapist.

At this time, his attitude toward his father changed: he now regarded him as a good man, in opposition to his previous opinion.

After the 11th session on dependence, he no longer requested further hypnosis sessions, and he felt that he could now manage with discussion sessions only. He was then transferred to the Post Behavior Therapy Club, but he only attended on a few occasions. He has lost all interest in taking drugs, but he still feels the need to have discussions with the therapist about twice a year. He has been told that he may have an interview with the therapist at any time, without having to make a specific appointment, which is reassuring to him and has the effect of decreasing his need to see the doctor. A follow-up of 2 years shows that his improvement has been maintained.

Case 2: An 18-year-old, single, male patient was admitted to hospital with a 4-year history of Drinamyl addiction (5). He had a disturbed relationship with his mother, and they frequently had arguments in which they shouted at one another, and these often led to their hitting each other. He had a much better relationship with his father, who acted as an intermediary between mother and son.

The patient can remember being disobedient as a child and frequently being sent to bed, though he cannot remember the individual incidents which led to this form of punishment.

From the age of 13 to 15, he was often absent from school, and he would spend the time in one of the local cafes, feeling a sense of achievement. Despite this, he became head prefect, but was expelled later for setting off the fire alarm as a prank. On leaving school, he became an apprentice electrician, and he has a good work record, enjoys the work, and has passed the first official examination.

He started taking Drinamyl at the age of 14½, having bought the tablets from a friend. On the first occasion, he bought 5 tablets, and after taking them, he felt "fantastic." He had never felt so well before, and he felt extremely happy and could not stop talking, an effect which persisted for 8 hours before wearing off. At this stage, he would buy Drinamyl tablets once a fortnight. At the age of 15, he started increasing the dose and found that he now had to take 10 tablets to obtain an equivalent effect of the original 5. At the age of 16, he started smoking cannabis, and though he enjoyed the "floating sensation" induced by smoking this, he preferred the effects of Drinamyl.

From the age of 16 to 18, he gradually increased the dose of Drinamyl, particularly after losing his girl friend, 2 months before his admission to hospital. He estimated that he was taking about 45 tablets of Drinamyl each day. In order to pay for these drugs, he would steal an average of £10 ($ 24.00) a week from the public house where he worked, and on one occasion, he stole several hundred cigarettes, which led to prosecution and a fine.

From the age of 14 onwards, he has had outbursts of aggression in which he either hits other people or injures himself, by hitting his head or his hand against the wall. These outbursts seem to occur only with his parents or girl friend. On several occasions he has beaten his girl friend severely, and on four occasions he has attempted to strangle her. The relationship with his girl friend ended after a stormy holiday together, in which the police were called in and the patient was sent home. After this, her parents had forbidden her to continue seeing him.

He became aware of difficulties in talking to people at about the same time as he started drug taking, but he had not connected the drug taking with his social difficulties. He found that he had trouble in mixing with young people in the 14 to 21 age group, and he found greater difficulty with girls than boys. He felt out of place, in that he could not hold a conversation, except with the aid of drugs, and on such occasions, he felt embarrassed, started to blush, broke into a cold sweat, and developed nausea. Merely discussing this in the history taking was sufficient to give rise to vomiting (3).

He started having headaches at the age of 16. At first, they would occur about once a month, but gradually they increased in frequency, until, by the time he was admitted to hospital, he suffered from daily headaches, which could be relieved only by Drinamyl.

He required a total of 52 hypnosis sessions, 26 being devoted to the first stage and a further 26 sessions for the second stage. Treatment was completed within 5 months.

After the first session, although finding the idea of hypnosis rather strange, he liked it and felt very happy. After the treatment session, the patient found that he could talk quite easily to one person at a time, but, when confronted with two people, he developed nausea. In fact, throughout his treatment, nausea was a warning signal that he was becoming anxious.

After the second session, he enjoyed going to the cinema with the first patient, but in the evening, when his parents visited him, he developed nausea and headache.

After the fourth session, he managed to talk to three patients on the ward, but when a fourth patient started shouting across the ward, he developed nausea again.

In the eighth session, he wished to discuss a female patient on the ward, who reminded him of his former girl friend. They found that they could talk to one another without any difficulty, and he enjoyed dancing with her at the hospital social. Soon he became friendly with her and enjoyed kissing her. Unfortunately, she soon lost interest in him and said that she wished to discontinue the relationship. This proved very disturbing to the patient so that he cried and banged his head against the wall. At this point in the treatment, he wanted to discharge himself from the hospital, but she managed to dissuade him from doing so, which was followed by intimacy. This was very similar to the relationship he had with his former girl friend.

In the 14th session, he said that he could now talk to a group of 5 people when there were 30 people on the ward. In the 19th session, he rehearsed the idea of the hospital social, and he subsequently enjoyed going to the dance, feeling well throughout the evening.

At this stage, although feeling competent within the hospital, he showed great reluctance to go outside the hospital, especially to the West End of London. He commented that he had never been so scared of the outside world as he was now, and it was explained to him that he was doing all these activities for the first time without the assistance of drugs. In the 22nd session, which he now equated with 40 Drinamyl tablets, he rehearsed the idea of going to a public house with the first patient, and, when achieving this in the evening, he found it difficult to speak for the 1st hour but then settled down and felt more comfortable. Later, they went to a coffee bar, where they talked with some girls.

After the 25th session, the patient walked all around the West End of London without feeling anxious, and, in particular, he went to those areas where he had previously been searched for drugs by the police.

In the first session on dependence, he was given a highly structured program over the weekend. He found this part of the treatment extremely difficult, and there were times when he developed a strong desire for drugs, though he did not take any.

After the 15th session on dependence, he returned to work for 3 days a week. He found

211

the 1st day back at work very difficult indeed and was relieved that, still being an inpatient, he could return to the hospital at the end of the day. At this stage, he was receiving two hypnosis sessions and one discussion session during the week. Gradually, he increased the hours worked each week, and his firm allowed him to make a gradual return to full time work. At the end of his course of treatment, he felt very well indeed. He only occasionally felt depressed, and he no longer has any desire for drugs.

After completing treatment, his former girl friend came to visit him at the hospital, and she was so impressed with the change, though finding it difficult to put into words, that she decided to return to him, against her parents' wishes. They are very much happier than before treatment and are now happily married. A follow-up of 2 years shows that his improvement has been maintained.

DISCUSSION

The treatment, originally devised for treating alcoholics (6–8), is based upon the likelihood that the drug addict has difficulties in communication and that, once these difficulties have been resolved, he will no longer require the support of drugs.

While the two young Drinamyl addicts had, to some extent, been conscious that the use of the drug had removed their social anxieties, at least temporarily, they had not connected their difficulties in communication with their addiction.

The second patient was terrified when he was told to venture outside the hospital, for phobic symptoms had emerged, of which he had previously been completely unaware. It may well be that the young addict takes a drug because he cannot tolerate his severe neurotic symptoms, and that the addiction serves as a protective guard against such painful stimulation (1). Possibly cultural factors in Western society determine the higher incidence of drug addiction in the male, reflecting a greater need for the young males to hide from their own neurotic symptoms.

Although no conclusions may be reached from only two case studies, preliminary results seem encouraging, and it suggested that desensitization of patients' social anxieties might be investigated as one method of treatment for young drug addicts.

SUMMARY

A new method of treatment for drug addiction, developed by the author, aims at correcting the personality disorder underlying the patient's addiction. The method uses two stages, first removing the patient's social anxieties, and secondly counteracting dependence on the therapist. Two young Drinamyl addicts have received this treatment and appear to have made an adequate recovery so that they no longer require their drug of addiction.

REFERENCES

1. Fenichel, O. In *The Psychoanalytic Theory of Neurosis*, pp. 385–386. Routledge & Kegan Paul, London. 1946.
2. Kraft, T. A post behavior therapy club. Newsletter. Association for Advancement of the Behavioral Therapies. 2: 6–7. 1967.
3. Kraft, T. Social anxiety and drug addiction. Brit. J. Soc. Psychiat.. 2: 192–195, 1968.
4. Kraft, T. Successful treatment of a case of Drinamyl addiction. Brit. J. Psychiat.. 114: 1363–1364. 1968.
5. Kraft, T. Treatment of Drinamyl addiction. Int. J. Addict.. 4: 59–64, 1969.
6. Kraft, T. and Al-Issa, I. Alcoholism treated by desensitization: A case report. Behav. Res. Ther.. 5: 69–70. 1967.
7. Kraft, T. and Al-Issa. I. Desensitization and reduction in cigarette consumption. J. Psychol.. 67: 323–329. 1967.
8. Kraft, T. and Al-Issa. I. Desensitization and the treatment of alcohol addiction. Brit. J. Addict.. 63: 19–23. 1968.
9. Lesser, E. Behavior therapy with a narcotics user: A case report. Behav. Res. Ther.. 5: 251–252, 1967.
10. Liberman, R. Aversive conditioning of drug addicts: A pilot study. Behav. Res. Ther.. 6: 229–231. 1968.
11. Raymond, M. The treatment of addiction by aversive conditioning with apomorphine. Behav. Res. Ther.. 1: 287–291. 1964.
12. Wolpe. J. Conditioned inhibition of craving in drug addiction: A pilot experiment. Behav. Res. Ther.. 2: 285–288. 1965.
13. Wolpe. J. In *Psychotherapy by Reciprocal Inhibition*, pp. 139–165. Stanford University Press, Stanford, Calif.. 1958.

COMMENTARY ON "TREATMENT OF DRINAMYL ADDICTION"

JOSEPH WOLPE, M.D.[1]

An especially interesting feature of Dr. Kraft's article is the very detailed account of the manner in which his two patients established their habits of taking Drinamyl repeatedly. However, in my view, no real drug addiction was involved. That, of course, is in the first place a matter of definition. But if addiction is to be distinguished from other habits, it seems to be a necessary criterion that the subject continues taking the drug even after the original reason for taking it has disappeared. A person who takes morphine for months on end for the relief of severe pain can be said to have a drug-taking habit, but he can no more be labeled an addict than a person who may habitually take aspirin to alleviate a less severe pain. Addiction can be positively asserted only if there is a compulsive urge to ingest a drug after removal of the symptom that caused its use.

Kraft's cases no longer had any need for Drinamyl when their unadaptive anxiety habits were overcome. The therapist had very properly addressed himself to removing the "underlying disorder responsible for the patients' addictions," and then the drug no longer had to be taken. But if so, on the analysis given above, their drug habits were not addictions.

A question of interest is whether these two subjects showed such very favorable symptomatic responses to the barbiturate-amphetamine combination because of some definable feature of their personalities, such as, perhaps, high extraversion. It would be quite a considerable practical advantage to know in advance what drugs are most likely to be symptomatically helpful to patients with particular features of personality. This important area of research has only begun to be explored (1).

An unusual feature of the desensitization program that Kraft employed was the recapitulation at each session of hierarchy items that had already been successfully dealt with. This is a time-consuming activity, and my own observations do not indicate that it would facilitate change; nor on theoretical grounds would I expect it to do so.

Although Kraft found that after his patients had been deconditioned to anxiety they became extremely dependent on the therapist, it would be a mistake to infer that this is usual. I have hardly ever known such a consequence to develop. It may perhaps be another feature of the kind of personality who responds well to the barbiturate-amphetamine combination of drugs, or possibly in some way a consequence of prolonged use of this combination.

---

[1] The Editorial Board felt that the general issues treated in Doctor Kraft's paper were worthy of more discussions, and we invited this commentary by Doctor Wolpe.

REFERENCE

1. Eysenck, H. J. *Experiments with Drugs*, Pergamon Press, London, 1963.

THE TERMINATION OF AN LSD 'FREAK-OUT' THROUGH THE USE OF RELAXATION

RICHARD M. SUINN AND JACKIE BRITTAIN

Users of lysergic acid diethylamide (LSD) are subject to an acute psychological experience referred to as a 'freak-out' or a 'bad trip'. Among the characteristics of this freak-out are feelings of fright approaching panic and heightened tension. This case report involves an individual who was in such a state when seen. Although Thorazine is often used to bring about recovery, this had been refused by the S. The directions for achieving deep muscle relaxation [1] were used as an alternative mode of treatment. To our knowledge, this is the first time such a procedure has been used for this purpose.*

Background History. The S is a 19 year old New Yorker with a slight stammer and a tic, consisting of frequent rolling upward of the eyeballs. He attended a junior college for one semester, then dropped out because "It was too much like high school, I missed the college life, the people were too wrapped up in themselves." He intends to return during the coming school year since he aspires to be a physical education teacher. He has always been athletic, having competed in swimming and diving meets in high school. Besides, he said he "likes kids and wants to develop their minds." The S's father was a vice president of an advertising firm; his mother works as a social worker. They appear to be financially well off. The family includes two older brothers both of whom "finished the college thing".

The subject has been an LSD user for three years, his highest dosage being 3,000 micrograms, his typical dose being 300. He has used the drug on the average once a week, but during the week in question he had taken 'acid' three to four times. He had never experienced a bad trip before, and considers that "Acid is a very beautiful thing."

The Freak-out Experience. During Halloween week, S used LSD three to four times. On Wednesday (Halloween night), one girl went on a bad trip; on Friday a second girl experienced one; on Sunday the S had his traumatic experience. The total duration of the experience was six hours.

Two factors were important as possible events precipitating the experience: Acid of an undetermined amount was taken by injection, and two of the users were strangers to the S and made him uncomfortable. Within ten minutes, the S reported feeling strange and a desire to "get out". He left, borrowed a car, and drove apparently randomly. He had visual distortions ("the road moved upward"), but he was aware of the fact that this was an illusion. He found himself at the home of one of the authors (J. B.), stayed for a brief moment, cried, then felt compelled to leave. On the drive back alone, he "screamed, felt sick inside, nauseous, yelled." Upon his return to his place, he began to experience the frightening stage of the trip: "My friends came in and really scared me . . . faces like a bad dream . . . ugly." He refused Thorazine, insisting that he wanted to work it out. His dog entered his bedroom causing more panic, "I screamed and threw a pillow." He curled in a corner, "like things were coming towards me." In a lucid moment, he asked for J. B. and was reassured that she would be called. He began to feel suspicious at how long it was taking, and "all of a sudden she appeared, and I froze, and she sat on the bed, and I jumped." He shivered, cried, and remained tense.

The Treatment. J. B. instructed the S in the deep muscle relaxation technique, using modified directions for contraction and relaxation of muscle groups. The S reported following the directions and feeling somewhat better, "then all of a sudden

---

*The authors have subsequently replicated this application of desensitization/relaxation training on another LSD case with similar success.

214

I got tense again." The relaxation directions were started again and "All of a sudden I felt relaxed, I wasn't scared, I knew who she was and what was happening, my head started setting down." Within minutes after the instruction was first started, the S was completely clear, calm, and able to converse realistically. He was amnesic for much of his experience which occurred earlier in the evening.

DISCUSSION

There are several possible reasons for the S's recovery. It is possible, although not probable, that the LSD effects had worn off by themselves. The S suspected that he had taken two separate doses of the drug; six hours seems too short a period to account for the recovery without the introduction of a tranquilizer. Psychological factors may be a plausible explanation. The S sought out J. B. and feels a sense of confidence in her; her presence may have been sufficient to reassure him. Her presence alone, however, must have been different in some way from the presence of the S's other friends (who frightened him rather than relieved him). Finally, it may well be that the relaxation directions were in fact able to counter the panic and muscle tension. This technique is used by behavior therapists [2, 3, 4] as the preliminary phase in the treatment of anxiety and phobic states. Since the freak-out has many of the characteristics of a severe anxiety state or a fear reaction, the relaxation technique could be a very valuable method for the reduction of the tension.

REFERENCES

1. JACOBSEN, E. *Progressive Relaxation.* Chicago: Univ. of Chicago Press, 1938.
2. ROBINSON, C. and SUINN, R. M. The use of massed sessions in the desensitization of spider phobias. *Behav. Res. Therap.*, 1969, in press.
3. SUINN, R. M. The desensitization of test-anxiety by group and individual treatment. *Behav. Res. Ther.*, 1968, *6*, 385-387.
4. WOLPE, J. *Psychotherapy by Reciprocal Inhibition.* Stanford: Stanford Univ. Press, 1958.

MANAGEMENT OF "BAD TRIPS" IN AN EVOLVING DRUG SCENE

Robert L. Taylor, MD; John I. Maurer, MD; and Jared R. Tinklenberg, MD

"Bad trips" arise out of an increasingly complex drug scene. Rational therapy must consider completely, social, psychological and physiological factors. Complexity results from the development of new drugs, indiscriminate ingestion, contamination, and adulteration. Drug-induced psychological changes occasionally lead to fatal behavior. Bad trips from anticholinergic compounds may be seriously worsened by phenothiazine treatment. Protection of the patient from dangerous behavior is fundamental to treatment. A clear history is invaluable but should be augmented by physical and mental examinations. Treatment begins with establishment of verbal contact without the use of tranquilizers, if possible. Reassurance and reality defining are often sufficient. With severe ego disruption, medication in combination with verbal interaction may be required. Administration of phenothiazines or sedatives helps to reestablish the observing ego with rapid dissolution of perceptual distortion and reestablishment of the premorbid ego functioning in most cases. Optimal treatment includes a follow-up visit.

Psychedelic drugs produce perceptual and cognitive distortions which, in the majority of instances, are experienced by an individual as strange but tolerable, if not pleasant or even exhilarating. Although the exact reasons for a person's feeling threatened by these changes are unknown, periodically, the necessary mix of factors occurs, and a state of anxiety varying from mild apprehension to panic evolves.

The crisis created in an individual when he perceives himself in a threatening situation following psychedelic drug usage is commonly known as a "bad trip." It arises out of an extremely complex drug scene, making effective management an increasingly difficult problem. Attempts at therapeutic intervention should take into account such complicating factors as the increase in the number of drugs available, impulsive use of unknown compounds, adulteration and contamination of drugs, and the lethal potential of psychedelic agents.

Complications of the Drug Scene

The rising incidence of psychedelic drug usage is paralleled by the evolution of new drugs. The ever-increasing list of "mind expansion" drugs now includes lysergic acid diethylamide (LSD) ("acid"), peyote, mescaline ("cactus"), psilocybine ("magic mushroom"), marihuana ("pot"), 2, 5-dimethoxy - 4 - methyl - amphetamine (STP), dimethyltryptamine (DMT), methylenedioxyamphetamine (MDA), N, N-dimethylthyptamine (DMA), trimethoxyamphetamine (TMA), methoxymethylene + dioxyamphetamine (MMDA), thiocarbanidin (THC), the amphetamines ("speed"), phenylcyclidine (Serny) [PCP], and various solvents.[1] Recently, reports have appeared describing the use of cough syrup, cold tablets, sleeping pills, heart stimulants, nasal inhalants, insecticide aerosols, asthma remedies, throat disks, and aerosol refrigerants to create the mind-expanding kick (*Medical World News* 9:24-26, 1968). The rapid expansion of this psychedelic pharmacopoeia is accounted for by several factors: (1)

the ease with which derivative compounds can be synthesized, (2) the availability of numerous proprietary agents containing potential psychedelics, such as atropine, scopolamine, and various solvents, (3) the desire of an increasing number of people for the psychedelic experience, (4) the prevalence of naturally occurring psychedelic agents, such as mescaline, belladonna, and marihuana, and (5) the large profit that can be realized through the sale of these drugs.

The growing number of psychedelic agents results in changing drug fads as the popularity of one drug gives way to more recent arrivals on the drug scene. The medical director of the Haight-Ashbury Clinic has recently commented on this evolution in psychedelic drug usage.

For better or for worse, San Francisco was the "acid" capital of the world for a long time, and now it has become the "speed" capital of the world.[2]

The tendency of drug users to ingest indiscriminately adds further complexity to an already complicated drug problem and creates a significant danger. Research in the hippie community shows that almost one half of the persons interviewed had taken unknown drugs. At a San Jose, Calif, rock festival, 4,000 unidentified pills were taken! In addition, mixing of various drugs is common, resulting in combinations such as LSD and methamphetamine hydrochloride (Methedrine) and marihuana "cut" with a variety of substances including amphetamines, heroins, mescaline, cocaine, and opium. Contamination of marihuana with tincture of camphor containing 2.2 gm of opium per ounce has been reported in California.[3]

The mixing of cheap psychoactive agents with more expensive psychedelic drugs can greatly increase profits and thus has become common practice. Unfortunately, such adulteration can create serious treatment problems. For example, the central anticholinergics, particularly the belladonna alkaloids, are frequently used for "spiking," thus making treatment of bad trips with phenothiazines potentially hazardous. The anticholinergic effects of these alkaloids are enhanced by the addition of a phenothiazine, and this combination may lead to coma and cardiorespiratory failure. The undesirable consequences resulting from the interaction between anticholinergic agents and phenothiazines have been adequately demonstrated in clinical studies. Patients receiving an anticholinergic agent treated with a representative phenothiazine showed marked central nervous system (CNS) depression.[4]

The psychedelic drugs have established their lethal potential. Although deaths have been reported following the ingestion of STP (probably adulterated with belladonna alkaloids)[5] as a result of cardiovascular and respiratory effects,[6] death from the physiological effects of these drugs is rare. The psychological changes and their behavioral manifestations represent a greater threat to life. Feelings of omnipotence or panic, with an associated increase in irrational risk-taking have led to deaths resulting from such things as leaping from high places with the intention of flying, or standing in front of oncoming vehicles in an attempt to push them back. Heavy usage of methamphetamine has been associated with an increase in paranoia and violent behavior.[7]

Evaluation of the "Bad Tripper"

Protection of the individual from dangerous behavior either to himself or others should be a fundamental concern in treating the bad trip. For this reason, the patient should not be left unattended while he is awaiting medical attention. An attempt should be made to provide a quiet place, away from unnecessary stimulation, since the patient is already overwhelmed by external and internal input. His main task is to reassemble and control this input overload, and extraneous data can only aggravate the situation. After initial safety is established, treatment of the bad trip should include an attempt to clarify the situation. Frequently, bad trippers are brought in by friends who have already unsuccessfully attempted to alleviate the condition. Usually some knowledge of what has happened can be elicited from them. Most importantly, the physician should try to determine what drug was taken, the amount involved, and the approximate time the patient took the drug. Knowledge of the amount of drug and when it was taken will determine to some degree the course of the trip and may give the treating physician a rough idea of the amount of intervention that will be required, assuming he possesses a certain familiarity with the dosage, range, and duration of the common psychedelic agents. This area has been thoroughly covered in a recent review.[8] The experience of other drug-taking participants should be determined. This information may allow the examiner to determine whether he is dealing with an effect that is primarily the result of the unusual susceptibility of one person.

Any attempts to treat the bad trip prior to the patient's being brought for help should be explored, particularly in terms of medication that might have been administered. Accompanying friends often cannot give reliable information, either because of the drug effects they are experiencing, or because they simply do not know what has happened. A clear history is the exception—not the rule. Fear concerning the possible legal implications of drug ingestion may block history taking. Emphasizing the confidentiality of this information may be helpful. A history of the patient, obtained in order to facilitate medical treatment, comes under the rule of privileged communication and should not be shared with authorities.

Sometimes bad trippers are brought in alone by the police without any history. In such situations, a physical examination may yield some clues as to what drug was taken. Because of the ever-increasing problem of drug contamination, even a straightforward history which identifies the drugs should be substantiated, if possible, by physical findings.

The hallucinogens, such as LSD and mescaline, generally produce dilated pupils and reflex hyperactivity. Accompanying anxiety may mimic moderate sympathomimetic signs such as mild increase in pulse rate and blood pressure, sweaty palms, and tremor.[9] Anticholinergic agents produce somewhat similar physical findings which usually cannot be distinguished from those of other psychedelic agents. Excessive dryness of the mouth and absence of sweating, however, may be useful clues in establishing that an anticholinergic drug was involved. Amphetamines such as speed produce marked sympathomimetic effects such as rapid pulse rate, moderately elevated blood pressure, and excessive sweating, as well as increased motor activity. Miosis is a symptom of opiate usage. Marihuana causes dilatation of conjunctival blood vessels, creating a reddened appearance similar to that seen in conjunctivitis. There is no dilatation of pupils[10] (Table).

A wide variation of mental states ranging in severity from mild apprehension to severe panic may be seen in persons undergoing bad trips. With high doses, a picture, best described as a toxic acute brain syndrome with disorientation and clouded consciousness, is present. Perceptual changes, such as illusions and hallucinations, are usually present and can be terrifying. A person may feel that he is going to "lose control" or "never come back." Severe feelings of depersonalization or even total loss of one's sense of identity may appear. Gross distortions of body image may be present such as the sensation that one's "brain is melting." But these same sensations that are experienced by one individual as extremely frightening and threatening may be experienced by another as mystical or beautiful.

An important indicator of the severity of psychological disruption is the amount of observing ego present. The degree to which an individual is able to "get outside" this experience, seeing it as apart from himself and the result of taking a drug, can be of important prognostic significance. The individual who develops the awareness that what he is experiencing is drug-induced and time-limited generally reintegrates successfully at the end of the experience. The absence of observing ego, however, indicates severe dis-

Physical Findings	
Agent	**Effects**
Hallucinogens (LSD, mescaline)	Dilated pupils Reflex hyperactivity Anxiety symptoms
Anticholinergics	Dilated pupils (with cycloplegia) Reflex hyperactivity Anxiety symptoms Dry mouth Absence of sweating

Amphetamines	Rapid pulse
	Increase in blood
	  pressure
	Increased sweating
	Increased motor activ-
	  ity (variable)

Opiates	Miosis
Marihuana	Dilation of conjunc- tival blood vessels Rapid pulse No pupillary dilation

ruption; if it fails to reappear as treatment proceeds, the possibility of functional psychosis triggered by the drug experience should be considered.

Treatment of the "Bad Tripper"

Establishment of verbal contact with the minimum use of tranquilizers should be a fundamental rule in the management of "bad trips." In cases of apprehension or even panic where contact with reality is maintained as evidenced by the presence of observing ego, reassurance and repetitive defining of reality often prove to be adequate treatment. In defining reality, the physician should emphasize statements which attribute the distortions and frightening feelings of the experience to the drug. It is often useful to get the individual to put into words the experience he is having. Patients who are able to grasp and verbalize these experiences may thus be able to bring them under control rather than feel overwhelmed by them. One therapist found it helpful to pick up simple concrete objects such as a book and say to the patient, "This is a book; feel the book." Simple repetitive concrete statements about person and place

are useful. The temporary nature of what the patient is experiencing should be repeatedly emphasized. For a panicked "bad tripper," it can be very reassuring to be repeatedly told his name, that he is in a hospital bed, and in such and such a city. Concrete labeling helps the patient reassemble his reality, allowing him to firmly establish that he is indeed a real person experiencing a drug-induced "bad trip" that is time-limited.

While a person "comes down," he experiences a phasic "in and out" alternation of mental clarity and confusion. This should be expected and predicted by the therapist. Reassurance should include making explicit this waxing and waning of awareness. Caution should cause the physician to make certain that a patient who evidently has come down is truly "all the way down," not just in a temporary or transient clear spell.

The verbal "talkdown" with continuing reassurance and reality-defining is usually effective when given an adequate period of time. The treating physician, however, may not have sufficient time or staff. In these instances, medication should be used, and in the majority of cases will result in rapid dissolution of perceptual distortion and reestablishment of premorbid ego functioning. If medication is used, initially, it should be administered in a dose related to the size of the individual, not to the extent of the toxic effects. Subsequent doses, however, will depend to some degree on severity of symptoms and response to initial medication. Most experience has been with chlorpromazine. A 70-kg (154.3-lb) person could be given a first dose of 50 mg of chlorpromazine (instrumuscularly) (100 mg of chlorpromazine should be given initially if the oral route of administration is used). The intramuscular route is preferable for its rapid onset of action and because bad trips are frequently accompanied by gastrointestinal disturbances such as nausea and vomiting. If, after 45 minutes, no symptom improvement has occurred and blood pressure has been adequately maintained, the initial dose can be repeated. This treatment can be continued every 45 minutes until a favorable response is achieved, but usually after the second dose, oral medication can be substituted. The physician should exercise caution in administering repeated injections of phenothiazines. Orthostatic hypotensive episodes can occur. If this happens, the medication should be discontinued and the patient placed in a reclining position. Levarterenol may be given, but is usually not indicated.

The main contraindications for phenothiazine medication are previous allergic reactions to phenothiazines, the presence of significant hypotension, and the suggestion of an anticholinergic drug etiology.

Treatment of the bad trip should include caution concerning the possible development of excessive anticholinergic effects. A large dose of a centrally acting anticholinergic agent such as scopalamine (commonly found in proprietary sleeping medication) or the combination of a centrally acting anticholinergic compound and phenothiazine may result in an "anticholinergic crisis." This medical emergency can be effectively handled with quick reversal of symptoms by the oral or intramuscular administration of 2 to 4 mg physostigmine salicylate. Since physostigmine has a short duration of action, the patient must be closely observed

for recurrence of symptoms. Additional doses in one to two hours may be necessary. This treatment regimen must be undertaken with considerable caution, however, so as to avoid over-treatment and a resultant cholinergic crisis.[11] Although extensive experience with chlorpromazine supports its efficacy, it should be used only when support and reassurance are ineffective or time is a primary consideration, such as might be the case in a busy city-county hospital emergency room.

Clinical experience has suggested to the authors that the therapeutic affect of the phenothiazines in the treatment of bad trips may not be related to their antipsychotic properties, but rather to their sedative qualities. This observation has led to the use of such sedating drugs as paraldehyde, diazepam, and the short-acting barbiturates, thus avoiding the possible complication of anticholinergic potentiation. Results of initial clinical trials have been promising.

Most patients with adverse drug reactions respond favorably to supportive psychotherapy with or without medication to the extent that hospitalization is not needed. If the perceptual distortions have subsided and the patient feels comfortable in returning home, this is a reasonable disposition. The patient should be with a responsible person for the next 24 hours. Thus, if he lives alone, he should only be released if he is able to stay with a friend or relative.

Certain exceptions to this disposition should be considered. Prolonged use of speed often results in severe depression with increased suicidal risk when the person is "brought down." Hospitalization may be required. In addition, complicating medical problems such as abscesses and hepatitis are present in some patients treated for adverse drug reactions, particularly where the intravenous route has been used. Patients should be carefully screened for medical problems and hospitalized if indicated. Overnight hospitalization is advisable in those cases where observing ego fails to return or contact with reality is tenuous so that the individual does not appear in control of his thoughts or impulses. If these deficits persist beyond 24 hours, the diagnosis of functional psychosis is strongly suggested. It is good practice to avoid the use of phenothiazines as a sleeping medication when the patient is hospitalized overnight. They may mask a psychosis and falsely reassure the physician that the individual is reintegrated the following morning.

Once the acute reaction is over, the physician may be tempted to investigate the reasons for drug use. He should be cautious about this, however. Patients just recovering from a bad trip are unlikely to be able to discuss more general issues such as continued drug use or underlying emotional problems at this time. Decisions about future use of drugs are likely to be in reaction to the bad trip rather than based on rational thought and therefore easily reversible. The physician should confine his treatment to the immediate situation that prompted the request for medical help. He should encourage the patient to return for a follow-up, and at that time, when the patient is far more likely to be receptive and open, a discussion of drug use and possible underlying emotional problems could be started. Questions about drugs and the possible need for continued counseling can be explored. If there are no signs of continuing ego disruption and the person feels no need for counseling, further follow-up is not indicated.

Nonproprietary and Trade Names of Drug

Chlorpromazine—*Thorazine hydrochloride.*

References

1. Smith DE, Fort J, Craton DL: Psychoactive drugs, in *Drug Abuse Papers 1969.* Berkeley, Calif, Continuing Education in Criminology, University Extension, University of California, 1969, p 10.

2. Smith DE: Changing drug patterns on the Haight-Ashbury, *Calif Med* 110:151-157, 1969.

3. Unwin JR: Illicit drug use among Canadian youth. *Canad Med Assoc J* 98 (pt 2):449-454, 1968.

4. Gershon S, Neubauer H, Sundland DM: Interaction between some anticholinergic agents and phenothiazines. *Clin Pharmacol Ther* 6:749-756, 1965.

5. Snyder SH, Faillace L, Hollister L: 2,5-dimethoxy-4-methyl-amphetamine (STP): A new hallucinogenic drug. *Science* 158:669-670, 1967.

6. Solursh LP, Clement WR: Hallucinogenic drug abuse: Manifestations and management. *Canad Med Assoc J* 98:407-410, 1968.

7. Unwin JR: Illicit drug use among Canadian youth. *Canad Med Assoc J* 98 (pt 1): 402-413, 1968.

8. Smith DE (ed): *Drug Abuse Papers 1969.* Berkeley, Calif, Continuing Education in Criminology, University Extension, University of California, 1969.

9. Hollister LE: *Chemical Psychoses.* Springfield, Ill, Charles C Thomas Publisher, 1968.

10. Weil AT, Zinberg, NE, Nelson JM: Chemical and psychological effects of marijuana in man. *Science* 162:1234-1242, 1968.

11. Crowell EB, Ketchum JS: The treatment of scopolamine-induced delirium with physostigmine. *Clin Pharmacol Ther* 8:409-414, 1967.

Use of the Television Monologue with Adolescent Psychiatric Patients

BY HARRY A. WILMER, M.D., PH.D.

Each patient admitted to the youth drug study unit, a therapeutic community for adolescents with drug problems, is asked to make a videotape monologue. The tape is replayed to him immediately, and he can choose to have it erased or to review it with his therapist. The author describes the monologue technique as a unique form of clinical record and revelation about the patient; it also opens new vistas for self-observation.

IN MAN'S inner speech and inner dialogue (3, 10, 15), his ego identity and his social identity are continually preparing him to present himself to others. In social discourse, instantaneous transformations are constantly taking place in response to the feedback from social perception of the self.

How it is possible to give man a tool to externalize his inner speech and make it available to himself and others, and to experience this free of the contamination of human interaction, is the subject of this paper. The method I am going to present is that of the television monologue or soliloquy. This technique involves a patient sitting alone in a room talking to a television camera for a short period of time.

This self-encounter or self-confrontation is not familiar to the patient from any previous experience and provides us with a new dimension for the study of personal and individual social perception. At this particular time of technological development, such self-examination by closed-circuit television is a totally unfamiliar experience. Within a short time, however, with the probable widespread use of new, inexpensive videotape equipment, this may no longer be true. Therefore, we have at present a unique opportunity.

Evolution of the Television Monologue

This technique has been described previously in four presentations(18-20, 23). The introduction of the audiotape recorder allows new flexibility in the study of human monologue or dialogue. The development of high fidelity stereo audiotapes played through stereo headphones adds to its dramatic and realistic impact(17). Yet this lacks the visual image and remains essentially a one-dimensional sensory experience. Clinical observation through one-way mirrors in addition to the audiotape improves the set but leaves a major defect, for the participants cannot themselves reexperience and reexamine the audiovisual transaction.

Moreover, there is another factor, almost entirely ignored: namely, that the observer sees through a transparent window, but the participant sees a mirror on the wall. A mirror is a conscious or preconscious remainder of past ways of looking at oneself from early childhood. At some level of consciousness, it evokes the "looking glass self," where to see ourselves we look to see how we are reflected in the reactions of others. The other in the mirror may not be perceived as the self. In the one-way mirror experience, the mirror is, so to speak, "behind the patient's back." From one side, it is sophisticated snooping; from the other it is expectant play: "Mirror, mirror, on the wall . . . ."

Videotape playback gives us a valuable tool for the exploration of human interac-

Read at the 125th anniversary meeting of the American Psychiatric Association, Miami Beach, Fla., May 5-9, 1969.

This work was supported by grants from the Rosenberg Foundation, San Francisco, Calif., the Harris Foundation, and the Division Fund, Chicago, Ill.
The author wishes to thank Mr. Laurence Grunberg, television and film coordinator on the youth drug study unit staff, who made all of the videotapes.

tional behavior. Clinical studies of self-confrontation(1, 4), as well as studies of interviews, group and individual psychotherapy, supervision, training, and teaching, are appearing(13, 15). The motion picture has obvious research value, but its usefulness is limited because of expense, delay in viewing the performance, frustration of production retrieval, and projection. It has an added psychological factor influencing the performance: the sense that what is being recorded is "printed" indelibly, irrevocably. This intensifies the feelings of anxiety, paranoia, and fears of loss of part of self into a machine.

Much effort was expended in early film and television work to disguise or hide the camera in the hopes of getting a more or less natural picture(2, 6, 9, 11, 12). It has been my experience that the undisguised open camera (and even cameraman in some instances) provides a more authentic and better picture because of greater camera flexibility; moreover, it causes less suspicion because of the openness and lack of deception(16, 22).

In five years of videotape experience with open cameras we have had no problems with paranoid and psychotic patients. We never make a videotape without the patient's consent and without fully explaining to the patient beforehand what is being done and why. When minors are involved, consent is also obtained from parents or guardians. With informed consent, there is no intrusion of privacy. The only possible breach of confidence would be the misuse of tapes by showing them to persons other than select professional audiences, and no ethical person would permit this.

For the first time the supervisor can actually see and hear what is taking place, eliminating the distortions of the therapist's verbal reconstructions. Several factors are painfully obvious: The therapist's anxiety is generally greater than the patient's and influences the transaction in gross to subliminal ways; young patients who have grown up in the television world are more at ease than their therapists, are more spontaneous, natural "performers." It is also evident that what is taking place is a form of intrusion into the privacy of the therapist. Therapists' reactions suggest that Glover was perhaps correct when he said that psychotherapists often choose their field precisely to avoid self-examination(8).

By sensitive supervision it is possible to win the trust and confidence of the interviewer and to get reliable videotapes of dyadic relationships. It is our experience, however, that the videotapes of groups of three or more persons are more valuable for therapy and for the teaching of group technique than for person perception research. The complexities of group social interaction, the low definition of the television picture (an essentially close-up medium), and the limitation of the number of people who can be seen at one time on a screen restrict its value as a research tool.

The Nature and Distortion of Television Interview Evidence

In our experience in videotaping interviews and psychotherapy it is obvious that the patient presents himself differently to different interviewers. Since we are concerned primarily with obtaining and perceiving clinical evidence about the patient, we devised an experiment that demonstrates the two major variables in videotaping dyadic relationships—the camera angle and the interviewer.

In the television studio of the university, where quality broadcast equipment was available, we simultaneously recorded interviews with four cameras, one at each corner of the room, while the same patient was interviewed serially by five different persons in ten-minute sequences. The identity of the interviewers was not known to the patient before. Each interviewer asked the same four questions in his own words and style. The interviewers were a professor of criminal law, a psychoanalyst, a newspaper reporter, a policeman in plain clothes, and a policeman in uniform.

At the end of the 50 minutes, the four videotapes were played back simultaneously in a block of four monitors to all participants. The same transaction appeared strikingly different from each camera angle, as well as with each interviewer. The patient behaved and responded in a significantly different manner, either conforming to, in subtle defiance of, or resistant to the interviewer's manner, style, and person(19). In all instances, it was obvious that both people

224

were interviewing each other, a fact that Sullivan noted long ago(14). These findings are significant for clinical psychiatry as well as forensic psychiatry, now that television is being used in courts of law(5).

We decided, therefore, that we might obtain reliable, replicable audiovisual records of an individual if we recorded the patient talking to the television camera with no one else in the room. At first this was undertaken as a psychotherapeutic technique in which the patient made three 20-minute videotapes by himself, one every other day, and showed either parts or all of the tapes to his therapist in a one-hour weekly session. Because of the difficulty of evaluating this from the point of view of therapy, we decided to study a fairly large sample of short patient monologues. One hundred such videotapes are the basis of the observations in this paper.

The Setting of This Study

A patient's performance before a television camera alone is affected by the setting and the purpose. The subjects in this study were adolescent patients (mean age, 18) in a therapeutic community for the treatment of problems attendant upon the use of dangerous drugs, but excluding narcotic addicts. This ward is only nine blocks from Haight-Ashbury and has been in operation since 1967(20, 23).

The monologue was used as a method of patient self-confrontation and as a way of the patient's presenting himself to his doctor. These monologues are relevant in this therapeutic community because here television media are used in all group transactions as a part of the feedback process. In this particular setting there is a great deal of enthusiasm for the monologues. Half of our patients were diagnosed as acute schizophrenics. Many of our patients, when they first come to us, are withdrawn, find it difficult to relate verbally to others in groups, and are overwhelmingly preoccupied with themselves and "their own head hassles." I suspect that they welcome this TV experience because at these moments they become the center of the ward "universe."

Moreover, monologues have a symbolic meaning in the therapeutic community, which is more or less an extended family, as a ritual resembling a rite of passage of marginal persons from one status to another, from one culture to another(7). Since this is a multimedia community that relies heavily on television, film, and audiotape, the monologue is also a symbolic ritual of initiation into the new electronic informational environment.

Staff as well as patients are invited to make monologues. For them, the "initiation" is voluntary. Only a small fraction of the staff have taken advantage of this technique, and this only after long periods of internal debate, hesitation, and fear of exposure. This is revealed in their tapes. Many staff members choose to erase their tapes, but only two patients have asked to do this. Some staff members have used the monologues as a psychotherapeutic exercise in which they act as their own therapists, saying to the camera variations of "I have a problem I want to discuss. . . ."

Technical Procedures for Making a Television Monologue

On admission to the ward the patient is told about the monologue and within the first two or three days he is asked by the television technician, who is a full-time member of the ward staff, to make his monologue. By the time the patient makes his monologue, he will already have had several television group experiences.

The technician schedules and arranges for monologue production. Instructions are minimal. The patient is merely told that he can say or do whatever he wishes, that he is "to do his own thing" for 15 minutes before a camera alone, and that after watching the replay alone he may have the tape erased if he wishes. Any further explanation is strictly in response to the patient's questions. The videotapes are made either in a room on the ward or in a small television studio adjoining one of the doctor's offices, so the setting is informal and is a part of the living treatment milieu. Figure 1 shows a patient making her monologue.

The camera is placed before a comfortable chair in which the patient sits, and it is focused on the upper half of his body. Until recently we used lavaliere microphones hung around the patient's neck, but now we prefer to use an overhead microphone on a boom so that the patient's movements are not re-

stricted and he is not physically attached to the machinery. The technician, having arranged the setting, leaves the patient, telling him he will be back in 15 minutes. He goes into the adjoining room and starts the videotape recorder.

At the end, the technician returns to the room and, with minimal conversation, turns off the camera, turns on the monitor, then rewinds the videotape, and plays it to the patient, again alone in the room sitting in the same chair. If the patient requests that the tape be erased, this is done with no attempt to persuade him otherwise.

The patient and his psychiatrist almost always review the monologue together within a day or two. The patient may elect to show the monologue to other patients or to the community. His monologue is also used for supervision 'and in formal case presentations to consultants. The patient is also told that he may make subsequent monologues if he wishes, but he is not urged to do so. Recently, we have been experimenting with monologues of ten-minute duration. After the replay, the patient is videotaped again, talking about his monologue, or continuing it for another five minutes; this five-minute commentary is then replayed to him.

Excerpts from Sample Patient Monologues

This is how one patient began her monologue, looking directly into the camera:

Hello everybody. This is my film. This is my thing, and you'll soon know what value this film has. If I talk to you people through a camera, nobody understands. Makes it kind of frustrating if you direct your energies in any direction because you have no direction, so here I am, and [pointing to the camera] so there I am. There's the camera, and I don't know, but I'm kind of freaky. I'd like to bring up one thing, that's that I'm in this room all by myself.

She removed the microphone, walked away, got an autoharp, returned to play it, then, after a pause, began to talk about her problems.

A young girl chose to use her monologue to make a confession. She began by saying:

I would like to talk about . . . [long pause] . . . times I've taken dope since I've been here [on the ward]. I'd like to talk about it alone before I tell the group. One of the reasons I took it . . . and why I go down to Haight Street . . . it excites me so much I just naturally want to get dope when I'm around it. . . . I wanted to get dope because it makes life beautiful, makes me like myself and accept myself. . . . During the heavy taking of dope I lose all my desire to ever commit suicide, to kill myself again [sic]. . . .

A young girl who was hallucinating sat before the camera, forlorn, head hanging down, hands loose at her side. After two minutes of silence, she began her monologue, almost under her breath, in a singsong way. The voices that spoke to her were articulated:

Lies . . . lies . . . lies . . . [silence]. Lies . . . lies . . . lies . . . lies. You're lying. You are a liar. You talk too much. [long pause, whistles as if to ignore the voices, then] You are lying!

An attractive young girl sat before the camera. She began her monologue with a big yawn, but used it to sing, to search:

Wow . . . oh, wow. I get to be all by myself for a while. [In a childish voice. She smiles, stares at the camera.] Wow, well, I think a lot of the time I'm a really sad person. I was thinking about it this morning, like going back and being with my father, the urge I have to go back, in being and time. It's a strong feeling, but I don't know. [She begins singing a Dylan song.] How many roads must a man walk down before they call him a man . . . . [Then a while later she says] My friends away from here are having babies.

All my friends are away from here. God damn it! My scene is all screwed up. [Looks long at camera.] I would like to say that all I am saying is a bunch of bullshit . . . but I would like to say . . . I just feel really lonely. I just feel really scared. I'm paranoid about the big world. I don't want to get shot down. [She sings from "Porgy and Bess"] Your daddy's rich and your mamma's good lookin' . . . .

Another patient, a young man, used counterphobic techniques to experience the monologue as a sensory trip. He started by lighting a cigarette, looked up and down, threw his hands down to his sides, said:

Fuck. [Then he recites a clinical history beginning with where he was born. He speaks fast until he abruptly stops and, head down, says] Trying to help myself. See if I can't get something out of it. I feel like leaving, but I'd better not. [He takes a glass prism from his pocket, holds it over his right eye, looks at the camera lens through the prism, as if doing to it what it is doing to him, and therefore, neutralizing it.] All my life I feel nobody ever paid any attention to me. Something wrong somewhere. I guess it's me. . . . I feel like nobody cared for me all my life. Now I'm seeing colors: blue, purple, red, yellow. Everything is hazy looking. Looking freaky. Strange trip I'm on. Not a trip by drugs. A self trip. . . . Fuck. I'm scared. I wish it was over. I guess I wouldn't be here if I didn't think something. The whole place is a dream to me [still looking through prism]. Things aren't real. Things aren't happening. Colors are beautiful, the way I wish everything was.

Another patient regressed to a very little girl. She stretched at the beginning, looked at the camera, and whispered:

I wish I could whisper all the time . . . [stretches again; pushes the microphone out of the way]. Or yell. [Her eyes turn up, she looks gingerly around the room, stares innocently at the camera, licks her lips, mumbles something inaudible, then holds the microphone to her lips.] Why aren't you here to help me, pixies? [Now, with microphone pressing her lips.] Where are you, pixies? [She bends over, picks up a mask she has brought with her, and holds it in front of her face. Then, embracing a pillow, she calls her own name plaintively . . . repeats her name, then] Where are you? [Now on her knees] It's so easy to love you because you're a pillow and you won't love back and it's so easy to love an image of someone [pause] who isn't here anymore. [The rest of the monologue is really a dialogue between herself and her imaginary persons until, at the very end, she holds the pillow, which is very big, over her abdomen so that all you see is her

head and arms around the pillow. She looks at her watch and knows the time is over—then softly rocking says, at the very end of the tape] Baby.

One patient made the following comments on her monologue:

I was afraid of it at first. I didn't like the camera when I first sat here. I really had this thing about being really ugly, you know, and I didn't want the camera on me at all. Like in the meetings I'd hide my face or something because, you know, I really thought I was horrible looking and I didn't want it on tape or anything. The monologue was like my mom always said, "Someday you're going to wake up and see yourself like you really are, and then all these little things you are doing." Wow. Everything I did was wrong to mom. It drove me out of my mind. I wanted to make another monologue later to see if I had improved. I had. I can't explain it, but I didn't feel like I was ugly any more.

Another patient had this to say:

At first I didn't want my doctor to see the tape. I wanted to have it burned. I was going to have it erased. When I was thinking of the camera on me, I was thinking, oh, God, you know, I've got to look at it and see, you know, how tough I could be. It was like a test of guts. Well, now I really like the idea of the monologues, you know, because I really learn from them. I couldn't think of anything to say, like the camera reminds me of my mother, I mean this just occurred to me. Not like an interview where I'd be either playing a game with my doctor warding off his questions or I'd be giving "yes" or "no" answers or something like that, you know. But in a situation like this, no one's telling you what to do or say, and no one, you know, is doing anything to you.

Overview of the Patient Monologue

After reviewing all the patient monologues, as I tried to describe, catalogue, and conceptualize what I had seen, I found it extremely difficult to commit to print what was an electronic all-at-once experience, richly varied, and evocative of memories of these patients in their community life. At this time, it is like describing the exploration of heretofore unknown territory. Until its boundaries are relatively well known and its field defined, it is best to give a clinical, subjective report.

The monologues are primarily intriguing revelations of patients. They would be invaluable clinical evidence for other psychiatrists who, at a later date, might want to review the case material or who would be subsequently called on to treat the patients. They are a unique form of clinical record supplementing the written record.

They are also a fascinating revelation of the patient's inner speech. One has the opportunity to see what a patient might say in a 15-minute period with no psychiatrist present to prod, to question, to say, "Go on," or "What are you thinking?" in moments of silence: in short, when the patient has only himself and a silent participant observer camera(21) to cope with.

In some tapes we see remarkable examples of free association; in others, we see clearly regressive behavior. In some, the patient is willing to talk freely about painful material that as yet he finds impossible to discuss with his therapist or in groups. Some people will tell a camera personal, intimate, or historical material that they will not yet tell a therapist. The monologue facilitates the expression of transference feelings or confrontation with the doctor or any member(s) of the staff. There is, I think, within the limits of the patient's internal censorship, a kind of immunity in the monologue procedure, for the patient has the stage all to himself, with no human parental surrogate facing him.

Some patients use the monologue as a pantomime experience; for others it is a kind of psychodrama that incorporates whatever props they choose to bring. One patient used the monologue as a means of loosening her "uptight straight" psychiatrist by taking off her clothes and doing a topless dance. Needless to say, when her doctor sat down to discuss her monologue with her and pushed the button, he sat popeyed and dumbfounded. Yet this videotape, our most spectacular one to date, revealed, in more ways than one would expect, a great deal about her.

A few patients, in monologues, said nothing. Then, the physical behavior was the domain of the experience and was highly revealing. Sometimes it exemplified an overwhelming sense of inhibition and phobic reaction. More often, it was a defiant and rejecting act toward the doctor and the community. Such patients generally did poorly in the community, so pervasive was their withdrawal and their commitment to deviant, nonrevealing behavior. In one such patient, this was clearly a reenactment of his dominant childhood behavior, when he dared reveal nothing intimate for fear of being hurt, rejected, or given the silent treatment by his parents. Others, in their silence, act like little children reverting to a kind of sign language, using playful self-distortion as they once did before mirrors.

Some patients talk excessively to avoid self-revelation. Others rely on objects and clinging to objects to establish relationships. The most commonly used objects are books and musical instruments. Some read prepared autobiographies, and some read from books. One withdrawn schizophrenic patient read poetic essays from a book. When he saw that his time was running out, he proceeded to finish the book by turning page after page, reading only one line from each page. The total effect was Joyce-like, almost an epic poem.

Another patient talked about his homosexuality. Another about her love for her therapist. One patient knitted throughout her monologue, as we heard her inner speech: feelings about a friend's pregnancy and her own feelings about wanting a baby. Another patient sang a song she had written. One patient came high on acid and showed us what a trip was like.

Monologues present the patient in ways that, for practical purposes, may be classified as follows: 1) predictive, diagnostic; 2) informational, historical; 3) behavioral representation of self; 4) psychotherapeutic effect; and 5) record of the patient at a given time and place.

Dimensions of intimacy may be revealed by body movement, eye contact with camera, movement toward and away from the camera, or total removal of oneself from the camera's view. Social skills, such as humor, imagination, and creativity, are revealed in the tapes.

This technique lends itself to objective measurement. Time of eye contact with camera, speech nonfluencies, repetitive gestures or metaphors, specific references to time, persons, places, events, speed and volume of speech, silences, and opening phrases, body touching, etc., can be tallied.

Summary

The monologue, a method of using the television experience with adolescent users of dangerous drugs, has been described. It is a short videotape experience of the patient talking in a room all alone to a television camera and then watching the replay all alone. This is subsequently examined by the doctor and patient together.

Adolescence is a time of high visibility, of ego identity crises and self-consciousness. The monologue, as part of the videotape experience with its immediate playback, is a new form of metaphorical experience. The first task of science is to register objectively and describe reliably the material one wishes to study. In social perception and interpretation it is of the utmost importance to be as free as possible from theories and subjective interpretations. Evaluation must carefully take into account the position of a social action within that unit to which it actually belongs.

The monologue opens new vistas for self-observation in often poetic and creative ways. In it, each in his own way is exploring his own version of the most famous monologue of all: "To be or not to be: that is the question."

REFERENCES

1. Alger, I., and Hogan, P.: Enduring Effects of Videotape Playback Experience on Family and Marital Relationships, Amer. J. Orthopsychiat. 39:86-93, 1969.
2. Benchoter, B. A., Eaton, M. T., and Smith, P.: Use of Videotape to Provide Individual Instruction in Techniques of Psychotherapy, J. Med. Educ. 40:1156-1161, 1965.
3. Benjafield, J.: Evidence that 'Thinking Aloud' Constitutes an Externalization of Inner Speech, Psychonomic Science 15:83, 1969.
4. Cornelison, F. S., and Tausig, T. N.: A Study of Self-Image Experience Using Videotapes at Delaware State Hospital, Delaware Med. J. 37:229-231, 1964.
5. Evidence: Getting It on Tape, Time Magazine, December 22, 1967, p. 49.
6. Geerstma, R. H., and Reivich, R. S.: Repetitive Self-Observation by Videotape Playback, J. Nerv. Ment. Dis. 141:29-41, 1965.
7. Gennep, A. van: Les Rites de Passage. Paris: Noutry, 1909.
8. Glover, E.: Psychology of the Psychotherapist, Brit. J. Psychol. 9:1-16, 1929.
9. Moore, F. J., Chernell, S., and West, M. J.: Television as a Therapeutic Tool, Arch. Gen. Psychiat. 12:217-222, 1965.
10. Ostwald, P.: Inner Speech of Psychotherapy, Amer. J. Psychother. 21:757-766, 1967.
11. Ruhe, D. S., Grundle, S., Laybourne, P. C., Forman, L. H., Jacobs, M., and Eaton, M. T.: Television in Teaching of Psychiatry, J. Med. Educ. 35:916-927, 1960.
12. Schiff, S. B., and Reivich, R. S.: Use of Television as an Aid to Psychotherapy Supervision, Arch. Gen. Psychiat. 10:84-88, 1964.
13. Suess, J. F.: Teaching Clinical Psychiatry with Closed Circuit Television and Videotape, J. Med. Educ. 41:483-488, 1966.
14. Sullivan, H. S.: Psychiatric Interview. New York: W. W. Norton & Co., 1954.
15. Wilmer, H. A.: Practical and Theoretical Aspects of Videotape Supervision in Psychiatry, J. Nerv. Ment. Dis. 145:123-130, 1967.
16. Wilmer, H. A.: Television: Technical and Artistic Aspects of Videotape in Psychiatric Teaching, J. Nerv. Ment. Dis. 144:207-233, 1967.
17. Wilmer, H. A.: Use of Stereophonic Audiotape Recording in Supervision of Psychotherapy, Amer. J. Psychiat. 123:1162-1165, 1967.
18. Wilmer, H. A.: The Use of Television Videotape in a Therapeutic Community for Adolescents Involved with Drugs, read at the western divisional meeting of the American Psychiatric Association, Los Angeles, Calif., October 21, 1967.
19. Wilmer, H. A.: Drugs, Hippies, and Doctors, J.A.M.A. 206:1272-1275, 1968.
20. Wilmer, H. A.: Innovative Uses of Videotape on a Psychiatric Ward, Hosp. Community Psychiat. 19:129-133, 1968.
21. Wilmer, H. A.: Television as Participant Recorder, Amer. J. Psychiat. 124:1157-1163, 1968.
22. Wilmer, H. A.: The Undisguised Camera in Psychiatry, Visual/Sonic Medicine 3:5-11, 1968.
23. Wilmer, H. A.: The Vibes Are Good Doc, Mayo Alumnus 5:1-8, 1969.

Innovative Uses of Videotape
on a Psychiatric Ward

HARRY A. WILMER, M.D.
Langley Porter Neuropsychiatric

AT THE Langley Porter Neuropsychiatric Institute, we are using television videotape with instant replay as a treatment modality, a learning experience, a means for staff and patients to scrutinize their behavior and relationships, and a training and research tool. Transactions of all types, including ward community meetings, psychodrama sessions, individual interviews, and random activities, are televised and immediately replayed for the participants.

The ward on which we are using the videotape technique is a therapeutic community ward for adolescents and young adults whose presenting symptoms are related to drug abuse. They include day, night, and full-time patients of both sexes. Because of our proximity to the Haight-Ashbury district, the ward has a number of hippies. They are seriously disturbed young people whose problems are expressed in and accentuated by their use of such drugs as LSD, the amphetamines, and marijuana. They

This article is based on a paper he presented at the Western Divisional Meeting of the American Psychiatric Association on October 21, 1967, in Los Angeles.

are the misfits, the rejected, the lost and wilting flower children. Having withdrawn conspicuously from society, they are often bent on oblivion, seeking rebirth and mystical existence, even death or madness. Some are schizophrenic; most have character disorders.

The philosophy of our treatment program is to

give these patients self-awareness, yet leave them free to "do their own thing," whether it is to become involved, silently or actively, or to remain apart. We neither preach the evils of drugs nor attempt to force adjustment to the world; we try to let the patients see themselves through their own eyes, our eyes, and the eyes of television. The experience of confronting one's own image on the television screen produces what I call "self-awakedness," a sudden turning-on of the self; it differs from ordinary social awareness, in which the individual may turn to others for verification. We hope that, through self-awakedness, these young people may find internal strengths to help them endure the suffering of their lives, and thus to renounce escape through self-destructive behavior and drugs.

Dr. Wilmer, right, listens intently to Eric Hoffer, the longshoreman-philosopher, one of the many eminent guests videotaped during the ward's weekly seminars.

When we started using videotaping on this ward, we had the benefit of four years of experience with closed-circuit television at Langley Porter. I have reported elsewhere on the advantages of using open, undisguised cameras and cameramen,[1] the artistic and technical aspects of television in psychiatric teaching,[2] the practical and theoretical aspects of television supervision of psychiatric residents,[3] the television camera as a participant-recorder,[4] and its research value in studying concomitant verbal content and behavior.[5]

[1] Harry A. Wilmer, "The Undisguised Camera in Videotape Teaching of Psychiatry," *Visual-Sonic Medicine* (in press).

[2] Harry A. Wilmer, "Television: Technical and Artistic Aspects of Videotape in Psychiatric Teaching," *Journal of Nervous and Mental Disease*, Vol. 144, March 1967, pp. 207-223.

[3] Harry A. Wilmer, "Practical and Theoretical Aspects of Videotape Supervision in Psychiatry," *Journal of Nervous and Mental Disease*, Vol. 145, August 1967, pp. 123-130.

[4] Harry A. Wilmer, "Television as Participant Recorder," *American Journal of Psychiatry*, Vol. 124, March 1968, pp. 1157-1163.

[5] Harry A. Wilmer, " 'You Know': Observations on Interjectory, Seemingly Meaningless Phrases in Group Psychotherapy," *Psychiatric Quarterly*, Vol. 41, April 1967, pp. 296-323.

As a condition for admission to the ward, the patients are required to sign a legal consent to be videotaped, and minors must have written consent from their parents or guardians. No applicants have ever refused. We use two legal forms, which were prepared in collaboration with patients after the first group rebelled against the usual blanket release used by other departments of the university. That release gave the university unlimited freedom to use the videotapes, even for public broadcasts. The first of the two new forms we use, and the one all patients sign as a condition of admission, permits us to televise patients for tapes to be used only in the institute, with the condition that the tapes will be erased.

The second form allows us to keep the tapes for study or to use in making training films for professional audiences. We use the university form to obtain permission for public showings, such as on educational television. We never try to persuade patients to be televised, even though they have signed permission forms, and we take care to preserve the privacy and dignity of patients and staff.

The television camera, which is kept on the ward, is mounted on a dolly so that the TV technician can move it freely about the ward to take shots. We have two portable Ampex videotape recorders, one in the nurses' station off the ward and the other, with its own camera, in a small soundproof and specially lighted studio that is adjacent to my office. When replaying the videotapes, we can use a control device to stop the tape and replay portions for closer examination. Videotapes may be reviewed again by staff or patients, or both, at designated times in the studio adjoining my office. When we need special effects, such as superimposed shots or split screens, we use the studio of the university medical school, which has broadcast-type television equipment and a staff of skilled technicians and directors.

WE PREFER to tape and show brief sequences; although occasionally we elect to videotape an entire session of up to one hour, replay is usually

233

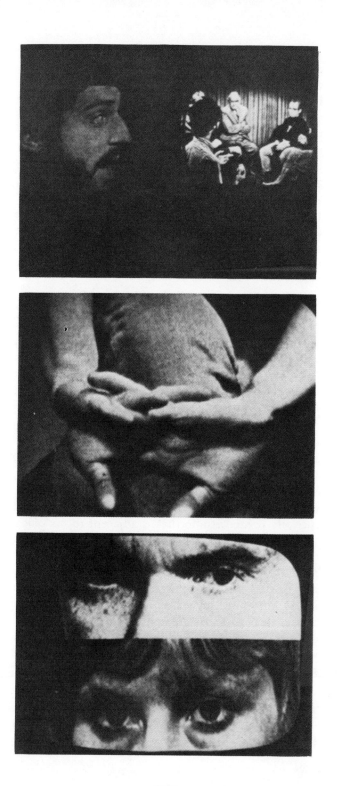

The special effects that can be achieved with video-tape are shown in these three photographs of video-tape monitors. Above, two monitors placed side by side simultaneously show a close-up of a patient talking and a group shot of the other members' reactions to what he is saying. Center photograph of a patient's hands demonstrates how close-up shots can highlight unconscious gestures. At bottom, the split-screen technique can be used to study pupillary reactions of patient and therapist during psychotherapy.

limited to segments of 5 to 15 minutes. Someone is designated to keep track of the crucial transactions, by using the tape meter or by jotting down the time they occur, to permit a selective playback. That avoids the monotony of having to watch uninteresting sequences and eliminates the confusion of trying to come to grips with an overload of audiovisual information.

We videotape the first 15 minutes of one community meeting and one multiple-family group session each week, and then we play the tape back at the end of the hour-long meeting; the playback and discussion last about 30 to 45 minutes. Immediately after one community meeting each week, we hold a 90-minute psychodrama session and often tape it for selective replay of 15-minute segments at the end of the session. We also videotape small group meetings on request, but not more than once a week. Patients sometimes operate the camera so that we can see the group through their eyes.

During a patient's first week on the ward, we videotape an interview between him and his doctor so that together they can explore their relationship as revealed on the tape. The playback is intended to be a collaborative experience, not one in which the expert tries to awe the patient with interpretations of behavior. The only adverse reactions to this procedure have occurred when patients correctly perceived that the therapist was insensitively pressing for information in the interview or trying to gain the upper hand during the playback. The tapes sometimes reveal that the interviewing resident failed to respond to obvious clues of reticence or counterphobic exhibitionism in a patient.

R ESIDENTS are assigned to the ward in their first year of residency. We have begun to videotape ten-minute samples of each one's initial interview with different patients. The taping will be repeated at six-month intervals throughout his residency, with a total of six patients, providing him with a kind of videotape scrapbook of his development as a therapist over the three years of residency.

Because we use individual psychotherapy only in unusual cases or in crises, we usually record only the individual sessions that are to be presented at a weekly conference with a consultant, at which the patient is not present. Close-up shots can be used to show eye movements and pupillary reactions and to highlight gestures. Split-screen effects can be used to show the expressions of therapist and patient simultaneously.

Once a week a guest lecturer attends the ward community meeting and afterward holds an hour-long informal seminar with patients and staff. Visitors may be invited to the seminars, which are held in a classroom if the audience is too large for the ward to accommodate. Often the lecturers are famous persons, and we usually videotape the entire seminar and keep the tapes for the ward or institute.

On one occasion the TV technician spent a day on the ward taking random shots for a three-hour tape of patient activities. We have experimented at times with improvisational artists. For example, a member of a well-known improvisational drama troupe sat in with a group and reacted as a spontaneous and uninhibited commentator.

Another group meeting was videotaped in the television studio while a jazz pianist in another room improvised musical responses to the group's actions as he watched them on a monitor. The music was fed into the videotape, but the group did not hear it until the replay. They reacted adversely to the musical critique, largely because it made them painfully aware of their awkward, unspontaneous group behavior. We are carrying out further experiments with the pianist, who is a psychiatric resident at the institute; we believe that musical improvisation has interesting possibilites for making our young patients aware of themselves, because so much of the adolescent's social expression is through improvised music.

In another experiment, we asked several patients to spend time alone in a room three times a week talking to the camera. After the TV technician set up the camera and left the room, the patient would begin talking or acting for 20 minutes. Then

237

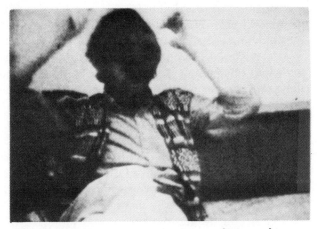

A hippie patient mugs and gestures before the camera while he is being videotaped in a room by himself, a procedure routinely used for new patients.

the technician replayed the videotape for the patient, to view it by himself and decide whether to keep all or part of the recording or to have it erased. Once a week the patient would meet with his psychiatrist for an hour and show him whatever portions of the videotape that he chose to.

Our hypothesis was that some patients would talk more freely to the camera than to their therapist, and indeed some patients talked as if releasing a torrent of suppressed thought. However, one hippie, dressed in the typical fanciful garb, was practically mute in front of the camera. He mugged and gestured, and mumbled about not knowing a friend's address. He appeared on the tape as a forlorn child, bewildered and lost. He was constantly touching his face and body, as if to reassure himself of his objective existence. It was a tactile performance, a mimicry of a child whose mother had left him.

That use of television has been so successful and so stimulating to patients that we have made it part of the routine admission procedure. Each new patient spends 20 minutes alone before the camera during his first or second day on the ward.

In any audiovisual portrayal, one inevitably questions how natural is the performance of the person being recorded as compared with his unrecorded self. It is my opinion that the recorded self is neither an artifact nor a false self, but a special aspect of the total personality, the social self. It is not, of course, the same as is revealed in individual personal encounters, but a magnification of the self-conscious state. The videotape performance brings into sharp focus elements of personality that might otherwise be hidden from the therapist unless he is unusually perceptive. Moreover, it accentuates perceptual distortions and brings them to the attention of both therapist and patient.

A frequent objection to videotape recording of groups is that a single camera cannot always record the entire process. The replay is sometimes frustrating to the viewer, who is forced to see the group from the perspective of the camera rather than of the group itself. It is possible to videotape both sides of a group with two cameras and to show them simultaneously on a split screen. However, that seldom is satisfactory, because the pictures lose detail when compressed onto a single screen.

To solve that problem, we have developed a technique using at least two cameras to videotape groups of 6 to 25 members. We place a camera and directional microphone on each side of the group and record simultaneously on two separate videotapes and sound tracks. They are replayed to the group on two monitors placed side by side, which gives stereophonic sound effects from the two videotape recorders. The viewer may elect to watch himself or others at any given moment. At first the experience is confusing—more so to staff than patients, because the latter can more readily adopt new modes of perception and also are more attuned to today's electronic world. However, as the viewer becomes accustomed to the situation, he feels less as if he is watching a tennis match and becomes absorbed in a total audiovisual experience.

Another innovation we have developed is to videotape a group viewing the playback of a session and, using a split screen, simultaneously show the session itself and the group's reactions to it as they witness the playback.

After we had been videotaping on the ward for two months, we gave the patients and staff a questionnaire about the experience. All patients responded positively, saying that it had helped them learn about themselves and others. Four of the 16 staff members felt that it was obtrusive or valueless, saying that the equipment was distracting. Perhaps they projected onto the machinery their discomfort about being exposed to the critical gaze of patients. After all, the patients come to the unit to learn about themselves, and so they have more to gain and less to lose by having their behavior exposed on videotape. The patients correctly perceived that many of the staff were being stiff, impersonal, and unresponsive and were hiding behind clichés and psychiatric jargon.

A month later we distributed a second questionnaire. By then the staff members were comfortable about the videotaping, and the patients were critical of the technical problems and the machinery. Only one person, a patient, expressed a preference for hidden cameras, and he also wanted videotaping to be limited to doctor-patient interviews. Most of the patients still felt that the videotaping was useful or even valuable, but one patient considered it a bother.

Both patients and staff commented that the videotapes gave them new awareness of their mannerisms and appearance. As one patient said, "My personal appearance was not at all how I imagined it to be. I also saw myself from all angles, in action, and I was never aware of my entire appearance before." A staff member said, "I became painfully aware of qualities I don't like, but maybe with time can change—especially rigidity of posture, lack of spontaneous movement, and a monotonous verbal quality that seems rehearsed." Another commented, "During one particular community meeting when I thought I was listening to someone objectively, I discovered on replay that I had a very tight-lipped, disapproving expression on my face."

240

OUR USE of videotaping (which is supported by grants from the Harris Foundation and the Division Fund of Chicago and the Rosenberg Foundation of San Francisco) gives the participants a highly involving experience through an objective, uninvolved machine. The playback is a paradigm of the feedback that is the heart of the sought-for open communication in a therapeutic community. It induces and intensifies self-confrontation, for the videotape offers irrefutable evidence of the transactions that have occurred. Videotaping is, therefore, an excellent medium for studying human behavior. Its measurable effectiveness as a learning or therapeutic device is being determined by carefully controlled experiments to obtain precise data.

Video Recordings

Sheldon H. Griffiths, RMN, SRN

In January 1969, the Cardiff and District Hospital Management Committee received a video tape recording machine and accessories. The equipment was donated by Tenovus, and the chairman of the committee, in accepting this gift, expressed the sincere gratitude of the recipients. This equipment is used in the treatment of patients suffering from alcoholism or drug dependency, and it is installed in Adfer—the Regional Alcoholic Unit at Whitchurch Hospital.

Although most lay people are relatively uninformed about psychotherapy—that is, the psychological treatment of dependency—it is not difficult to understand that a video tape recorder would be an extremely powerful aid. Interviews, discussions and lectures can be video taped, replayed when they are needed and as many times as required. Staff, patients and family members would be able to see themselves, study their own reactions and discuss any notable points that arise.

Here, briefly, is how the venture originated. A small group of dedicated people met to discuss the possibilities of using television recordings in treating alcoholics. This group included, amongst others, those in the field of television who were able to give expert technical advice as to the necessary requirements. This group then approached Tenovus and put forward their recommendations. Tenovus considered the ideas and implications of this scheme before accepting it and kindly supplying the equipment. The original group of people has continued to support and participate in the venture throughout.

This is not all, however, for Industrial Video Systems Limited, the suppliers of the equipment, were themselves donors of accessories to the basic equipment, which will enhance its usefulness to both medical and nursing staff. Indeed, Mr. J. M. Leonard, a director of the company concerned, travelled down from London especially to spend the whole day with the staff in demonstrating the techniques and principles used.

A video recorder, such as this, is the only way in which a visual recording can be made and replayed at will. For the first time, this will enable the therapist to confront the patient with himself. The patient may then be able to appreciate the personality changes which alcohol, or dependence on alcohol, has produced in him. Obviously, this process of self-confrontation will have to be supervised most carefully. If not, the patient's reaction to the situation would be uncertain and possibly quite disturbed. It is essential that the patient consents to the interview situation prior to recording. This is clearly a very private and intensive kind of therapy and it is therefore necessary that the strictest rules of confidence be applied to the tapes at all times.

Sony Videocorder : Model CV-2100E

The most important part of the equipment is the actual videocorder. The one used here is the Sony Videocorder: Model CV-2100E. This is a complete picture and sound recorder and reproducer, and, when used in conjunction with the camera mentioned below and the television monitor, reproduces, from tape, a recording comprising vision and sound. This videocorder uses a 12·7 mm wide tape, and the playing time amounts to 40 minutes of continuous recording on each tape. High quality heads, videotape, and rotary head system produce a picture with excellent resolution and with high signal-to-noise ratio.

The videocorder can be operated on AC 240 volts, 110 volts and 100 volts. The set is, however, factory pre-adjusted in two types of voltage: AC 240 volts or 220 volts. To look at, the videocorder is very much like an ordinary tape-recorder, although a little larger and with wider tapes. Its operation is quite simple: an automatic recording level control system ensures perfect recording, although a manual override can be used ·if necessary. Additional features are, editing capability during reproduce-mode, picture insertion and sound dubbing on· recorded tapes. Also, an automatic shut-off switch functions when the tape reaches the end of the reel.

The camera used with the Sony Videocorder is the Sony Videocamera Kit VCK-2100A. This camera and microphone supplement the Videocorder system to give live action with sound-recording and playback immediately. Sharp and crisp pictures are ensured by the use of a high-performance video-signal amplification system. The solid-state· circuitry of 30 transistors and 20 diodes is designed for rugged continual use. The camera

adapts itself to a wide range of lighting conditions, from dark indoor to bright outdoor light. It is extremely compact and easily portable.

It is not only suitable for recording purposes but also for all conventional closed-circuit applications, such as surveillance, exhibits and communications. The operating voltage of the camera is adjustable, these being AC 100 volts, 117 volts, 220 volts or 240 volts. The usual f 1·8 25 mm. C-mount lens has been supplemented by an f 2·5 20 to 80 mm. model VCL 20 zoom lens. This zoom lens can move a subject closer or farther away on a screen, as is desired. The lens travels a full range from 20 mm. wide angle to 80 m. telephoto with a smooth manual zooming. The television set used is an ordinary 19-inch receiver which has been adapted for use with the Videocorder.

Lighting is by means of four wall-mounted variable-focus and ·beam spotlights and two portable wide-angle lights. Each spotlight is attached to a bracket on the wall and is approximately 10 feet from the floor. Two spotlights are to the front of the staging area and are placed at each side; the other two are slightly to the rear of the staging area and, again, are placed to each side. The two front lights are approximately 18 feet from the staging area, while the rear ones are 12 feet away. The portable lamps can be used as required and depend on angles of subjects and camera. Normally, they are used in front of the staging area and at a distance of 14 feet.

Operating Technique

The entire recording equipment can be set up in 15 minutes. This entails the connection of the camera and television receiver to the Videocorder, plus adjustment of the focusing and beam of the lighting. The furniture or equipment used in the staging area might also require some minor adjustments. It is also necessary to make minor adjustments to the Videocorder and camera according to lighting and distance of camera from the staging area.

First the Videocorder. After

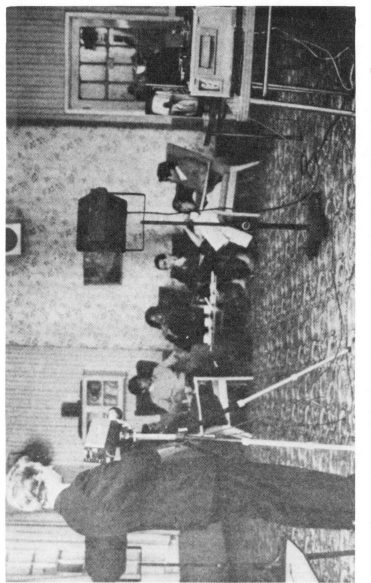

The author focuses the camera during a recording session. Two of the four fixed spotlights and two standing spotlights are in use. At right on tables, the monitor screen and videotape recorder

threading the tape through the machine, the tape counter re-set button is pressed in order to set the tape counter to the starting position. The power to the Videocorder and television receiver is turned on, and after allowing a short period for the equipment to warm up, it is now ready to record or replay as required.

Before recording begins, it is necessary, first, to adjust the camera according to lighting and distance from the subject. This is done by using the equipment as for the closed circuit application. The camera is switched on and when the record button on the Videocorder is pressed, a picture will appear on the screen. The camera should be pointed towards the subject and the lens aperture and focusing adjusted according to distance and lighting. Normally, when used indoors, with full lighting available, the aperture setting is f 5·6, and distance is around 12 feet from the subject. When a satisfactory picture has been obtained on the screen, the equipment is ready for recording.

The right or wrong way to film a subject or an interview has been learned by varied experience. It is not, for example, the best technique to film from directly in front of the person, as this may well distort the reproduction on the screen. The face may look too fat or too thin or maybe even too long, depending upon lighting, shadows, the position of the face and other factors. It is much more satisfactory to shoot at an angle of approximately 30 degrees from the person, in order to get a good reproduction.

When recording, it is essential to move the camera slowly and gently, as any sudden jerk will be exaggerated on the screen. Use of the zoom lens will depend on what is being discussed and also on the patient's reactions to the conversation. Usually, at the start of a sequence, a full-shot view of the patient is taken. The camera is then gradually zoomed in to pick up, perhaps, a close-up of a particular facial expression, exaggerated tremors or other manifestations. For a dramatic effect, when a patient shows a marked response to a particular point in the interview, the camera should be zoomed in quickly. When the interview has been completed, the camera is then switched off and the tape on the Videocorder is rewound to the starting position. The recording is now ready to be replayed.

An important asset when replaying the recording with this equipment is that the tape can be stopped in any desired position and a still picture of the recording can be reproduced on the screen. A slow-motion effect can now be used by slowly winding on the tape by hand. This is particularly important when one wishes to see some special mannerism, for example, raised eyebrows or even a wrinkled nose.

Therapeutic Values

The main use of the equipment is, of course, to improve methods of treatment, although there are many other fields in which it has distinct advantages.

One of the projects being undertaken in the therapeutic situation is research into the 'self-concept' of alcoholics and drug dependents. This entails the recording of a highly confidential interview between the consultant and the patient, where the patient is asked such questions as how he sees himself and how he would like to see himself. As with every other use, careful thought must be given to the possible consequences of self-confrontation.

Another important use is the replay of family therapy sessions. The recording can be replayed to: (a) the family as a whole,, in a prepared session with the therapist, (b) individual members of the family, (c) the therapeutic team as a whole, (d) individual members of the treatment team, (e) various groups of students, for example, medical, nursing, social work, etc. These same principles can be used in recording and replaying group therapy and drama therapy sessions.

The teaching uses of the equipment are also numerous. It can be used to illustrate: the teaching of interview techniques, the replay of lectures and demonstrations given by visiting experts, and the preparation of fifteen minute teaching and training tapes.

The potential of the video recorder used, not only in this field, but in the hospital service as a whole, is unlimited, and if it were not for the generosity of Tenovus, this hospital would have been denied a valuable and sophisticated aid in the treatment of alcohol and drug dependency.

Research

LSD Research: The Impact of Lay Publicity

BY CHARLES C. DAHLBERG, M.D., RUTH MECHANECK, M.A.,
AND STANLEY FELDSTEIN, PH.D.

An inquiry was sent to 29 investigators conducting research involving the use of LSD or other hallucinogens, in an effort to determine what effects publicity about LSD may have had upon their research. Nineteen of the investigators reported that the publicity had negatively affected the recruitment of "appropriate" subjects, the attitudes of already participating subjects, the behavior of research personnel, and the continuation of several research projects.

THE EFFECTS OF value-laden information upon attitudes, while a topic of continuing concern for its political, social, and psychological implications(1, 2, 3, 4, 5, 6), have become of particular interest in psychopharmacological research where drugs such as LSD have been receiving sensational and often unfavorable attention in the press. The investigators became interested in this problem as a result of their own observations of subjects in an LSD research project during a period of widespread adverse publicity, and they became concerned about the effects of publicity upon similar research projects.

A short review of the history of publicity that LSD has received will perhaps highlight the problem facing research involving this drug. There has been much interest in LSD throughout the 1950s and 1960s in research, psychotherapy, literature, and the popular press because of its psychotomimetic characteristics and because of its reputedly "mind-manifesting" or insight-enhancing properties. This, however, was not a topic of concern until 1962, at which time a scandal ensued at Harvard University involving the uncontrolled use of the drug.

The scandal was the source of much sensational publicity at the time in such magazines as *Playboy, The Reporter,* and the *Saturday Evening Post.* In addition, an LSD black market began to flourish. Unfortunately, press coverage was practically nonexistent for articles about LSD appearing in popular medical magazines, professional journals, and periodicals such as the *Medical Tribune.* LSD, which previously had been available to individual investigators, was no longer obtainable for private research. However, government research grants were available to study the drug's effects, and LSD continued to be supplied to authorized researchers by Sandoz Pharmaceuticals, the sole company that manufactured it.

After this period there was very little publicity until March 1966, when *Life Magazine* renewed the notoriety by publishing an article with considerable sensationalistic emphasis. Shortly thereafter, newspaper, magazine, radio, and television coverage abounded —lurid reports of a child accidentally swallowing the drug, a murder connected with LSD, inquiries by a district attorney, etc. Recall of the drug by Sandoz followed. The New York County Medical Society made formal recommendations to the state legislature asking for more stringent penalties for illicit manufacture and distribution of the drug, which was followed in April 1967 by the enactment in New York State of laws controlling the sale, possession, and use of hallucinogens.

The authors were beginning recruitment for a study investigating the effects of LSD upon communication in psychotherapy at the time of the unfavorable publicity.[1] This

This study was supported by Public Health Service grant MH-11670 from the National Institute of Mental Health.

[1] Supported by PHS grant MH-11670 ("Effects of LSD-25 on Psychotherapeutic Communication") to the William Alanson White Institute, New York, N. Y. Drs. C. C. Dahlberg, S. Feldstein, and J. Jaffe are the principal investigators.

study involves patients who are seen in private psychotherapy sessions and are given LSD in small doses at regular intervals during the course of their therapy, over a period of about a year and a half. The therapist in the project, when speaking to prospective patients for the study, began to notice a degree of anxiety on the part of several of them which contrasted markedly with the response of patients to similar situations at previous times. Because of this change in patient response, it seemed worthwhile to inquire about the effects of adverse publicity on other research projects which were employing LSD.

It should be noted that the data of the present study were collected by the last month of 1966. The data collection phase occurred, therefore, during the period of adverse, sensationalistic publicity and prior to the appearance of any articles or publicity concerning LSD and chromosomal changes. The question of whether such changes do, in fact, occur as a function of LSD ingestion is obviously of considerable moment and is still under investigation (by the authors as well as others). The important point is that this question was not a public issue at the time the present study was completed.

It is also worth noting that there was a significant difference between the stories in the popular press before and after the discovery of possible chromosomal damage by LSD. Before the first report of chromosomal damage, the stories were about sensational activities of illicit drug users and included claims of nirvana, insights, and personality change as well as claims of psychosis, suicide, and other psychic damage. These reports gave little rational reason for avoiding carefully controlled scientific study of the drug. When the reports of chromosomal damage appeared there was, for the first time, a tenable argument for persons being more concerned about being subjects in an experiment on LSD than on another drug.

This report concerns the effect of publicity which did not give a rational reason for avoiding carefully supervised experimentation with LSD. It has been the authors' experience that subsequent to public attention to the possibility of LSD-caused chromosomal damage, the recruitment of

subjects became considerably more difficult. Informal conversations with other researchers using LSD have tended to confirm this finding. Moreover, other scientists have raised questions about the propriety of conducting any research with humans which involved the use of LSD.

Procedure

Identical letters of inquiry were sent to 29 researchers in the United States and Canada who were known to be conducting studies involving the use of LSD or other hallucinogens, or who, at previous times,

TABLE 1
Letter of Inquiry Sent to Investigators

Dear —————:

My associates and I are currently engaged in a research project investigating the effects of LSD on communication in psychotherapy. We are in the midst of recruiting subjects for the project and have become concerned about the effects on patient attitudes of the tremendous amount of adverse publicity which LSD has been receiving of late.

It is my impression that the anxiety being expressed by patients about the drug contrasts markedly with the attitudes I have previously observed in my work with patients using LSD. We have noted, for example, that although our current patients have not, on the whole, been deterred from participating in the study, there has been an increasing tendency on their part to turn to others (friends, relatives) for advice. Because of their lack of any other source of information, it is these people who tend to be most persuaded by distortions and sensationalism in the press and, in turn, instill apprehension and concern in the patients.

The degree to which these attitude changes may affect not only the willingness of future patients to participate in the study, but their reactions to the drug as well, is unknown at this point. However, I feel it is a problem of major importance to investigators in the field. For this reason I am contacting you and several other people currently working with LSD. I would be extremely interested in hearing from you about your impressions, or any data you may have, regarding the effects of the recent publicity on attitudes and recruitment of subjects in the past few months as compared with your work prior to this time. I would be particularly interested in specific descriptions of individual reactions that have been noted. In this way I hope to be able to pull together the experiences of various people and begin to obtain an over-all perspective about this issue.

I would appreciate receiving your reply and will be happy to send you the results of this inquiry when they are compiled.

Sincerely,

had conducted such studies. The letter (table 1) presented the senior author's observations and concern about the amount of adverse publicity LSD was receiving, and it solicited the recipient's opinions and, in addition, any available data or information about the effects of such publicity upon the attitudes and recruitment of subjects in and for the recipient's research.

Of the 29 investigators, 25 replied, although only 19 of the replies were pertinent to the study. The remaining six investigators expressed either a disinclination to respond to the specific request or reported that they were not currently involved with such research. Thus the results reported below are based upon the responses of 19 investigators.

Results

Letters of response were divided into three categories on the basis of the issues with which they dealt. These categories were: 1) the effects of adverse publicity on recruitment of subjects; 2) changes in attitudes of subjects already participating in a study and any impact these attitude changes may have had upon drug reactions; and 3) the effects of adverse publicity upon scientific investigation, its impact on hospital personnel, and its effect upon research endeavors in general.

Because this inquiry was not intended as a formal investigation, no statistical analyses were performed. Instead, the number of responses falling into each of these categories and the descriptive comments which accompanied them are presented.

1. *Subject recruitment.* Fifteen of the 19 responses were relevant to the first category of effects of adverse publicity upon subject recruitment. Most studies did not actively seek to recruit subjects but used volunteers instead. Eleven respondents reported that volunteers were as numerous or more numerous subsequent to the outburst of publicity than prior to it. Only one respondent reported considerable difficulty in recruiting desirable subjects, and three replied that they felt there was a somewhat, though not totally, negative reaction. One of these respondents felt that relatives were interfering with patient volunteers: ". . . subjects who had not taken the drug were becoming more difficult to convince, especially their rela-

tives." Another felt that the occasional dropouts from projects were often the result of family pressure. A third, using LSD to treat alcoholism, reported some reluctance on the part of alcoholic patients, though none with normal volunteers.

The majority of respondents commented upon the change in the type of subjects volunteering for the project. Although more volunteers were noted as applying for participation in the projects, they were reported as being less "appropriate." As one investigator stated:

. . . it may be speculated that the motivation of persons who seek out and are willing to participate in LSD experiments may have changed as a result of the recent publicity, as it is likely that such participation is now viewed more as a potentially dangerous experience.

Another stated: ". . . in spite of our recruitment efforts we have had considerable difficulty in securing subjects of the type in whom we are interested for our experiments." Many volunteers have been lured by the "promise of nirvana," which was the expression used to describe the effects of publicity.

2. *Attitude change.* The reported change in the attitude of subjects was most marked. Of the nine responses which were relevant, all spoke of the increased fears of subjects (and their relatives) in the study and their increasing need for reassurance. This need was expressed by a tendency to postpone scheduled sessions and by an increased number of inquiries about potential dangers as a result of taking the drug.

Several investigators expressed fears that this increase in anxiety on the part of the subjects might result in an increase in the number of panic reactions under LSD, and one stated, "I feel all the notoriety will induce variables we will not be able to recognize or identify—let alone measure or control for the next five years." No documentation of this possibility could be offered by any of the respondents inasmuch as there had been no reports of bad reactions which could be readily attributed to the publicity. One investigator reported that ". . . the flood of mass media coverage had increased favorable attitudes among the previous skeptics or fence sitters, but with those negative or uninterested to begin with the publicity has served to reinforce their fears concerning adverse effects. . . ."

3. *Scientific investigation.* Several investigators offered information that was not specifically requested, i.e., that the publicity affected their scientific endeavors adversely. Three who had previously conducted research privately were prevented from continuing their studies because of the recall of the drug. Three others who were conducting research in mental hospitals were forced to discontinue their work. One was relatively noncommittal about his superior's reason for stopping, except for noting his concern about working with LSD "at this time"; another reported bluntly that he was in a state hospital and was particularly vulnerable to political investigations; and the third stated that the administrative authorities and he had decided to "temporarily" stop research because of the present difficulties in obtaining LSD.

Two respondents from hospitals noted that although their research was not discontinued, there were additional problems. One said that his staff had become more frightened and ambivalent; and the other, that hospital personnel began to treat the research as "shady," which had the effect of rendering the therapists in the project overcautious and fearful.[2]

Discussion

Although the results are relatively informal, they do suggest that the adverse publicity associated with LSD has had generally negative effects upon certain aspects of research concerned with the drug. It has reputedly led to: 1) a decreased number of "appropriate" volunteers, 2) an increase in the anxiety of participating subjects, 3) the premature demise of several LSD projects, and 4) increased ambivalence and cautiousness of personnel participating in other LSD projects.

The first two effects should probably be

considered interactive. It seems likely, that is, that the decrease in "appropriate" volunteers reflects the arousal of fears similar to those reported by participating subjects. The "inappropriate" volunteers presumably represent a group that is attracted to the drug and sees the research as a legalized method of obtaining it and, perhaps, a safe way of taking it. Presumably, too, the characteristics and expectations which make for the attraction of such individuals would severely limit the generalizability of whatever experimental results their participation yielded.

With respect to the reactions of participating subjects, it may be of interest to present several detailed illustrations drawn from the project (see footnote 1) which generated the present inquiry. The illustrations are of five patients in treatment with the psychoanalyst of this project. All had been in analysis for at least a year prior to the beginning of the project, and two had had prolonged prior analyses.

In each case the therapeutic relationship was quite good at the time the patients were approached for participation in the project. Before the spring of 1966 when the publicity began, two patients had been asked to participate, and although both had quickly agreed, only one had been started. Patient 1, who was well into the study when the publicity began, reacted only with an expression of sympathy about the position of the research team and with some pride at being part of such an important project.

Patient 2, who had been mildly apprehensive and in the unfortunate position of having a rather prolonged waiting period from the time she agreed to go into the project until the time when she could actually start, became very anxious. She talked to a number of people about LSD including members of her family, some of whom expressed strong opposition. She had originally expressed mild concern about LSD precipitating a psychosis or suicide, and these concerns increased. She stated that the publicity had made her think much more seriously about LSD than she had previously, when it had not seemed quite real. After some thoughtful consideration, she decided to accept the risk.

Patient 3 reacted very much as patient 1,

---

[2] Subsequent to the completion of this report it was learned that two other LSD research projects (not among the original 29 queried) had been discontinued during the data collection phase of the present study and prior to their completion. One of these projects utilized human subjects; the other, nonhuman mammals. Their discontinuation was attributed to the adverse publicity.

with an attitude which could be described essentially as, "If you think it's the thing to do, let's go ahead."

Patient 4, who had more than the usual amount of knowledge about the drug, reacted with intense anxiety for about three days. Her roommate said, "You may be crazy enough to do that, but I wouldn't." Other persons with whom she spoke gave more considered responses, but she became fairly obsessed with fantasies of psychosis. Analytic exploration led to a decrease in her anxiety and an eagerness to participate in the project.

Patient 5 also had fantasies of disorganization and spoke to many professionals about LSD, some of whom strongly opposed it. She was, however, fascinated by the drug and could not let go of the idea, although eventually she refused to take it.

The reactions of the participating subjects, institutions, and investigators described by the respondents might be interpreted as a conjoint effect of the communications and communicators to which they were exposed and the groups to which they belonged. Klapper(5) contended that mass media, used as agents of persuasion, are capable of inducing neutrally disposed individuals to develop an attitude in the direction intended by the propaganda. Mass communications concerned with the effects of drug use have primarily relied upon emotional rather than rational appeals, and have associated LSD use with mental illness, crime, mass orgies, and the like. It seems understandable that such publicity aroused the anxieties of subjects and potential "appropriate" subjects, few of whom presumably had any prior knowledge or opinions about hallucinogenic drugs.

On the other hand, subjects participating in an LSD project who are also patients have another source of information, i.e., their therapist, with whom they have usually established a relationship based upon some degree of trust. A patient does not tend to believe that his therapist would ask him to submit to a procedure that is harmful or potentially harmful. The therapist will, therefore, often be considered a more reliable communicator than mass media, and the patient will elect to join or remain in the project in spite of his fears.

The reported institutional and investigator responses to the adverse publicity appear to be primarily in compliance with actual or imagined pressures by publicity-sensitive agencies, both political and professional.

These responses indicate that research involving LSD has suffered from the adverse sensationalistic publicity received by the drug. Thus the acquisition of possibly important information about the drug has been prevented or retarded.

It is of additional, if peripheral, interest that the survey might be viewed as a field examination of persuasibility. Laboratory studies have suggested a number of variables which appear to determine the effectiveness of such persuasive communications. Among such variables are: 1) the role, affiliations, and intentions of the communicator or message source; 2) the content and presentation style of the communication; and 3) the characteristics and reference groups of the audience that receives the communication. It seems likely that the results of the present survey might be reasonably understood within the conceptual framework outlined by these variables.

It should be mentioned as a limitation of the study that the wording of the letter of inquiry sent to the investigators may have exerted some influence upon their responses. The extent of such influence, if it occurred, is difficult to assess.

REFERENCES

1. Hovland, C. I., and Janis, I. L., eds.: Personality and Persuasibility. New Haven: Yale University Press, 1959.
2. Hovland, C. I., Janis, I. L., and Kelly, H.: Communication and Persuasion. New Haven: Yale University Press, 1953.
3. Janis, I. L., and Freschback, S.: Effects of Fear Arousing Communications, J. Abnorm. Soc. Psychol. 48:78-92, 1953.
4. Kelman, H. C.: Three Processes of Social Influence, Public Opinion Quarterly 25:57-78, 1961.
5. Klapper, J. T.: The Effects of Mass Communication: An Analysis of Research on the Effectiveness and Limitations of Mass Media in Influencing the Opinions, Values and Behavior of Their Audiences. Glencoe, Ill.: The Free Press, 1960.
6. Siegal, A. E., and Siegal, S.: Reference Groups, Membership Groups and Attitude Change, J. Abnorm. Soc. Psychol. 55:360-364, 1957.

Conference on Drug Abuse

Implications for Research

Daniel X. Freedman, MD

The abuse of drugs is not solely a medical problem. It is an array of different social, behavioral,
and physiological problems in which the manufac-
turer, distribution, and use of medicinals is involved. While clinical practice presents an incessant
panorama of behavioral issues to which the perceptive physician is privy, he usually is only minimal-
ly expert or influential in behavioral treatment and
legal policy. This certainly is the case in the area
of drug abuse.

Hopefully, physicians will sharpen the focus of
their interest, develop appropriate skills, and seek
the expertise of others whose competence is clear.
For reliable knowledge, the traditions of scientific
medicine require explicit definition of a number of
quite different aims. What do we need to know to
prevent the spread of drug abuses—about those motives and forces which initiate drug intake, those
sustaining it, and those leading either to uncon-

Read before the 14th Annual Conference of Mental Health
Representatives of State Medical Societies, sponsored by the
AMA Council on Mental Health, Chicago, March 16. 1968.

trolled or controlled intake? What do we need to know about the determinants of stopping the intake of drug or the relapse potential? These different issues call conceivably for different answers; eg, legal and educational means may be more salient for prevention and self-help programs (aided by drug-detection devices) for preventing relapse. What does the abuse of these drugs require of legal, psychotherapeutic, and social science research, and of pharmacology and toxicology? However these questions come to be answered, they truly require special study of discrete problems rather than instant global prescriptions.

Intrinsic Problems in Research

Contemporary concern is provoked not by crime, but by youthful rebellious behavior which appears to be irresponsible and to lead to varying degrees of sudden or insidious loss of productivity. The children of the culture-bearing elite have in increasing numbers—especially over the past eight years—turned to drugs. We are now asked to develop information both for those who must design laws and for those treating the abusers of opiates, hallucinogens, marijuana, various stimulants (generally the amphetamine derivatives), and sedatives. Our task would be simple if all of these drugs led inevitably to perdition, or more neutrally, if each were lethal! Yet some are users without apparent harm, others with some cost to their physical or personality functioning, and others at great cost. Our job is to present the information we have or need to develop and to share with the public what the physician always assesses: the probability of one or several kinds of hazards as well as specific programs most apt for particular patients.

In doing this, we can note that drugs always evoke irrational images of power—either to poison or to enhance potency (physical, mental, or sexual). Given the prevalence of these underlying irrational beliefs we should not be surprised to find physicians acting as passionate advocates of one or another social position concerning what it is that people do with their bodies. Most of the early leaders in psychiatry were fervent prohibitionists; they had confronted the end result of alcohol abuse sufficiently to provoke this posture, although we could question the extent to which they were equipped to tailor specific and useful social policies. Different experts are bound to emphasize what they see. Thus law enforcement agents watch already-delinquent experimenters become addicted criminals; severe personality disorganization is referred to the psychiatrist; educators must cope with other people's misbehaving and untutored children; and writers may see special visions of man's basic nature as exposed by drugs. Each approach generates questions—if not methods—for research.

That rational discourse will be achieved with difficulty is underlined by another fact. There are a number of modes by which people can "turn off" for a period of time—a process which generally involves a redirection of attention. This is true of a hobby, or physical exercise, or the taking of drugs in culturally ritualized ways. Yet fundamentally we know little about the psychobiology of recreation or of man's successful ways of achieving episodes of well-being. Such research would begin with the observation that we try in many ways to relieve the sense of isolation engendered in our everyday struggles with drab reality. Apparently the need to transcend limits and the search for a wider or different communion to "turn to" easily evokes a universal wish for omnipotence—an urge to transcend all physical and social limits. History notes that utopian dreams are recurrently generated and that drugs frequently play a part in group or individual quests for escape, salvation, and transcendence.

Specific Drug Responses

To conduct research on this ancient link of drugs with behavior, we must first recognize that almost any peripherally or centrally acting drug can produce the perception of a change of bodily state; this "ego disruption"—this holiday from ordinary reality—can in itself produce a state in which euphoria is a consequence. This *potential* is a general response to quite different drugs. What is so fascinating to the biobehavioral scientist is that there are molecules which can specifically compel altered periods of mental functioning. Etched upon the variabilities of personality, expectation, suggestibility, and setting, specific patterns of chemically induced behavioral change can be discerned. Study of dose effects will discriminate different categories of drugs as the dose is increased.

The psychotomimetic indole or phenylethyl

amines produce a relative loss of controlling structures (habits, categories, boundaries, abstractions) through which the flood of input is normally ordered such that familiarity, stability, focus, and constancy are achieved. This "dehabituation" leads to a heightened sense of vividness, an absorption in novelty, in the irrelevant details which we normally suppress in order to achieve efficient functioning. Events seem boundless and portentous. The *sense* of truth is enhanced, but there is a diminished capacity to test the truth of the senses; meaningfulness is more important than the object that is meant, and an array of sensorially vivid inputs take on an uncanny patina. This order of consciousness, operative in dreaming, is normally suppressed, but the *waking* dreamer is starkly and simultaneously confronted with both orders of consciousness. Hence these "de-suppressive" drugs are called mind-manifesting or psychedelic. Input is increased while control over input is reduced; the nonrational aspects of experiencing are expanded but logical thought and judgment—while present—are shrunk! Acute nondrug psychoses are often seen with these characteristics of mental functioning.[1] This is quite different from the delirious confusional reaction produced by cholinolytic drugs such as atropine or the dream-like contentment and reduction of anticipation produced by opiates. Each family of drugs requires extensive behavioral and subjective response profiles.

Biobehavioral Research

Thus researchers seek methods for the study of altered perception, mood, and affect. They attempt to study the genesis of these odd drug-induced experiences—the neural and chemical mechanisms as well as the kinds of behavioral controls which are operative.[2] The strategy is to understand the functioning of the brain and its normally covert biochemistry. The use of specific drugs to unearth important neurochemical pathways could lead to some degree of chemical control of abnormal behavioral states encountered clinically. Indeed the role of norepinephrine and serotonin in brain is being elucidated by the study of different classes of psychoactive drugs which differentially affect amine metabolism at specific sites.[3]

As different substituents are placed upon the phenethylamine molecule, it is possible to observe

256

slight differences in the pattern or in the intensity of the psychedelic effects. This structure-activity approach promises another method of dissecting the organization of abnormal states at the neural and the behavioral levels.[4] Pharmacological, psychological, and temporal factors are involved in accounting for differences among similar molecules. We should find out why it is that the acute effects of methamphetamine are more hazardous than those of amphetamine and why the chronic use of both leads to insidious mental changes which may differ from those produced by the related structure, mescaline.

A chemist can not only devise related molecules which could block one or another effect of psychoactive drugs which the addict finds reinforcing (and thus aid in treatment programs), but, by recently making available the active molecules in marijuana, he can lend precision to research. Methods can emerge which will allow identification of these structures in body tissues and study of their metabolism and neurochemical effects. This controlled knowledge of biological processes can form the basis for discrimination of mechanisms of effect as well as toxicology. We know that marijuana and its active ingredients can produce a combination of the effects of psychotomimetics, alcohol, and sedatives. With low doses a euphoriant, relaxed and somewhat disinhibited state with altered time sense is seen; and with higher dosages, hallucinatory and unpleasant effects are followed by drowsiness.[5,6] Yet we know very few clear-cut facts about the chronic toxicity of potent marijuana, in spite of a wealth of moralizing anecdotes. All that seems evident is that the drug can be used in other countries very much as our "skid row" alcoholics abuse alcohol. If society wants the well-sifted facts, if we are to answer the question of whether there is or is not brain damage from continued use of high doses, teams of internists, neuropathologists, psychiatrists, and social scientists will have to sort the data at first hand. We can recognize that the less-potent American marijuana presents a lure away from the acquisition of competence but not one which all people accept; many can control its use for relaxation. Others report loss of control over intake and confusional states, but these accounts need careful evaluation and reporting.

Prevalence and Scope of Abuse

While alcoholism continues unabated, new and younger populations are involved in drug abuse. Because of the rapidly changing social mores in our various subcultures, today's study may be quite irrelevant tomorrow. There is a distinction between casual trial, episodes of experimentation, and dedicated and uncontrolled drug use and the forces sustaining these patterns, as well as their quite variable consequences. We should, incidentally, wonder why it is that a difficult question about which society wants authentic data is usually left to the frequently untutored and skewed views of policing agents without the aid of an expert social science team.

It would be valuable in planning legal steps if it were possible to determine in advance exactly who —in the growing population of users—might be vulnerable to dangerous effects. Yet even if one could identify a population at low risk of drug-related problems today, could we predict whether or not there would be loss of control over intake two or three years hence? Observation of alcohol addiction indicates that individuals are variably at risk at different periods of their life and that this cannot be predicted. Could historical research show that prohibition reduces the total population at risk? (I suspect it would.) Does a single dose of alcohol carry a differential dependence liability compared with a single dose of marijuana? If there are differences, on what basis do they occur? Does the presence of identifiable motor impairment, gastritis, and odor prove to be a check on consumption by some alcoholics and a signal to society that a person is drugged—and if so, is this kind of signal to the self and others available with marijuana?

In any event we can cite conditions and dosage schedules as well as consequences of differential drug intake and evaluate a variety of hazards. With lysergic acid diethylamide (LSD) the risk is clearly enhanced when the dose is increased, when motives are confused, and when the purpose for consumption is to solve problems for which the undrugged mind is far more reliable and efficient. There is enough loss of anchors to reality to make self-exploration and attempts to divine secret motives and virtues the most dangerous of motives in psychedelic drug use. The hazards drastically shift when as many stabilizing forces as possible (authentic religious groups, medical supervision) can guide and structure the LSD experience. With research, the appropriate conditions and hazards for a wide variety of drugs can be specified. Whether or not the young of a society could be tutored in judging these and safely taking drugs in unsupervised situations is another question.

Drug-Behavior Interactions

Surprisingly, we do not really have sufficient knowledge on the role of the subjective effects of a drug in determining its habitual use. In the range of low dosages of many drugs, it is clear that surrounding environment and expectations can determine the emotional response[7]; small doses of barbiturates can be intoxicatingly euphoric or sedative depending upon intentions and the setting. Response of the uninitiated to mild marijuana may be interpreted as dizziness, while with slight tutoring, attention can center on the euphoric mental effect which can then be indulged. It may be that drugs which tend to cause a "turning in" of attention could reinforce (though *not* compel) further exploration through drugs for such experiences. In any event the fundamental question is whether certain drugs are potent reinforcers to different kinds of aims and ends. The disinhibiting but socializing effect of low doses of alcohol conceivably enhances certain group aims which marijuana might not.

There are differences in the patterns of sensitivity to and modulation of input from the environment between the sexes.[8] Whether or not this might account for the more frequent abuse of drugs by males is not known. We have yet to understand the basic mechanisms by which the LSD experience can so enhance the interaction of the drug state and surrounding events and then so compellingly but variably alter subsequent behavior patterns. Chronic LSD users may appear to be more open to input from the environment and less discriminating about what they tend to be occupied with. With LSD, competitive and angry feelings are quite aversive, while cosmic and magically omnipotent thoughts may be augmented and pleasurable. The carry-over may be manifest in less aggressiveness and ambition and greater reliance on magical and wishful thinking after the drug state. Nor do we know the mechanism of the "flashback"—the dry drunk or trip without the drug. Whether this is an hysterical reaction, a traumatic neurosis, a specific drug effect on habitual defenses, or an effect on the "switch" controlling waking and dreaming thoughts, or on temporal-lobe mechanisms is entirely unknown. The point is that events occurring during the drug state, their immediate management as well as their subsequent interpretation, are potent factors in the outcome.

Group Processes and Psycotherapy

Group processes not only enhance drug cults but form around the therapy of the addict. For the large proportion of addicted persons, the sharing of therapeutic experience, reinforced by frequent actual contact with peers, seems to be important. The reformed addict must put aside his false autonomy (centered around his power to take drugs and feel immunity in the drug state). He often must relax his pride and thoroughly respect his vulnerability, which can be managed often more easily with peers than with even benign authority. In working with authorities it is reassuring to the addict if his actual temptations are understood and if the deceits of his drug-taking behavior are comprehended. The extent to which treatment must be prolonged is not known. It may be for a lifetime. Unlike the neurotic, the addict can learn clearly to identify his temptations and vulnerabilities, and as he seeks constant group support he is really little different than those neurotic patients who maintain some kind of community of memories if not activities (such as referring friends and family) related to their therapy long after its termination. We have much to learn about psychotherapy generally as specialists focus upon the psychology of different addicts and the meaning of their searches for cure. The fact that addiction involves a habit may provoke more focused interest in the psychology of dependence and the extent to which all men rely upon ritual for stability and familiarity while seeking novelty and escape through a variety of techniques.

Research on Treatment Programs

Medicine can claim little credit in the treatment of any of the addictions from alcohol to food. We have not as yet discerned a sound profile of an addictive personality in spite of years of speculation, even though there are many features common to

260

persons who orient their lives around one or another addiction. It is only recently that the scientific community has overcome prejudice and begun to support a variety of different goals and treatment procedures in narcotics addiction. A treatment which socially rehabilitates a person who remains dependent on a drug supply (methadone[9]) might be achieved where total cure might be more difficult. Urinary monitoring for evidence of drug intake might achieve more reliable behavioral control to prevent relapse than any number of mandatory incarcerations. If we could anticipate that there will be people who will remain antisocial but give up drugs while others would be dependent but productive and yet others remain unproductive, we can begin an effective test of a variety of treatment programs, because we will have stopped supposing that blanket diagnoses of motives and global prescriptions for treatment are effective. The effectiveness of different legal sanctions (such as commitment can also be evaluated in terms of relative costs and effectiveness for specific aims. Society may have to resort to legal proscriptions in order to manage a problem it cannot tolerate, but open research in such management and therapeutics should proceed.

Motives for Drug Use

Psychedelic drugs have been advertised freely by sensationalism in our supposedly sober and proper press. This arouses curiosity and contagious episodes of drug experimentation which can then terminate as supplies dry up and as the young people observe for themselves what the risks in fact are. Since a variety of motives lead to drug taking, it is interesting but rarely useful to probe for "motives." For LSD they have clearly been variable, although a "need to feel," to escape a sense of personal constriction, was frequently noted in early studies of college users. Sociologists rightly point out that a society which does not underwrite a future for its children and does not promptly recognize true competence, which has little regard for and little skill in the uses of tradition, and which is vulnerable to sudden fads and fancies enhanced by the media, is going to have problems with its youth. This is a developmental period in which transition is of the essence, in which separation from the past and some form of continuity with it is fashioned as youth

261

begins impatiently to shape its future. Yet one would caution against mythologizing the motives of youthful drug abusers, since many of our sociological slogans do little more than glamorize actual events. They may provide us with transiently useful or useless generalizations, but they do not identify the range of personal experiences and environments which lead to drug abuse or experimentation. The ideologies of youth are as vulnerable to the accusation of rationalization as are the aphorisms of the establishment they attack.

Research and Social Control

One implication of research in drug abuse is that we should not use it prematurely to control people's behavior. It is fair enough to warn people about what we in medicine know: that there is always the unexpected which occurs with drugs and that they are never given without weighing the risk. We have recently seen a number of conflicting reports on the "dangers" of chromosomal damage. These treat a laboratory finding as if it were a disease and evoke unsubstantiated and sensational inferences concerning health and reproduction. Normally in medicine we take care to evaluate our techniques and methodology and approach the problem of predicting disease or defects with firm data in hand. If we lend our premature findings to the current of sensationalism, a credibility gap grows in an era where sanity might be gained from honest communication.

Publication of suspicions about LSD certainly offended the pride of youth who believed that there were drugs and experiences which were their civil right to have with impunity. They expected parental but not biological recrimination! Perhaps in five years we will be able to evaluate the extent to which chromosomal damage occurs (after tests of a variety of molecules and not simply those which give rise to "kicks") and the meaning—if any—for health. In the meantime it appears appropriate that we emphasize what we know.

It seems to me that what is at stake in many arguments about the use of drugs for recreation and self-enhancement is the arrogance of those who simply do not believe that drug dependency *can* occur and think that adverse reactions are an invention of the moralistic medical people. This posture is pitted against our wish to find simple and absolute control over those behaviors which bring us troubled people (and their parents) with whom we must cope.

No society can thoroughly regulate what a population of 2-year-olds, adolescents, or depressed people can put in their mouths. It can try to regulate personal "vice"—but not successfully. It cannot avoid establishing stabilizing (or harmful) customs surrounding the recreational use of drugs. Society may very well wish to regulate the spread of indiscriminate self-medication and advertisements which lure the unwary. But it is not the business of research to provide flimsy rationalizations for issues that require value judgments and public choice. With appropriate support, the data which are required can be generated, evaluated, and shared with those who will arrive at means for social control. It will be of more enduring value to drug-takers and both the opponents and proponents of wider use of psychoactive drugs if medical research is not diverted to produce a quick answer and if the community generally will sanction its researchers to have both the tools and the time to discriminate.

References

1. Bowers, M.B., and Freedman, D.X.: "Psychedelic" Experiences in Acute Psychoses, *Arch Gen Psychiat* **15**:240-248 (Sept) 1966

2. Freedman, D.X.: On the Use and Abuse of LSD, *Arch Gen Psychiat* **18**:330-347 (March) 1968.

3. Freedman, D.X.: "Aspects of the Biochemical Pharmacology of Psychotropic Drugs," in Solomon, P. (ed.): *Psychiatric Drugs*, New York: Grune & Stratton, Inc., 1966, pp 32-57.

4. Snyder, S.H.; Faillace, L.; and Hollister, L.: 2,5-Dimethoxy-4-methylamphetamine (STP): A New Hallucinogenic Drug, *Science* **158**:669 (Nov 3) 1967.

5. Isbell, H., et al: Effects of (−)Δ⁹-trans-tetrahydrocannabinol in Man, *Psychopharmacologia* **11**:184-188 (June 9) 1967.

6. Hollister, L.E., and Gillespie, H.K.: Similarities and Differences Between Tetrahydrocannabinol and Lysergic Acid Diethylamide, read before the Rutgers Symposium on Drug Abuse, June 4, 1968.

7. Schacter, S.: "Interaction of Cognitive and Physiological Determinants of Emotional State," in Liederman, H., and Shapiro, D. (eds.): *Psychobiological Approaches to Social Behavior*, Palo Alto, Calif: Stanford University Press, 1964.

8. Silverman, J.: Variations in Cognitive Control and Psychophysiological Defense in the Schizophrenias, *Psychosom Med* **29**:225-251 (May-June) 1967.

9. Dole, V.P.; Nyswander, M.; and Kreek, M.J.: Narcotic Blockade, *Arch Intern Med* **118**:304-309 (Oct) 1966.

AUTHOR INDEX

KEY-WORD TITLE INDEX